Historical Association Studies

China in the Twentieth Century

Historical Association Studies

General Editors: Muriel Chamberlain, H. T. Dickinson and Joe Smith

China in the Twentieth Century

Second Edition

Paul J. Bailey

The right of Paul Bailey to be identified as author of this work has been asserted in accordance with the Copyright, Designs and Patents Act 1988.

First published 1988
Second edition published 2001

2 4 6 8 10 9 7 5 3 1

Blackwell Publishers Ltd
108 Cowley Road
Oxford OX4 1JF
UK

Blackwell Publishers Inc.
350 Main Street
Malden, Massachusetts 02148
USA

British Library Cataloguing in Publication Data

A CIP catalogue record for this book is available from the British Library.

Library of Congress Cataloging-in-Publication Data

Bailey, Paul John, 1950-
    China in the twentieth century / Paul J. Bailey. – 2nd ed.
        p.   cm. – (Historical Association studies)
    Includes bibliographical references and index.
    ISBN 0-631-23030-0 (alk. paper) – ISBN 0-631-20328-1 (pb.: alk. paper)
        1. China – History – 20th century.   2. Communism – China – History.
    I. Title.   II. Series.

DS774.B27 2001
951.05 – dc21

2001025244

Typeset in 10.5 on 12 pt Times
by Best-set Typesetter Ltd., Hong Kong
Printed in Great Britain by TJ International Ltd, Padstow, Cornwall

This book is printed on acid-free paper

Contents

Author's Note

Abbreviations used in the main text are:

CQ   *China Quarterly*
FEER   *Far Eastern Economic Review*
SCMP   *South China Morning Post*

The *pinyin* system of romanization is used for all Chinese names and words, with the following three exceptions:

Sun Yatsen (*pinyin* equivalent is Sun Yixian)
Chiang Kai-shek (*pinyin* equivalent is Jiang Jieshi)
Manchukuo (*pinyin* equivalent is Manzhuguo)

Map

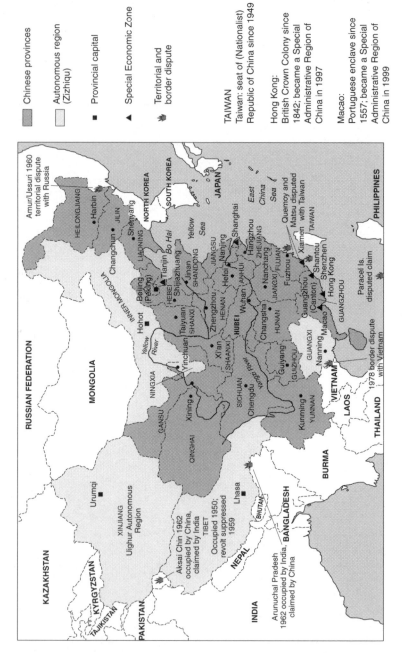

Map 1 The People's Republic of China. From Patricia Buckley Ebrey, *The Cambridge Illustrated History of China*, Cambridge University Press: Cambridge 1996.

Introduction

When I arrived in China in September 1980 to begin a year's postgraduate study at Beijing University (*Beida*) the Chinese Communist Party (CCP) had just begun to embark on its programme of economic reforms. The changes that such reforms ushered in over the subsequent fifteen years completely transformed the face of Beijing. In 1980, apart from the cars used solely by high-level officials and cadres and a small number of taxis (access to which was extremely limited), the traffic mainly comprised buses, *sanlunche* (a rather 'basic' three-wheeled motor-cab), bicycles and the horse-pulled carts of peasants bringing their goods into the city. I remember cycling from the university (situated to the northwest of the city) to the centre (about a one hour's trip) without coming across a car; moreover, the area between the university and the outskirts of the city was virtual countryside, the tranquillity of which was broken only by the few outdoor free markets that had recently received official sanction and the hawking of an occasional 'street entrepreneur' (offering bicycle repairs for example) camped along the dusty roadway. I also recall cycling back at night to the university from the offices of United Press International in the foreign embassy quarter of the city, where I worked part-time translating news stories from the Chinese press, and crossing Tian'anmen Square in glorious isolation.

By 1995 Beijing had three giant ring roads enveloping the city clogged with an increasing number of private cars and taxis; although bicycles were still prevalent, the *sanlunche* and the horse-pulled carts had all disappeared. The intervening years had also witnessed the construction of a bewildering array of Sino-foreign luxury hotels, restaurants and even discotheques, besides which the 1950s-built Beijing Hotel, Friendship Guest House and the International Club (virtually the sole focus of social life in 1980 for foreigners) looked exceedingly forlorn and seedy (although all have been given facelifts recently). As a recent study notes (Gaubatz 1995: 28–60) Beijing, like other cities, had acquired an increasingly differentiated landscape compared to the Maoist era. In Beijing this included the appearance of 'multifunctional' foreign commerce and residential districts concentrated in the northeast of the city (ibid.: 56–8).

Within the city the closely packed courtyard residences located in the traditional maze-like *hutong* (street alleys) were being demolished to make way for impersonal apartment blocks, banks, trading offices and department stores. In 1980 consumer items were scarce and limited in variety; the department store of Wanfujing, the main shopping street a few blocks east of the Forbidden City (the former residence of Chinese emperors), was attracting huge crowds daily as home-produced television sets and washing machines had begun to be put on display. Foreign consumer items were only available at the state-owned Friendship Store (*Youyi shangdian*) in which ordinary Chinese were forbidden to enter; moreover, such items could only be purchased with foreign exchange certificates (*waihui-piao*) rather than the domestic currency (*renminbi*). By 1995 this 'two currency system' had been dismantled and the monopoly of the Friendship Store well and truly broken. Beijing had become one vast shopping emporium in which increasing numbers of ordinary residents could marvel at (if not always afford to buy) a range of consumer goods unimaginable in 1980. In close proximity to the august Forbidden City Beijing residents could now also savour the delights of Kentucky Fried Chicken and McDonald's hamburgers – by August 1995 there were 12 McDonald's outlets in Beijing and 55 nationwide (Miles 1996: 318). The almost rural landscape between the city and Beijing University had metamorphosed into a densely built-up area crammed with hotels, shopping malls, computer stores and western-style fast-food restaurants.

The changes in these fifteen years were reflected in the different enquiries addressed to me on the streets during my various research visits. In 1980, with the CCP launching its 'open door policy' welcoming western and Japanese investment and sending Chinese students abroad to the West, I was frequently asked by passers-by if they could practise their spoken English with me; in 1990, with the winding down of the two currency system and growing interest in speculative activities (a stock market was soon to be opened in Shanghai) virtually the only enquiry addressed to me was whether I wanted 'to change money' (i.e. change my US dollars into *renminbi* at a 'very good rate'); in 1995, when one could buy a computer from a street vendor in a pedestrian underpass, the only question asked of me as I walked around Beijing University was whether I wanted to buy a CD-Rom.

These dramatic economic changes constitute only one ripple in the waves of turbulent, often violent, change that have broken over China's political, social and cultural landscape since the beginning of the twentieth century. The opening years of the century witnessed an ambitious attempt by China's last imperial dynasty, the Qing, to shore up the foundations of dynastic rule through the implementation of constitutional, military and educational reforms. Although such reforms did not prevent the overthrow of the monarchy and its replacement by a republic in 1912, they had set in motion long-term transformations, the significance of which transcended the disappearance of the dynasty itself. The Chinese Republic (the first in Asia apart from the abortive attempt to establish a republic by local leaders in the island province of Taiwan, which had been ceded by China to Japan following its defeat in the Sino-Japanese War of 1894–5, and the short-lived republic of the Philippines established by Emilio Aguinaldo in opposition to Spanish colonial rule in 1897 and ultimately suppressed in 1902 by the US, which had replaced Spain as the colonial power in 1899) was invested with high hopes of creating a new political order and improving China's international position, but gradually disintegrated through corruption and a lack of consensus. Although a central government continued to prevail in Beijing, political and military power gravitated towards provincial militarists and their civilian allies, while the country itself had to continue enduring the humiliation of the 'unequal treaties', a system of privileges and concessions enjoyed by the western powers and Japan in China which had been forcibly extracted during the latter half of the nineteenth century. In the 1920s a national revolutionary movement, preceded by a vigorous cultural–intellectual movement (known as the May Fourth Movement) and spearheaded by an alliance between the Guomindang (Nationalist Party) and the Chinese Communist Party (founded in 1921), embarked on a crusade to defeat the militarists, reunify the country and end foreign imperialism in China.

After brutally suppressing its communist allies in 1927, the Guomindang, under the leadership of Chiang Kai-shek following the death of the party's founder Sun Yatsen in 1925, succeeded in defeating the last major militarist in north China and announced the inauguration of the new Nationalist government in 1928, the capital of which was to be based in Nanjing. With the CCP's urban base smashed, leaders such as Mao Zedong retreated to the countryside and began the long and tortuous process of forging support amongst the peasantry in its bid to defeat the Guomindang and claim the mantle of national leadership. Meanwhile, in the late 1920s and 1930s, the Nationalist regime, committed (at least in theory) to the long-term implementation of full-scale democracy under the 'tutelage' of the Guomindang, oversaw a modest programme of social and economic reform. The regime, however, was always in a vulnerable position. Its writ did not extend throughout the country, especially as many provinces remained under the control of former militarists who (along with their armies) had simply been co-opted by the Guomindang and whose loyalty to the new regime remained ambivalent. The Guomindang itself was riven with corruption and factionalism. During the 1930s much of the regime's energies and resources were devoted to eliminating the communist rural base areas in central-south China and crushing rebellions led by former militarists and dissident Guomindang leaders. At the same time China faced a growing threat from Japan, increasingly suspicious that its economic stake in China might be undermined by both the Nationalist regime's rhetorical commitment to renegotiating the unequal treaties and growing Anglo-American hostility to Japan's economic influence in China. By 1932 Japanese military forces had overrun the northeast (Manchuria) and established the puppet state of Manchukuo (Manzhuguo). In subsequent years Japanese pressure on north China increased, culminating in a full-scale invasion in 1937. Throughout the 1930s Chiang

Kai-shek's appeasement of Japan (with priority being accorded to defeating the communists) aroused the opposition of intellectuals, students and the business classes already disaffected by Guomindang domestic policies. Following the retreat from its principal base area in central-south China in 1934 and the establishment of a new base area in the northwest (Shaanxi province) in 1935, the CCP called for another united front to confront Japanese aggression. Such a united front with the Guomindang was officially proclaimed in 1936, which meant that throughout the eight years of resistance against Japan (1937–45) the CCP and the Guomindang were formally allies; however, the relationship was marked by mutual suspicion, bitter recriminations, and an almost total lack of co-operation.

While the Guomindang retreated westwards from its capital in Nanjing and re-established its headquarters in Chongqing (Sichuan province) in 1938, the CCP from its principal base area centred at Yanan (as well as from other scattered base areas in north and central China) conducted guerrilla campaigns against the Japanese. This was also the period when Mao Zedong consolidated his ideological and political leadership of the party, and when a Maoist mythology began to take shape associating the history of the communist revolution exclusively with the realization of Mao's 'correct line'. By adapting its policies to the interests of both poor peasants and rural elites, and presenting itself as the genuine incarnation of nationalist resistance in contrast to the vacillating Guomindang, the CCP garnered increasing support so that by 1945 large areas of rural north and northeast China were under effective communist control. The end of the Second World War in Asia in August 1945, however, did not bring peace and stability to China. After fruitless negotiations mediated by the US, the CCP and Guomindang embarked on civil war in 1946, a war in which the Soviet Union and the US, the two new superpowers to emerge from the rubble of Japan's defeat in Asia, played a role (hence constituting the opening salvoes of the Cold War). CCP victory over the Guomindang resulted in the establishment of the People's Republic of China in 1949, the third dramatic change of political regime in less than half a century.

In its quest to achieve wealth, power and international respect, the new communist government set out to remake Chinese society, an ideal that had animated reformers and nationalists in different ways since the late nineteenth century. Under the increasingly arbitrary and erratic leadership of Mao, however, the ideological mass campaigns designed to usher in a society and polity shorn of individualism and elitism, and characterized by the virtues of asceticism and complete devotion to the collective interest, brought calamitous upheaval and turbulence for the Chinese people. In 1949 a gradual transition to socialism had been envisaged, with priority being accorded to land reform (which eliminated the landlord class and distributed land to poor peasants), marriage reform (allowing for free choice of marriage and extending equal divorce rights for women), and mobilizing the people in a patriotic campaign to support China's military intervention in the Korean War (1950–2). By the mid-1950s, however, all urban enterprises had come under state ownership and all of China's farmers had been organized into collectives. Campaigns were also launched against perceived enemies or critics of socialism, ranging from 'bourgeois elements' associated with the former Guomindang regime to non-party (and even party) intellectuals who were accused of taking advantage of Mao's invitation in 1956–7 to engage in 'healthy criticism' of party bureaucratism to question the legitimacy of CCP rule itself.

The pace and scope of change took a dramatic turn in 1958 when Mao and his supporters launched the Great Leap Forward. Reflecting Mao's dissatisfaction with the Soviet model of development (with its emphasis on centralized planning, heavy industrial development and bureaucratic hierarchies) that the regime had adopted in its early years, the Great Leap was both an ideological and an economic campaign to encourage the transition to a communist way of life and to utilize surplus labour power in the countryside to implement wide-scale rural industrialization. The irrational and incompetent actions of over-zealous party cadres and planners responding to Mao's encouragement were exacerbated by natural disasters that proved catastrophic for the peasants; the resulting famine in 1959–60 led to millions of deaths. During the Great Leap campaign, also, the simmering tensions that had frequently characterized the CCP's relationship with the Soviet Union, erupted. Although the new communist government had concluded an alliance with the Soviet Union in 1950 (which had done much to offset China's international isolation following the refusal of the US to recognize the People's Republic), clashes of ideological and national interests intertwined to produce publicly aired mutual denunciations in 1960.

The modification of Great Leap policies during the early 1960s convinced Mao (who had stepped down as Chairman of the People's Republic in 1959) that the ideological 'revisionism' he saw taking hold in the Soviet Union was beginning to affect China. By 1965 he was voicing suspicion that the CCP leadership itself was 'infected' with revisionism, which for Mao threatened his vision of creating a communist society. The stage was set for Mao's last major initiative. Beginning with an orchestrated attack on the party's cultural organs, Mao's Great Proletarian Cultural Revolution (officially launched in August 1966) called on the 'masses' (in particular high school and college students) to confront and denounce all those in authority (party, government, academic) supposedly sabotaging the revolution by 'taking the capitalist road' and/or adhering to 'feudal' beliefs and practices. For Mao the Cultural Revolution would help revitalize the party by purging it of 'impure' elements while also providing a younger generation with the experience of revolutionary struggle and sacrifice. It also witnessed the final flowering of a grotesque Mao cult (in which Mao's thought was invested with supernatural qualities) that had its origins during the Yanan period and which Mao had allowed to be assiduously cultivated within the army in 1963 as the prelude to his attack on the party leadership. The movement quickly degenerated into random and arbitrary violence (often the result of frustrations and resentments caused by official party policies in the 1950s), with thousands of party and government bureaucrats, teachers, intellectuals and artists being publicly humiliated, beaten and even killed, while competing factions of student organizations (known collectively as the Red Guards) each claiming to be the true supporters of the Maoist vision bitterly fought each other on the streets.

With the virtual dismantling of party rule and society tottering on the brink of complete anarchy in 1967 Mao stepped back from the abyss and sanctioned the intervention of the People's Liberation Army (PLA); in the short term this only resulted in further confusion and violence as factional divisions among Mao's radical supporters in the Cultural Revolution leadership were played out within the army and as armed clashes took place between PLA units and Red Guard organizations. The turbulence of these years also affected China's international situation. Condemning the US and the Soviet Union (and their respective allies) equally as enemies of world revolution, China became diplomatically isolated; Sino-Soviet tensions, in particular, reached a more dangerous stage in 1969 when a border war broke out in China's northeast.

The process of rebuilding the party began in 1969, by which time schools (closed in 1966) had been reopened and recalcitrant Red Guards sent to the countryside to undergo labour and ideological reform. The last years of Mao's life were marked by uncertainty and ideological confusion, with the party leadership virtually immobilized by continuing factional, personal and policy differences between those closely associated with Cultural Revolution policies and their opponents. On the international front, however, the country's diplomatic isolation was dramatically ended when *rapprochement* with the US was formalized in 1972 and the PRC allowed to take its seat in the United Nations (from which it had been excluded since 1950).

The years after Mao's death in 1976 witnessed a further change in direction as the CCP sought to relegitimize itself in the eyes of an increasingly disillusioned population by promoting policies that would enhance stability and economic prosperity. Over the next two decades much of the Maoist legacy was dismantled through a series of economic and political reforms that downplayed the importance of mass ideological campaigns, introduced elements of a market economy while loosening state controls, dismantled rural collectives, placed greater stress on academic elitism in education, sought professionalization of the party and army, encouraged investment from, and more extensive links with, the capitalist world, revitalized political institutions that had hitherto been moribund, and allowed for wider political participation through local elections and consultation with semi-official policy research institutes and 'think-tanks'. Ironically, however, the 1980s also witnessed the most ambitious attempt at state intrusion into people's lives with the implementation of the one-child policy designed to limit population growth.

The post-Mao reform process, however, has not been a smooth one. Demands for greater accountability, an end to corruption and more extensive democratic reforms animated popular protests in 1979, 1986 and, most dramatically of all, 1989 (when student demonstrators were brutally suppressed by the army). The party itself has waged controlled campaigns against what it perceives to be 'unhealthy tendencies' of 'bourgeois individualism' and 'spiritual pollution' in 1983, 1986, 1989 and, more recently (in July 1999), against religious superstition. During much of the 1980s reformers and conservatives within the party clashed over the pace and extent of market reforms; opposition to such reforms was still being expressed in 1997 on the eve of the party's fifteenth National Congress.

The reforms themselves have engendered serious problems. Whereas a 1980s study of the reform process (Harding 1987) stressed the underlying 'liberalization' of the reforms (e.g. in granting more autonomy from the state) and argued that the choice for the future would simply be how to arrive at the most appropriate 'blend of plan and market, political consultation and political control, individual entrepreneurship and state ownership' (ibid.: 303), more recent analyses of contemporary developments (e.g. Gittings 1996; Miles 1996) have been more prone to emphasize the growing economic inequalities (between the more developed coastal regions and the rural hinterlands, between south and north, and within regions themselves), social tensions and conflicts (urban unemployment, rural unrest, huge waves of uncontrolled peasant migration into the cities, increasing crime rates), and the massive corruption brought about by the reforms. The party also faces continuing ethnic unrest amongst 'minority' peoples (particularly in Tibet, Inner Mongolia and Xinjiang), exacerbated by an assertive Han Chinese nationalism that the CCP has itself encouraged (directly and indirectly) in a bid to bolster its legitimacy by highlighting its patriotic credentials. Ironically this has meant that although the party has regularly fulminated against the resurgence of 'feudal superstitions and practices' brought about by the loosening of state controls (e.g. secret society activity, religious cults, fortune-telling, extravagant wedding and funeral ceremonies), it has also associated itself with past traditions, praising, for example, the vigorous rule of strong emperors in Chinese history and Confucian ideals of harmony, appropriate deference and filial piety. In fact, the party, with its specious use of patriotism and manipulation of tradition, has, since the late 1980s, opened up a Pandora's box from which has emerged a whole range of discordant discourses and angst-ridden self-reflections amongst intellectuals on just what exactly constitutes a Chinese 'identity'.

The manifold problems and uncertainties that have emerged during the reform process lead one observer (Miles 1996: 4, 310–11) to note that despite the achievement of phenomenal growth and economic freedom the country is in 'growing disarray, deeply unsure of itself', a scenario that makes China less stable now than it was in the 1980s. Another commentator is sceptical that the economic development of the coastal regions will be the motor for nationwide prosperity, arguing that 'the whole country is more likely to become, on a vastly larger scale, another Third World country where city is ranged against countryside, wealth against deprivation, and technological wonders mask deep social ills' (Gittings 1996: 282). The most pessimistic overview of contemporary developments, written in the wake of the brutal crackdown on student demonstrators in 1989 (Jenner 1992), compares the present regime to the dying Qing monarchy at the turn of the century, both being ultimately 'unreformable'. The CCP is described as a conservative force, only willing to make changes that are essential for its own survival.

All this seems a far cry from the prediction made by Liang Qichao (1873–1929) at the turn of the twentieth century. In late 1901 Liang, a prominent reformer and pioneer political journalist, wrote in one of his journals that China would become one of the three superpowers (along with Russia and the US) of the twentieth century. For Liang the new century would usher in a new and modern China whose magnificence would surpass even that of Europe in the previous century (Tang 1996: 48). Yet in some ways Liang's prediction has been partly fulfilled. From being a declining monarchical regime beset by imperialist powers at the turn of the century, and an economically and socially devastated country in 1949 after years of foreign invasion and civil war, China in the 1990s, according to some observers, is approaching the rank of an economic superpower. Official Chinese figures indicate that Gross Domestic Product (GDP) quadrupled between 1978 and 1994, making it the fastest growing economy in the world during this period-although, paradoxically, in terms of infrastructure, welfare and education provision, rural incomes, productivity and environmental problems the country still bore the hallmarks of a 'developing nation' (Hunter and Sexton 1999: 3, 68). The average rate of GDP growth between 1993 and 1997 was 11 per cent (7.3 percentage points above the world average) (CQ June 1998: 461), while reports in early 1999 suggested a more than respectable GDP growth of 7.8 per cent for 1998 despite the economic crisis that affected much of Asia in this year (CQ March 1999: 259). In 1993–6 China became the world's largest single producer of cotton, cereals, coal and television sets, and in 1996 became the world's largest steel producer (CQ June 1998: 461). The World Bank in 1996 predicted that 'Greater China' (the term applied to mainland China, Hong Kong – the British colony returned to Chinese control in 1997 – and Taiwan, to where the Nationalist government under Chiang Kai-shek retreated in 1949 to establish the Republic of China) would soon constitute the world's largest economy (Miles 1996: 261).

In terms of foreign trade the changes have been even more striking. Since the reforms inaugurating the 'open door' policy in 1978 foreign trade (particularly with the West and Japan) has assumed a greater role in the Chinese economy. In 1997 36.1 per cent of China's GDP derived from foreign trade, compared to 9.8 per cent in 1979 (CQ March 1999: 264), and the value of its merchandise trade in that year made China the tenth largest trading nation in the world (CQ June 1998: 461). Since China's *rapprochement* with the US in 1972, and especially since the formalization of diplomatic relations in 1978, Sino-American trade has particularly mushroomed, totalling US$49 billion in 1997 (twenty times more than in 1979). In that year China became Washington's fourth largest trading partner, while the US ranked second (after Japan) among China's trading partners (CQ Sept. 1998: 718–19). Perhaps more significantly, the trade is in China's favour; thus in 1994 Washington's trade deficit with China amounted to US$29 billion (Miles 1996: 6), which had increased to US$57 billion by 1998 (FEER 22 April 1999).

Politically, too, the People's Republic of China has emerged as a significant power in Asia to rival the US and Japan, a development facilitated by the disintegration of the Soviet Union in 1991. A further boost to Beijing's sense of pride has been the return of the British colony of Hong Kong (ceded by the Qing dynasty in 1842 following the Opium War) in 1997; in December 1999 the Portuguese colony of Macau (dating from the 1550s) also reverted to Chinese control. Yet as the new millennium begins China's relations with its neighbours and with the US are characterized as much by niggling tensions and uncertainties as by positive interaction. On the one hand, Beijing has struck what has been termed a 'strategic partnership' with both Russia and the US (in 1996 and 1997, respectively); although it continues to insist that Taiwan is a 'renegade province' that must eventually return to mainland Chinese control, Beijing has allowed in recent years an enormous increase in economic links (both in terms of trade and inward investment) as well as sanctioning dialogue through semi-official organizations; and during the Asian economic crisis of the late 1990s China gained considerable kudos amongst its neighbours as a stabilizing force in the region (by, for example, not devaluing its currency). On the other hand, China is involved in territorial disputes over the Spratly Islands (in the South China Sea) with Japan, Vietnam, Malaysia and the Philippines, and over the Diaoyu (Senkaku) Islands (northeast of Taiwan) with Japan; although Japan is China's largest trading partner the question of Japan's war guilt remains a sensitive issue, as well as Beijing's opposition to the 1997 Japan – US defence agreement; recent developments in Taiwan (e.g. the election in 2000 of a non-Guomindang president, Chen Shuibian, whose party – the Democratic Progressive Party – is more open to the possibility of a formal declaration of Taiwanese independence) have been stridently condemned by Chinese government and party officials as a threat to its 'one China policy' (i.e. Taiwan as an inseparable part of China), a policy to which, paradoxically, the Guomindang government in Taiwan had subscribed after 1949 by its very claim to represent the 'real' Republic of China; and Sino-American relations continue to be dogged by mutual recriminations, with criticisms of China's human rights record and nuclear espionage being countered by Beijing's accusation that the US seeks to use organizations such as the UN and NATO (most recently in Kosovo) to assert its hegemonic role in the world.

Whether, in the judgement of a recent overview of China's modern history (Spence 1999a: 728), a combination of pragmatic economic policies and an apparent ideological openness bodes well for the future preservation of stability, or whether

CCP rule 'implodes' as it did in the Soviet Union, remains a moot point at the beginning of the twenty-first century. As the last major communist state in the world, however (the others being Vietnam, North Korea and Cuba), which will (in whatever form) exert increasing influence in the global economy, the continuities, disjunctures and turbulence of China's twentieth-century history demand our attention and understanding.

1

The End of the Imperial Monarchy

> The whole nation is now inclined towards a republican form of government. . . . By observing the nature of the people's aspirations we learn the will of Heaven. . . . We recognize the signs of the age, and We have tested the trend of popular opinion; and We now, with the Emperor at our side, invest the nation with sovereign power, and decree the establishment of a constitutional government on a republican basis. (Cited in Irons 1983: 35)

Thus did the Qing dynasty, which had ruled over China since 1644, pass from the scene as the regent, the Empress-Dowager Longyu, formally announced the abdication of the dynasty in February 1912 on behalf of the six-year-old emperor, Puyi. The downfall of the Qing had been presaged the previous October when an army mutiny in Wuchang (Hubei province) had rapidly ignited anti-dynastic uprisings and political manoeuvres in central and southern China. Henceforth China officially became a republic, thus signalling the end of an imperial tradition that dated from the third century BCE and which had ascribed enormous powers to the emperors. Unlike the English, French and Russian revolutions, however, there were to be no royal executions. The ex-emperor and his immediate family were allowed to continue residing in the Forbidden City, where the imperial palace was located, and were to be provided with an annual subsidy from the new republican government.

Recent studies (e.g. Rawski 1996, 1998; Crossley 1997) have greatly contributed to a more nuanced and sophisticated understanding of the Qing dynasty that so ignominiously disappeared in 1912. At the same time a growing body of work dating from the late 1960s (e.g. Wright 1968; Bastid 1980; Schoppa 1982; Duara 1988; Bailey 1990; Thompson 1995) has highlighted the long-term political, social and cultural changes during the dynasty's last few decades (and which transcended the disappearance of the dynasty itself) that were long masked by the dynasty's apparent failure to confront internal and external challenges during the nineteenth century and by its ultimately abortive attempt after 1900 to strengthen the foundations of dynastic rule through a series of reforms.

The Qing Imperium

The Qing was one of the most successful of China's dynasties. The Qing rulers were Manchus, originally a collection of semi-nomadic and hunting tribes known as the Jurchen that over time engaged in agriculture and long-distance trade in what is now known as China's Northeast (beyond the Great Wall that had traditionally separated China from its non-Chinese neighbours). Under the able leadership of Nurgaci (1559–1626) these northeastern tribes were united into a formidable fighting force. Nurgaci's followers and their families were enrolled in eight Banners (each headed by one of Nurgaci's sons) which served to provide recruits for Nurgaci's campaigns as well as fulfilling administrative tasks such as population registration; later, in the 1630s and early 1640s, sixteen additional Banners were created incorporating both Mongol and Chinese followers (the latter were recruited from among Chinese troops stationed in the northeastern frontier region). In an attempt to link his ambitions with the achievement of his Jurchen forbears, Nurgaci in 1616 styled himself emperor of the Later Jin (in 1122–1234 the Jurchen had established a dynasty in north China known as the Jin) and in 1625 created a capital at Mukden (present-day Shenyang in Liaoning province). During the reign of Abahai (1592–1643) the Jurchen tribes were renamed Manchus and in 1636 the new dynastic title of Qing (lit. 'pure') was adopted. While conducting ever more audacious raids across the frontier into China, Abahai gradually created a civil administration in his capital that was modelled on Chinese practice and employed captured Chinese.

The reigning Ming dynasty (1368–1644) was ill-prepared to meet the growing Manchu threat on its northeastern frontier. A succession of weak and indecisive emperors, corruption and factionalism within the bureaucracy, and increasing peasant unrest as a result of famine and burdensome taxes had severely weakened the dynasty. When a large-scale peasant rebellion led by Li Zicheng resulted in the capture of Beijing in 1644 and the suicide of the Ming emperor, the Manchus seized their opportunity and entered China promising to restore peace and stability. With the aid of Chinese military commanders, alarmed at the disorder and anarchy in Beijing and elsewhere, the Manchus defeated Li Zicheng and proclaimed the rulership of the Qing over all of China. It was not to be until several decades later, however, that the Qing was finally able to consolidate its rule over the entire country; Ming loyalist resistance persisted in the south until 1662 and on the island of Taiwan until 1683 (when it was incorporated into the province of Fujian).

In the initial establishment of their rule the Qing rulers were both harsh and accommodating. Their Chinese subjects, for example, were forced to adopt the Manchu hairstyle (shaving the forehead and wearing hair in a long braid, or queue, at the back). The Chinese population and the 'conquest elite' (comprising Manchu, Mongol and Chinese bannermen) were strictly segregated, with Banner garrisons housing the bannermen and their families located in key strategic areas to maintain military control; bannermen were not supposed to engage in local trade (they were supported by government cash stipends), while intermarriage between Manchu and Chinese was discouraged. By the mid-nineteenth century, however, most Banner garrisons were merely 'subsistence-level holding camps' (Crossley 1990: 120); Banner stipends were progressively reduced and after the 1860s Banner residents could apply to the government to enter trades such as carpentry and weaving. On the eve of the 1911 Revolution only 1 out of 20 registered bannermen was still trying to support himself as a soldier (ibid.: 148). Interestingly, the early Qing rulers also attempted to prevent Chinese migration to the fertile agricultural regions of the northeast (regarded as their ancestral homeland); population and migratory pressures were to make such a ban virtually redundant by the end of the nineteenth century.

At the same time, by insisting that they were the legitimate heirs of the Ming dynasty and promising to rule in accordance with Chinese government norms and practices, the Qing rulers gradually gained acceptance from indigenous elites. In particular the continued status of the scholar official class was guaranteed. This class derived its prestige from success in civil service examinations (dating from the Song dynasty 960–1279), which were based on classical texts associated with the philosophy of Confucius (551–479 BCE) and his followers and used to recruit members of the governing bureaucracy. In a wider sense the scholar-gentry perceived themselves as the learned and moral guardians of a Confucian tradition that emphasized the importance of humane government, education, social and ritual propriety, respect for the past and one's ancestors, and filial piety. The Qing promised to uphold Confucian orthodoxy and restored the civil service examinations in 1646, while also sponsoring large-scale literary works and sanctioning the establishment of Confucian academies (*shuyuan*). This co-option of the scholar-gentry class was paralleled by the employment of Chinese in the bureaucracy. In the capital, for example, the six administrative boards were each headed by both a Manchu and a Chinese. Over the course of the dynasty the posts of governor (in charge of a province) and governor-general (in charge of two or more provinces) were mostly held by Chinese or Chinese bannermen, while local official posts (such as the district magistrate) were entirely monopolized by Chinese.

Under three remarkable emperors – Kangxi (r. 1661–1722), Yongzheng (r. 1723–35) and Qianlong (r. 1735–96) – the Qing ushered in a period of stability and economic prosperity that endured throughout most of the eighteenth century. Agriculture probably attained its highest point of development with the introduction of new food crops (such as the sweet potato, maize and sorghum) and cash crops (such as cotton, tea, tobacco and sugar-cane), which met the needs of a rapidly growing population and contributed to the expansion of commercial trading networks and a sophisticated urban culture (particularly in the Yangzi delta). After a period during the reign of Kangxi when coastal trade had been banned (due to security fears at a time when Ming loyalist remnants were active along the southern coast) the eighteenth century witnessed a flourishing maritime trade that catered to a growing western demand for Chinese handicraft products (e.g. porcelain, lacquerwork) and tea; it has been estimated that half the amount of silver imported into Europe from Mexico and South America between the end of the sixteenth century and the beginning of the nineteenth century was used to purchase such products (Gernet 1996: 487). Throughout the eighteenth century, also, Chinese trading junks were a ubiquitous presence in southeast Asia. The fashion craze amongst European elites during the first half of the eighteenth century for Chinese *objects d'art*, furniture, and garden design (known as chinoiserie) was accompanied by exalted praise of China's rational and humane governance by notable savants such as Voltaire, heavily influenced by the positive letters and reports sent back from China by Jesuit missionaries who had first gone there at the end of the sixteenth century and during the reign of Kangxi had been employed at court as astronomers and cartographers.

During the reign of Qianlong Qing control was extended to Mongolia, Tibet and Turkestan (to become the province of Xinjiang in 1884), while neighbouring kingdoms such as Korea, Vietnam, Nepal and Siam acknowledged the political and cultural superiority of the Qing imperium by sending regular 'tributary' missions to the Qing court. At the height of its territorial extent in 1760, the Qing imperium thus constituted one of the largest and most sophisticated empires in the world at that time (along with the Ottoman and Mughal empires).

As a recent study notes (Crossley 1997: 8–10), it is misleading to think of the Qing simply as a Chinese or even a Manchu 'dynasty', since this masks the cultural and political complexities of Qing rule. In fact the Qing presided over a pluralistic and multi-ethnic empire in which peoples speaking non-Sinitic languages and adhering to different religious faiths were placed on an equal footing with ethnic (or Han) Chinese (Rawski 1998: 1–8). Furthermore, Qing success has conventionally been explained in terms of 'sinicization', whereby non-Chinese conquest dynasties that at various times throughout Chinese history have ruled part or all of China were perceived to have adopted Chinese forms and practices of government, and to have become absorbed by 'superior' Chinese culture. Newly accessible archival sources reveal, however, that Qing rulers did not think of themselves as Chinese but, rather, through their institutions and state rituals sought to preserve a separate cultural identity (Rawski 1996, 1998), although it should be noted that the emergence of a Manchu identity and culture was inextricably bound up with the growth of a Manchu state in the 1630s under the leadership of Abahai, and Qianlong's attempt in the eighteenth century to standardize the Manchu language and record genealogies (Crossley 1990: 5–7; 1994: 340–78; 1997: 6–8).

In fact the reason for Qing success is to be sought in the ability of Qing rulers to address different ethnic and religious constituencies. On the one hand, for example, they presented themselves as model Confucian rulers in order to gain acceptance from the Chinese scholar-official elites. Emperors such as Kangxi employed Chinese Confucian tutors, issued edicts calling for the enforcement of orthodox Confucian values (such as family harmony, filial piety and respect for education), and, in line with the Confucian injunction that rulers should pay heed to the people's livelihood, fixed land tax rates in 1712. Also, within China proper, Qing rulers sanctioned a Confucian 'civilizing mission' amongst indigenous minority peoples in southwest and central provinces (Rowe 1994). On the other hand, Qing rulers patronized and promoted Lamaist Buddhism, practised in both Tibet and Mongolia; the Qianlong emperor even portrayed himself as the model Buddhist ruler (*cakravartin*), whose actions in the name of the Buddha would propel the world towards the next stage in universal salvation.

Internal and External Challenges in the Nineteenth Century

By the early nineteenth century the Qing empire confronted a number of serious domestic problems. The last years of the Qianlong reign were marked by complacency and corruption at all levels of the bureaucracy. This led, for example, to embezzlement of government funds destined for the upkeep of public works such as irrigation channels and dykes, and greatly exacerbated the natural disasters of drought and floods to which China had always been susceptible (Wakeman 1975: 102–6; Mann Jones and Kuhn 1978). Also, since land tax rates had ben fixed (with provincial quotas to be raised only as new land was registered, something that was rarely done in practice), expenses for local government such as salaries for traditionally low-paid district magistrates were met by 'customary' sur-charges, often arbitrarily imposed and which tended to increase over time, thus adding to the burdens of an already hard-strapped peasantry.

Furthermore, the peace and stability of the eighteenth century had resulted in an enormous increase in population that far outstripped the amount of cultivable land available. It is generally agreed that the population doubled during the course of the eighteenth century from approximately 150 million to over 350 million; by the middle of the nineteenth century it had reached 430 million. By way of contrast, Europe's population increased from 144 million in 1750 to 193 million in 1800 (Ho 1959: 270; Hucker 1975: 330; Gernet 1996: 488). Competition for land resources placed incoming Chinese settlers in violent conflict with indigenous minority peoples in provinces such as Guizhou, Sichuan and Hunan. A series of revolts broke out in the late eighteenth and early nineteenth centuries, which drained government coffers (already seriously depleted by Emperor Qianlong's military expeditions to Burma, Nepal and Vietnam) and revealed the inefficiency of Banner military forces long accustomed to internal peace. The most serious was the White Lotus rebellion (the White Lotus was a Buddhist millenarian lay sect), which affected the provinces of Sichuan, Shanxi and Hubei between 1795 and 1805. Since Banner forces proved ineffective in crushing the rebellion, the Qing court was compelled to compromise its military monopoly by relying on militia forces organized by local gentry.

The Qing dynasty's problems were compounded by the emergence of a new and potentially far more dangerous threat, that of an expanding West aggressively demanding commercial and trading privileges. Although Portuguese and Spanish traders had appeared off China's southern coast in the sixteenth and seventeenth centuries, it was not until the early nineteenth century that western, particularly British, traders arrived in greater numbers. Since the mid-eighteenth century the Qing court had restricted maritime trade to the port of Guangzhou (Guangdong province) due more to security concerns and a desire to maintain close official supervision than to opposition to trade *per se*. A British diplomatic mission led by Lord Macartney was sent to Qianlong's court in 1792–3 with the aim of securing an extension of trade and an end to restrictions on the trade already permitted at Guangzhou. Since Macartney's requests were rejected out of hand, the encounter has conventionally been portrayed as a clash between an immobile, self-sufficient and culturally arrogant China and a newly rising power representing modern and dynamic ideals of industrial progress and free trade (Peyrefitte 1993). Other recent studies (Waley-Cohen 1993; Hevia 1995) have pointed out, however, that Qing rulers were not necessarily blind to the benefits of western technology (evidenced by their use of Jesuit expertise in cartography, astronomy and even cannon-casting); furthermore, Qianlong's attitude towards the Macartney mission and its requests was as much conditioned by internal political considerations (i.e. the need to maintain Qing credibility amongst the Confucian scholar-elite), as well as by Macartney's failure to observe appropriate protocol. In a sense the encounter might be better seen as a clash between two expanding empires, each with universalist claims of their own.

The forcible 'opening' of China began with the Opium War of 1840–2, caused by Britain's aggressive response to Chinese official attempts to stamp out the lucrative opium trade in which British traders were involved. The ensuing Treaty of Nanjing (1842) ceded the island of Hong Kong to Britain, opened five 'treaty ports' (Guangzhou, Shanghai, Ningbo, Fuzhou and Xiamen) for unrestricted British trade and residence, and obliged the Qing court to pay a large indemnity. A supplementary treaty one year later fixed import duties at an average of 5 per cent *ad valorem*, allowed British gunboats to be stationed in the treaty ports, granted British residents the privilege of extra-territoriality (i.e. they were subject only to the jurisdiction of their own consuls), and included a Most Favoured Nation Clause, obliging the Qing government to guarantee that any future economic concession granted to a single foreign power had to be extended to all. The US and France concluded similar treaties in 1844. Although in the early twentieth century Chinese nationalists were to condemn these and subsequent treaties as 'unequal' (because they were imposed by force, impinged on Chinese sovereignty, and granted rights and concessions that were not reciprocal), it is important to note that the Qing court in 1842 did not view them in this light,

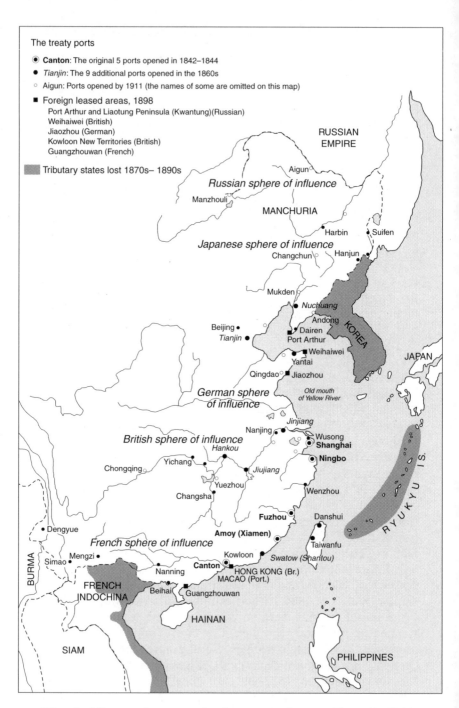

The treaty ports

⦿ **Canton**: The original 5 ports opened in 1842–1844

● *Tianjin*: The 9 additional ports opened in the 1860s

○ Aigun: Ports opened by 1911 (the names of some are omitted on this map)

■ Foreign leased areas, 1898
  Port Arthur and Liaotung Peninsula (Kwantung)(Russian)
  Weihaiwei (British)
  Jiaozhou (German)
  Kowloon New Territories (British)
  Guangzhouwan (French)

▨ Tributary states lost 1870s– 1890s

RUSSIAN EMPIRE

Aigun○

Russian sphere of influence

Manzhouli

MANCHURIA

Harbin ●   ● Suifen

Japanese sphere of influence

Changchun○   ●Hanjun

Mukden○

Beijing ●   ● *Nuchuang*
            Andong
Tianjin   ■ Dairen
            Port Arthur
KOREA

            ■Weihaiwei
            Yantai

Qingdao○ ■Jiaozhou

JAPAN

German sphere of influence

Old mouth of Yellow River

RYUKYU IS.

            Jinjiang
Nanjing ●   ○○Wusong
              ◉ **Shanghai**

British sphere of influence
Hankou

            ◉ **Ningbo**

Chongqing○ Yichang ● ● *Jiujiang*
            Yuezhou
            ● Wenzhou
Changsha○

            Fuzhou ●   ● Danshui

Amoy (Xiamen) ●

French sphere of influence

● Dengyue
            Kowloon ○ Taiwanfu
Mengzi ●   **Canton** ⦿
Simao○   HONG KONG (Br.) *Swatow (Shantou)*
            MACAO (Port.)
        Nanning ●

BURMA

FRENCH INDOCHINA
        Beihai● ○Guangzhouwan■

            HAINAN

SIAM

            PHILIPPINES

Map 2 Nineteenth-century foreign encroachments. From R. Keith Schoppa, *The Columbia Guide to Modern Chinese History*, Columbia University Press: New York, 2000.

rationalizing them as mechanisms to restrict western activity to a few ports in which foreigners enjoyed the generously granted privilege to trade.

Nevertheless, the western presence continued to grow throughout the nineteenth century. As a result of further hostilities with Britain and France between 1856 and 1860 the Qing court was forced to grant more concessions; additional treaty ports were opened, the right of inland navigation on the Yangzi was granted, missionaries were allowed to travel, proselytize and own land in the interior (as well as to enjoy the privilege of extra-territoriality), and permanent foreign legations were established in the capital. Earlier, in 1853, when the turmoil of the Taiping rebellion (see below) threatened to engulf Shanghai and affect western economic interests there, the western powers took over administration of the maritime customs service; this practice was then extended to the other treaty ports in the 1860s. Furthermore, in a number of treaty ports the powers were able to demarcate 'concession' areas in which they exercised legal jurisdiction and controlled local administration. The two largest such concession areas were the International Settlement (under British control) and the French Concession in Shanghai (Feuerwerker 1983b).

Meanwhile, the Qing had to contend with a series of internal rebellions during the mid-nineteenth century, the most serious of which was the Taiping Rebellion (1850–64). Led by Hong Xiuquan (1814–64), who came from an ethnic minority group in south China known as the Hakkas (descended from Chinese settlers who had migrated from the north after the twelfth century) and who established contact with Protestant missionaries in Guangzhou, the rebellion forged an ideology that amalgamated Christian doctrine with traditional Chinese utopian ideals. Initially drawing on the support of the Hakka community, the movement was soon joined by millions of landless peasants and unemployed handicraft and transportation workers. Hong called for the overthrow of the alien Qing dynasty and by 1853 had established in Nanjing the capital of the *Taiping Tianguo* (Heavenly Kingdom of Great Peace). The inability of Qing Banner forces to suppress the rebellion obliged the court to rely on regional militia armies organized and led by the Chinese scholar-official elite, who perceived in the Taiping's anti-Confucian propaganda and egalitarian ideals a threat to the

moral and social order (Kuhn 1978). As powerful provincial officials, these militia commanders were allowed to appropriate
central government revenue and even impose new taxes to
finance their armies. Although in one sense such a development
signified a loosening of central control, it did not portend a
full-blown regionalism. The provincial officials who commanded
the militia armies that finally defeated the Taipings in 1864 saw
themselves, and remained, loyal servants of the throne (it might
be noted that the most prominent of these officials, Zeng
Guofan, disbanded his militia army, known as the Hunan Army,
soon after the suppression of the rebellion); furthermore, the
court retained the power right up to 1911 to appoint, transfer
and dismiss provincial officials.

In response to the threat posed by internal rebellion – in
addition to the Taiping Rebellion, the Qing had to confront a
rebellion of roving peasant-bandits known as the Nian from
1851 to 1868 in north-central China and a Muslim rebellion in
the northwest from 1862 to 1873 – and continuing external
pressure, a number of court and provincial officials (many of
whom had been involved in the suppression of the Taiping
Rebellion) promoted various institutional and military measures (known as 'self-strengthening') with the aim of reinvigorating the socio-political order and shoring up the country's
defences. Thus as well as drawing attention to the necessity of
implementing traditional ideals of Confucian government
(especially in those areas devastated by rebellion), such as
reducing the burden of land taxes, ensuring the efficacy of public
works, and insisting on the moral probity of officialdom, the
Qing court sanctioned the establishment of a proto-foreign
office in 1861 (the Zongli Yamen) specifically to deal with the
western powers, the opening of foreign language schools in
Shanghai (1862) and Guangzhou (1864), and the building of
arsenals in Shanghai, Nanjing and Tianjin to manufacture
western-style armaments as well as a naval dockyard (with an
attached training school) at Fuzhou in 1866. Later, army and
navy academies were opened in Tianjin (1885) and Nanjing
(1890) respectively.

During the 1870s and 1880s the scope of this self-
strengthening movement widened with the creation of modern
enterprises that were overseen by officials and managed by merchants, such as the China Merchants Steam Navigation

Company in 1872; the recipient of official subsidies and bureaucratic protection, this company aimed specifically to compete with foreign steamship lines which at the time monopolized the coastal trade. Officials such as Li Hongzhang (1823–1901), a key commander of one of the anti-Taiping militia armies who became governor-general of the metropolitan province of Zhili from 1870 to 1895, emphasized the importance of economic development and championed the exploitation of mineral resources, the building of railroads, and the establishment of manufacturing industry. Modern coal-mining activity began in 1876, the first telegraph line was erected in 1879 linking Tianjin with the coast, the first railroad began operating from the Kaiping coal mine (opened in 1877) in north China in 1881, and the Shanghai Cotton Cloth Mill began producing machine-manufactured yarn and cloth in 1882.

At the same time the 1870s witnessed a significant change in official perceptions of overseas Chinese who had migrated to Southeast Asia and the Americas. In contrast to previous official attitudes that had equated overseas Chinese with rebels, pirates and traitors who had deserted the embrace of Chinese civilization, Qing officials in the 1870s evinced increasing concern for the plight of their compatriots, particularly that of indentured labourers recruited by westerners in the treaty ports to work in the mines and plantations of Southeast Asia, the British West Indies, Spanish Cuba, Australia and California. A Qing investigation into the living conditions of Chinese indentured labour in Cuba in 1873–4 led to the signing of a treaty with Spain in 1877 and the establishment of a Chinese consulate in Havana. The need to protect Chinese immigrant interests was also an important factor in the creation of China's first permanent diplomatic mission in the US (in 1878) and the subsequent opening of consulates in San Francisco and New York. Chinese embassies were also opened in Britain (1877), Japan (1878) and Russia (1879).

China's military defeats by France in 1885 (in a war contesting influence in Vietnam) and, especially, by Japan ten years later, which consolidated Japanese hegemony in Korea, are often cited as dramatic proof of the failure of self-strengthening. In general, it had been hampered by its uncoordinated nature and lack of long-term planning. Individual projects, for example, were mainly initiated and directed by a few provincial officials who might at any time be transferred or dismissed as a result of factional rivalries at court; such projects were also vulnerable to the vagaries of an inefficient fiscal system. Furthermore, the Empress-Dowager Cixi (who had assumed regency powers on behalf of her nephew, Emperor Guangxu, following the death of her own son, Emperor Tongzhi, in 1875), ever sensitive to the warnings of conservative officials that self-strengthening might undermine the traditional Confucian order, frequently wavered between support for change and defence of the status quo. A pioneering study of the 1860s and the 1870s (Wright 1957) argued that attempts at self-strengthening were ultimately doomed to failure because the requirements for modernization were fundamentally at odds with Confucian assumptions and practice (which, it was argued, had a limited notion of change and disparaged commerce, foreign trade and modern machines).

Since the 1970s studies have moved away from this deterministic assumption that Confucianism and modernization were incompatible, pointing out that other factors such as the impact of western imperialism or structural weaknesses in the economy affected the outcome of self-strengthening, or by taking issue with the view that Confucianism represented a static and homogeneous body of thought (Bailey 1998: 4–13). Recent studies are also less concerned with why the movement 'failed' than with analysing longer-term changes in reform thought, commercial development and modern state-building during the latter half of the nineteenth century.

Crisis and Reform in the 1890s

The 1890s represent a key turning point in the evolution of reform thought, a process that *predated* the western impact from the 1840s onwards. In the early nineteenth century, for example, scholars associated with the School of Practical Statecraft (*jingshi*) proposed a number of administrative reforms and insisted that government be judged by its usefulness and efficiency (Pong 1994: 16). By the 1860s and 1870s concern with the West's growing economic presence in China prompted officials and scholars in their reform proposals to use terms such as *shouhui liquan* (retrieval of economic rights) and *shangzhan* (commercial warfare), which referred to the need for China to compete with the West for economic benefits and to develop industry and commerce so as to drive out foreign economic interests. Some historians (Sigel 1976, 1992; Pong 1985) suggest that this demonstrated the beginnings of an economic or commercial nationalism that anticipated a more widespread nationalism in the early years of the twentieth century when gentry elites, merchants and students denounced the inequities of the unequal treaty system, foreign economic privilege and harsh treatment of their compatriots abroad (Iriye 1967; Wright 1968; Sigel 1985). This commercial nationalism was well illustrated by the writings of Ma Jianzhong (1845–1900), a Chinese Catholic reformer who studied in France in the late 1870s and later became an adviser to Li Hongzhang. Ma championed the increase of exports, development of railroads, and the exploitation of mineral resources in order to retrieve China's 'economic rights' and allow Chinese merchants to compete vigorously with western business; he was also the first to propose the creation of a professionally trained diplomatic service to enhance China's prestige abroad (Bailey 1998).

Other reform-minded scholars from the 1860s such as Feng Guifen (1809–74) called for greater participation by local elites in the administration of their areas (Kuhn 1975), while others such as Wang Tao (1828–97), the first Chinese scholar to spend an extended period in Europe (during the years 1868–70), drew attention to the virtues of western government institutions and practices in harmonizing the interests of rulers and people (Cohen 1974). In the early 1890s a number of reform writings referred positively to representative assemblies and parliaments in the West, as well as raising doubts about the suitability of traditional assumptions underpinning the Sinocentric worldview in an era of modern nation-states (Hao 1969; Hao and Wang 1980).

Two events in the 1890s, however, dramatically enhanced the sense of urgency felt by reformers. The attempt made by the Qing court to reassert its traditional influence in Korea led to conflict with Japan in 1894–5, which resulted in a humiliating defeat. The Treaty of Shimonoseki ending the war conferred on Japan the same privileges enjoyed by the western powers in China, as well as granting Japan the right to establish its own factories in the treaty ports whose products would be exempt from Chinese internal taxes (because of the Most Favoured

Nation Clause this right was automatically extended to the other powers). Furthermore, the island of Taiwan (administratively part of Fujian province) was ceded to Japan and it was to remain a Japanese colony until the end of the Second World War. Japan's dominance in Korea was confirmed and by 1910 the country had been formally annexed as a Japanese colony. All this represented a profound psychological shock for the Chinese scholar-official class long accustomed to viewing Japan in rather condescending terms as a respectful disciple of Chinese culture but now seen to be turning to western models for its modernization programme and participating in the western-imposed treaty system in China (Howland 1996: 1–3). For some scholars, also, defeat by Japan in 1895 graphically illustrated China's marginalization in the world; Liang Qichao (1873–1929), one of the most important thinkers of the early twentieth century, remarked that the war had 'awakened China from a slumber of four thousand years' (Yu 1994: 138).

The other traumatic event of the 1890s was the 'scramble for concessions' in 1897–8, which referred to the acquisition of leased territories (in which Chinese sovereignty was extinguished) along China's coast by the powers in a bid to enhance their political and economic presence and carve out 'spheres of influence'. The Qing court was especially vulnerable at this time since the huge indemnity imposed on it by the Treaty of Shimonoseki had necessitated dependence on foreign loans; the powers increasingly after 1895 were to use such leverage to demand railway and mining concessions. The process began when Germany, reacting to the killing of two German missionaries in Shandong province, coerced the Qing court in 1897 to grant a 99-year lease on the port of Qingdao (in Jiaozhou bay) and its surrounding area in Shandong. At the same time Germany gained the right to build three railroads (one of which would run from the provincial capital, Jinan, to Qingdao) and to exploit mineral resources along the routes. Against the geopolitical background of increasing imperialist rivalry in East Asia, other powers followed suit in demanding leased territories and railway concessions. Thus Russia, which had already in 1896 acquired the right to build a railroad across northern Manchuria (to be known as the Chinese Eastern Railway), obtained a 25-year lease on the Liaodong peninsula in southern Manchuria, as well as the right to construct a southern branch of the Chinese Eastern railway (to be known as the South Manchuria Railway); Britain secured a 25-year lease on Weihaiwei on the north Shandong coast as well as a 99-year lease on the New Territories, which adjoined the Kowloon peninsula (acquired by Britain in 1860 as part of the colony of Hong Kong); and France gained a lease on Guangzhouwan in Guangdong province. The acquisition of these leasehold territories was backed up by mutual agreement amongst the powers. It seemed to many Chinese officials and scholars that the country was about to be 'spliced up like a melon', and fears were expressed that China might become another Poland, which had been partitioned out of existence in the eighteenth century.

A group of radical reformers associated with Kang Youwei (1858–1927), a Cantonese scholar with a strong sense of moral mission, began agitating for fundamental change. Kang had already led a protest movement in 1895, when he and fellow candidates who were in Beijing to take the metropolitan degree examinations submitted a petition expressing their dismay over the terms laid down in the Treaty of Shimonoseki and urging continuation of the war. The petition also stressed the necessity for fundamental reform (Kwong 1984: 85–91). In the late 1880s and 1890s Kang produced a series of writings that radically reinterpreted Confucian teachings in order to justify political and institutional reform. In a work entitled *Kongzi gaizhi kao* (Confucius as an Institutional Innovator) completed in 1897–8, for example, Kang argued that Confucius himself was an innovative and forward-looking visionary (rather than the preserver of past traditions) who would have enthusiastically approved of radical change in order to 'adapt to the times' (Chang 1980: 287–9; Kwong 1984: 108–11). Citing a less mainstream commentary to a key Confucian text, Kang pointed out that Confucius had envisaged a progressive evolution of three eras that would culminate in a utopian world community (*datong*). Kang identified the second of Confucius's three eras (the 'era of approaching peace' in which harmony would prevail between rulers and ruled) with his own and maintained that constitutional monarchy was its political manifestation. In a memorial to the throne submitted at the end of 1897 Kang proposed that all affairs of state be turned over to a parliament for deliberation and decision (Hsiao 1975: 204). Kang's vision of the third and final era, the 'era of universal peace', was described in a utopian work that he began in the 1880s and which was not fully published until after his death in 1935 (Thompson 1958). Reflecting what one historian has referred to as a deeply held and consistent belief in a moral 'universalism' that transcended the national community (Chang 1987: 21–65), Kang portrayed a future world in which all national, racial and gender boundaries had been dissolved; concrete predictions included the establishment of a world government with its own army, the replacement of conventional marriage with renewable one-year 'contracts', the nurture of children in public institutions, and the physical amalgamation of peoples through intermarriage (Thompson 1958).

Some of Kang's followers, including Liang Qichao, had also been able to propagate radical ideas in the central province of Hunan in 1897–8. The provincial governor, Chen Baozhen, supported a number of modernizing projects such as the opening of a Mining Bureau and the construction of a telegraph line; he also sanctioned the establishment of the Academy of Current Affairs (*shiwu xuetang*) in 1897, which combined Chinese and western learning and employed Liang and other reformers as instructors (Lewis 1976: 43–56; Chang 1980: 301–5). The radical atmosphere surrounding the Academy soon aroused the suspicion and then the hostility of the more conservative local gentry elite. Liang, for example, promoted the concept of people's rights (*minquan*), which was linked to his developing notion of a national community (*chun*: lit. 'a grouping together') characterized by collective dynamism, and which represented a moving away from a Confucian cultural worldview and an attack on social hierarchy (Chang 1971: 98–107). Earlier, Liang had also suggested that schools and study associations might form the arenas for public discussion and thus serve as the institutional forerunners of assemblies and parliaments. Interestingly, Liang also suggested at this time (in the wake of Germany's seizure of Qingdao) that Hunan should declare temporary 'independence', thus enabling the province to play a pioneering role in reform and provide the basis for a reinvigorated nation in the future (Esherick 1976: 15). Tan Sitong (1864–98), another radical thinker associated with Kang Youwei, was also in Hunan at this time on an official assignment. Son of a provincial governor, Tan published a work entitled *Renxue* (An Exposition of Benovolence) in 1897 that criticized the social and gender hierarchies espoused by Confucian orthodoxy and espoused a radical egalitarianism that questioned the moral legitimacy of the ruler–subject relationship itself (Chang 1980: 299–300; Kwong 1984: 117–21; Chang 1987: 78–99). Tan's vision, drawing as it did on Buddhist ideas as well as on notions of western science (and implying a comparability of Chinese and western civilizations), was perceived by conservative critics as a dangerous cultural relativism.

By mid-June 1898 the Academy of Current Affairs had been closed down and Kang Youwei's teachings suppressed in the province, ironically at a time when the reform movement was beginning to take off in the capital. One of the long-term consequences of the abortive reform movement in Hunan was a split amongst the gentry elite. The alienation felt by those who had supported radical reform (such as the students at the Academy of Current Affairs) prompted a search for new ways to instigate change, which included militant action in alliance with traditional secret societies (Lewis 1976: 87, 97; Esherick 1976: 21–32) – a tactic that was to be adopted by Sun Yatsen in his anti-dynastic revolutionary movement (see later). The more conservative gentry elite in the province, meanwhile, was to become increasingly involved in a limited modernization programme designed to enhance its political and economic influence (Lewis 1976: 68–9; Esherick 1976: 18–19).

For a brief period in the summer of 1898 (known as 'The One Hundred Days') Kang Youwei and his followers gained direct access to the Guangxu Emperor, who had taken up personal rule in 1889 following the regency of his aunt, Empress-Dowager Cixi. Kang submitted three memorials in 1898 which, unlike those he had drafted earlier, reached the emperor personally. Kang urged the Guangxu Emperor to take bold steps and emulate the nation-building endeavours of Peter the Great in eighteenth-century Russia (Price 1974: 45) as well as the Meiji Emperor in Japan after 1868, and openly proposed the convening of a national assembly and the creation of a Bureau of Government Reorganization to prepare blueprints for administrative reform (Chang 1980: 323). On 11 June the Guangxu Emperor issued an edict declaring his resolve to remedy the dynasty's weaknesses, and on 16 June Kang Youwei had his first personal audience with the emperor. It has been argued that Guangxu's sense of powerlessness under the previous tutelage of Cixi may have bred a certain impulsiveness in his behaviour, and that a chance to amend for the disasters of 1895 and 1897–8 made the emperor particularly susceptible to Kang's proposals (Kwong 1984: 49–53, 58). Kang, even though occupying a minor official position in the capital after recently gaining the metropolitan degree, was now given a special appointment in the Zongli Yamen and allowed to send memorials direct to the emperor. In the ensuing weeks a flurry of reform edicts was issued by the throne calling for the creation of a deliberative assembly, the abolition of sinecure posts in the bureaucracy, the introduction of a modern school system that would incorporate the teaching of 'western' subjects, and the establishment of bureaux of commerce and industry to encourage innovation and enterprise (Chang 1980: 285–7; Spence 1982: 18–21; Kwong 1984: 169–71). By early September Tan Sitong and three other reformers had been appointed as secretaries to the Grand Council.

The reform cause was also publicized by gentry-led study associations (*xuehui*) that emerged in the 1890s (one of which was Kang Youwei's Self-Strengthening Society in 1895) and which represented an increasing public activism amongst local gentry elites begun in the wake of the Taiping Rebellion when they had established and managed semi-official bureaux assisting local administration and overseeing welfare and rehabilitation measures (Rankin 1986; Rowe 1989). These study associations – of which there were a reported seventy-six from 1895 to 1898 – were a new kind of voluntary association designed to mobilize elite patriotism and spread new ideas of western learning and social reform (Chang 1980: 332–3). Such gentry activism was to be even more marked after 1900.

Significantly, too, this period witnessed the beginnings of a political press. During most of the nineteenth century the new-style newspaper press (as opposed to the traditional gazettes issued by the court primarily to inform officials of imperial edicts) had been monopolized by foreigners in the treaty ports, and was designed to promote their religious and commercial interests; even the first (foreign-owned) Chinese language newspapers tended to be digests of trading and shipping news. The first new-style political journals aimed at promoting national self-strengthening and enlightening a wider audience were those published by Kang's Self-Strengthening Society; between 1895 and 1898 approximately sixty such newspapers appeared, many of which were published outside foreign-dominated centres. The number of newspapers increased from 100 in the late 1890s to over 700 by 1911 (Judge 1996: 20–3), thus anticipating the publishing boom of the May Fourth era (see chapter 2). In the words of a recent study this political press, spearheaded by 'cultural entrepreneurs' who saw themselves as mediators between government and the people, constituted a 'new middle realm' of discussion and debate that sought on the one hand to cajole and lobby officialdom in the cause of reform and, on the other, to introduce new political and social concepts (focusing on nation, popular power and public opinion) to a wider audience (ibid.).

The reformers at court, however, were always in a minority – although a recent study has pointed out that a number of Manchu officials were initially sympathetic to reform (Crossley 1990: 167–74) – and Kang Youwei in particular regarded as an upstart scholar seeking to undermine orthodox Confucianism. A hostile conservative reaction encouraged by the Empress-Dowager compelled the hapless Guangxu Emperor to issue an edict on 21 September 'requesting' Cixi to supervise government affairs; this marked Cixi's return to active rule after her 'retirement' in 1889 and the effective end of the One Hundred Days reform movement (Kwong 1984: 211). This was soon followed by the arrest and execution of several reformers (including Tan Sitong), although Kang Youwei and Liang Qichao escaped and eventually found refuge in Japan, where they continued to spearhead a movement 'to protect the emperor' (*baohuang*) and draw attention to the illegitimacy of Cixi's rule (ibid.: 15–16). Guangxu himself was placed under virtual 'house arrest' within the Forbidden City and played no further public role until his death in 1908 (ironically one day before that of the Empress-Dowager). Many of the reform edicts were rescinded, although one innovation survived: in 1898 the court had sanctioned the establishment of an Imperial College on the pattern of western universities (an idea first proposed in 1895). After 1912 it was transformed into Beijing University (*Beida*) and was to become one of the premier higher education institutions in the country.

The 1898 reform movement, although short-lived, was a significant stage in China's modern history – although one study has noted that the role and influence of Kang Youwei himself was much exaggerated by both Kang and his followers in later years (Kwong 1984: 101, 196–200, 228). Unlike the earlier self-strengtheners of the 1870s and 1880s, the aims of the 1898 reformers had focused on changing the nature of the bureaucracy itself (and, at least as far as Kang Youwei was concerned, encouraging a more activist role for the emperor) rather than implementing change through existing bureaucratic channels (Howard 1969: 7–8). In a wider sense the 1890s had also demonstrated a disillusionment with established institutions, introduced the concepts of representative government and popular sovereignty, and engendered a new journalism (ibid.: 14). Furthermore, one historian notes that in looking to western ideas of international law and relations and emphasizing the importance of protecting China's rights as a sovereign nation, Kang Youwei and his followers introduced a new approach to international affairs (through, for example, the establishment of institutions that would regulate or pre-empt future economic encroachments), described as a 'nationalistic foreign policy' (Schrecker 1969: 43–53). Such an outlook differed from earlier approaches that either sought to exercise some measure of control over foreign activity in China (by playing off the powers against one another or granting a role to foreigners in administration such as the Maritime Customs Service) or to reject any western innovations completely (except perhaps in the area of military technology) in the cause of preserving a 'pure' Confucian way of life (ibid.).

The Boxer Uprising

With the Empress-Dowager and her diehard conservative supporters controlling policy at court, a disastrous decision was taken in 1900 to support the activities of the Boxers (*yihe-quan*), groups of peasants practising martial arts, invulnerability rituals and mass spirit possession who attacked the foreign presence in China. Such a phenomenon had originated in the northwestern region of Shandong province in the spring of 1898 and subsequently spread to the metropolitan province of Zhili. Although an earlier view of Boxer origins (which drew on the observations of some contemporary Chinese officials) stressed the movement's links with a centuries-old sectarian tradition, recent studies (Esherick 1987; Cohen 1997) have emphasized its roots specifically in the popular culture of the north China plain and the socio-political context out of which it grew and expanded.

Shandong province was a notoriously poor agricultural region, susceptible to natural disasters such as drought and floods (in August 1898, for example, the Yellow River burst its banks resulting in the inundation of 3,000 square miles of farmland in the northwest part of the province) (Esherick 1987: 179). It was also an area indirectly affected by the Sino-Japanese War of 1894–5; on the one hand, troops were withdrawn from the province to fight on the front further north thus leaving a dangerous vacuum in the interior, and on the other, once the war was over, demobilization led to many of these same troops joining an increasingly unstable 'floating' population. The opening of Yantai (Chefoo) on the Shandong coast as a treaty port in 1862 had also exposed some areas of the province to competition from foreign imports such as cotton yarn, which adversely affected handicraft spinning (ibid.: 69–70).

More significantly, perhaps, Shandong witnessed increasingly aggressive Catholic missionary activity in the 1890s. The privileges gained by missionaries as a result of treaties imposed on the Qing by Britain and France in 1858 and 1860 (the right to own land and proselytize in the interior, and the enjoyment of extra-territoriality) had led to constant friction as missionaries appropriated land and destroyed native temples to build churches, and polarized village communities by using their influence (often backed up with the threat of force) to support and protect their converts in disputes with non-Christians as well as encouraging them to desist from participating in 'idolatrous' community festivals and rituals (Litzinger 1996: 41–52). In their educational and charitable work missionaries also directly competed with, and aroused the hostility of, local elites long accustomed to being involved in such areas of public life (in 1899, also, Catholic missionaries secured the right to be awarded official Chinese rank and thus were able to present themselves as the 'equals' of provincial and local officials).

German Catholics in Shandong (who established a new mission there in 1880) were particularly active since both they, and subsequently the German government itself, were keen to contest France's monopolistic control over Catholic activity in China (which included the role of sole protector of all Catholic missionaries) secured by the 1860 treaty (Schrecker 1971: 11–13). By 1895–6 a group known as the Big Swords Society (*dadao hui*), originally a self-protective organization led by landlords and wealthy peasants that co-operated with local officials in suppressing banditry, was actively involved in attacks on local Chinese Christians in southwest Shandong (Esherick 1987: 86–122). In the same way that conflict between locals and converts in other parts of China often originated in secular disputes (Sweeten 1996: 31–6), such attacks were as much to do with land disputes (e.g. tenants might convert to resist paying rent) or with the fact that bandits often claimed Catholic membership in order to escape suppression, than with hostility to Chinese Christians as such. Nevertheless, it was in this region that two German missionaries were killed in November 1897, thus providing the German government with the pretext to demand the cession of the Jiaozhou leasehold (it is interesting to note, however, that the Imperial German Navy had specifically marked out Jiaozhou bay as a suitable area for German occupation in 1896) (Schrecker 1971: 23–31).

Since the Big Swords were under the control of the landlord elite with close ties to local officialdom, they were easily dispersed once the decision was taken (under foreign pressure) to clamp down on their activities. Conflict between Chinese Christians and non-Christians, however, also broke out in the northwest of the province in 1898. It was here that a group originally known as the Spirit Boxers (*shenquan*) emerged; in contrast to the Big Swords, who claimed invulnerability to bullets through martial arts techniques and other rituals, the Spirit Boxers claimed such invulnerability through a form of mass spirit possession (*jiangshen futi*), by which individuals were possessed by gods drawn from popular opera (such as the Monkey King). In a sense, Boxers saw themselves as acting out the gods' righteous and heroic battles against deadly foes that were frequently portrayed in these popular operas. By mid-1899 the Spirit Boxers had changed their name to Boxers United in Righteousness (*yihequan*) and had adopted the slogan *fuqing mieyang* (uphold the Qing and destroy the foreigner). Since villages in this region were less cohesive and lacked a strong landlord/gentry presence (which facilitated the spread of heterodox beliefs and practices that had traditionally been pervasive in Shandong) (Esherick 1987: 38–46) these particular

Boxer groups were less amenable to official control; earlier attempts by the provincial governor to enrol them in local militia organization had failed, and although some of the original leaders were executed at the end of 1899 new leaders soon emerged and the movement continued to expand. Paradoxically, it was able to expand easily and quickly because it did not have a tightly organized hierarchical structure, mainly due to the fact that every individual could in theory experience spirit possession. Esherick (ibid.: 63–7) has also argued that precisely because many of the Boxers' heterodox practices were rooted in the popular culture of north China they could be accepted by large numbers of peasants, thus facilitating the spread of the movement.

A typical Boxer unit comprised 25 to 100 individuals in a village, practising their martial arts and other rituals at a 'boxing ground' (*quanchang*) invariably located near the site of temple fairs and village markets and where popular operas were performed. Since in northwest Shandong villages were home to a considerable floating population, such itinerants would often establish boxing grounds on returning to their home villages. Each unit was headed by a Senior Brother Disciple (*da shixiong*), but there was no established hierarchy of Boxer units. Interestingly, by the spring of 1900 unmarried teenage girls had also been incorporated into the movement. Known as the Red Lanterns (*hongdengzhao*), they formed separate detachments who, because of their magical powers (they could walk on water and fly through the air, as well as causing fires to break out), provided assistance to the Boxers by apparently gathering intelligence on the foreigners and destroying their buildings (Esherick 1987: 231–2; Cohen 1997: 39, 127–41). That the failure of Boxer magic (such as invulnerability to bullets) was often attributed to the 'polluting' influence of Chinese Christian and foreign women, however, clearly illustrated the persistence of traditional male anxieties over the effects of women's perceived powers.

By early 1900 Boxer groups had spread northwards into the metropolitan province of Zhili, and in May of that year had begun attacking the Beijing–Baoding and Beijing–Tianjin railway lines. They comprised for the most part itinerant poor peasants, particularly young males made idle as a result of a recent drought in the north (Esherick 1987: 235–6; Cohen 1997:

34–5, 68–77). In an atmosphere of fear, anxiety and suspicion the Boxers claimed that the drought was a manifestation of the gods' anger over the pervasive foreign influence and its undermining of indigenous customs and beliefs (Elvin 1996: 206–11); in early 1900 a missionary noted a Boxer placard as declaring:

> On account of the Protestant and Catholic religions, the Buddhist gods are oppressed and the sages thrust into the background. . . . The anger of Heaven and Earth has been aroused and the timely rain has consequently been withheld from us. But Heaven is now sending down eight million spiritual soldiers to extirpate these foreign religions, and when this has been done there will be a timely rain. (Esherick 1987: 282)

In such an atmosphere the targets of Boxer attacks soon widened to include not only missionaries, Chinese Christian converts and the visible signs of the foreign presence such as churches and railway lines – which were also condemned for destabilizing the unseen forces that guaranteed the natural harmony of the environment (known as *fengshui*, lit. 'wind and water') – but also many non-Christian Chinese suspected of having anything to do with the foreigners. A strict taboo was also placed on foreign articles and names.

The Boxer movement has interestingly been placed in a wider historical context, with one study (ibid.: 316–17) comparing it to the late-nineteenth century resistance by the Lakota Sioux (in the northern territory of the Dakotas, USA) against the white man's appropriation of their land and slaughter of the buffalo herds. Like the Boxers, the Lakota Sioux used invulnerabilty rituals (focused on the Ghost Dance and wearing of the Ghost shirt) with the aim of eliminating an alien presence and restoring a previous way of life. Another study (Wasserstrom 1987) compares the Boxers with early nineteenth-century English Luddites – weavers who destroyed new machinery. The targets of attack in both cases (western Christianity in the case of the Boxers, power looms in the case of the Luddites) were viewed as alien and disruptive presences, and both saw themselves as defending values and traditions held dear by their local communities. Finally, in the Chinese context, a number of intriguing parallels have been suggested between aspects of the Boxer movement and the Cultural Revolution in the 1960s

(Elvin 1996: 225–6). In both cases initial support from elements at the top was crucial, scapegoats for perceived crisis (in an atmosphere of near hysteria) were conjured up and targeted for attack, confidence was evinced in the willpower of the masses, rituals (in the case of the Boxers) and ideology (in the case of Mao Zedong Thought in the Cultural Revolution) were invested with magical qualities and held out the promise of superhuman achievement, enthusiastic youth were at the forefront, and, once unleashed, the mass movement became difficult to control.

When the foreign ministers in Beijing decided in May 1900 to reinforce their legations by calling up troops from the coast, thus exceeding the number of legation guards permitted, Cixi and her supporters became increasingly sympathetic to the Boxers. In any event, Cixi's earlier ambivalence demonstrated by her instructions to officials in January to distinguish clearly between 'sincere' martial arts practitioners and unlawful bandits had provided scope for continued Boxer activity. With Boxer units pouring into Beijing itself in May and June tension increased; an international force that left Tianjin for Beijing (without Qing authorization) was attacked and forced to retreat by both regular Qing troops and Boxers. On 20 June the legations in Beijing were besieged and the following day Cixi issued a declaration of war against the powers. The Boxers were formally enlisted in the militia under the command of Manchu princes, although relations between Boxers and local authorities were not always smooth. The attempt, however, by the court to use Boxer units in its resistance against the foreign powers has been cited by one historian as an example of 'conservative radicalism', i.e. faith in the power of the mobilized masses (under suitable control) to overcome adverse objective circumstances (in this case, the technological superiority of the foreign powers). Ironically, 'the first attempt at mass mobilization in modern Chinese history was thus the work of reactionaries' (Elvin 1996: 220–1).

It was indicative of the dynasty's inability to impose its will on the rest of the country, however, that the declaration of war was not supported by a number of provincial governors, particularly in the south. Anxious to avoid disorder and military catastrophe, governors such as Zhang Zhidong (1837–1909) in the Yangzi region negotiated informal agreements with foreign diplomatic representatives on the spot which avoided the spread of conflict through the guaranteed protection of foreign lives and property. In Shandong province, too, where Yuxian (who had been relatively tolerant of the Boxers) had been replaced as governor by Yuan Shikai (1859–1916) in December 1899, agreement was reached to prevent foreign intervention. Yuan's strict clampdown on Boxer activity, in fact, had been one of the contributory factors in the Boxers' move into Zhili. Boxer-related violence and disorder did, however, spread to the northeast (Manchuria) and to the west in Shanxi province.

The siege of the legations was eventually lifted when an allied expeditionary force of 20,000 men (mainly comprising Japanese, Russian and Indian troops under British command) entered Beijing in the middle of August 1900. The day before foreign troops entered the city the court had fled westwards to Xian (Shaanxi province), the second time it was forced to do so in the wake of foreign invasion (the other time being in 1860 when British and French troops occupied Beijing). The humiliation of the dynasty seemed complete, graphically confirmed by the terms of the Boxer Protocol of September 1901. A number of officials deemed responsible by the powers for encouraging and supporting the Boxers were executed (such as Yuxian, the former governor of Shandong and current governor of Shanxi, where many missionaries and their converts had been killed) or sentenced to internal exile. The court also had to send official missions of apology to Germany and Japan for the killings of the German minister and Japanese legation secretary in Beijing by Qing soldiers on the eve of the siege. The number of foreign legation guards was increased, and foreign troops were to be stationed between Beijing and the coast, a strip of territory that became a virtual no-go area for Qing military forces. The powers also insisted that local gentry elites be punished and in some areas the civil service examinations were postponed for five years.

Perhaps the most significant aspect of the Protocol was the imposition on the Qing government of a huge indemnity of 450 million *taels* (US$333 million), to be paid in 39 annual installments along with 4 per cent annual interest on the unpaid principal. The indemnity was divided among the powers in accordance with the amount of property destroyed and numbers of nationals killed (the main beneficiaries were Russia with 29 per cent, Germany 20 per cent, France 15.75 per cent, Britain 11.25 per cent, Japan 7.7 per cent, and the US with 7.3 per cent). It was later admitted by the US government that its claim for damages (US$25 million) had been overstated by nearly US$14 million. The excess was remitted to the Qing government in 1908 on the understanding that it be used to finance Chinese overseas study in the US (in the negotiations over its possible use Qing officials had argued that the decision should be left to the Qing government itself) (Hunt 1972). Such use of Boxer indemnity funds was perceived in Washington as an ideal way to enhance US cultural and economic influence in China, as well as confirming in the minds of many American politicians, educators and missionaries that the US pursued a uniquely altruistic policy towards China (in contrast to the self-interested policies of the other imperial powers). This 'special relationship', as it came to be seen in the US, had supposedly been earlier demonstrated by the Open Door Notes that Washington had sent to the other powers in 1899 and 1900. Although calling on the powers to respect China's territorial integrity, the motivation behind the Notes was as much to do with ensuring that no one power use its sphere of influence in China to gain monopolistic economic benefits at the expense of the other powers (Hunt 1983: 153, 198). It might also be noted that 'special relationship' rhetoric notwithstanding, it was precisely at this time (from 1882 on) that the US government, responding to increasing hostility to Chinese immigrants amongst white workers (especially in California), passed a series of draconian immigration laws (known as the Exclusion Acts) specifically aimed at eliminating Chinese immigration to the US altogether – and which were not to be repealed until 1943 (ibid.: 76–94; Tsai 1983: 67–98).

The impact of the Boxer uprising had three major consequences. First, it demonstrated to the powers the dangers inherent in excessive demands, while the disorder and chaos in its wake confirmed that dismemberment of the Qing empire was not in the powers' interests. Second, given the fact that the Boxer indemnity represented four times the government's annual revenue and that annual payments would constitute one-fifth of the national budget (Esherick 1987: 311), the dynasty after 1901 was compelled to seek new sources of domestic revenue; in so doing it contributed to the beginnings of modern state-building (Duara 1988: 1–2; Cohen 1997: 55–6). Such efforts were, in fact, part of a wider programme of reform called for by the court in January 1901 and designed to shore up the foundations of dynastic authority in the wake of the disasters of 1900 (which included the refusal of southern governors-general to obey the court's war declaration and the outbreak of a number of abortive revolts in central and southern China during the spring and summer associated with reformers such as Kang Youwei and revolutionaries such as Sun Yatsen). Third, the Boxer uprising proved to be a traumatic shock for most of the scholar-gentry class, who saw in Boxer beliefs and rituals dramatic proof of the essentially 'backward' nature of the ordinary people and their 'superstitious' culture. The perceived need to 'reform' the masses and 'improve' popular culture was to be an important motivation for gentry support of educational reform after 1901 (Bailey 1990: 64–6).

It was not only in the minds of the scholar-gentry that the Boxers conjured up images of irrational and abnormal behaviour. 'Boxerism' entered the English language at this time as a synonym for dangerous xenophobia and 'oriental barbarity', and helped perpetuate stereotypical western images of the 'Yellow Peril' that had taken root at the end of the nineteenth century (with public hostility in North America to Chinese immigrants), and which persisted throughout the twentieth century in popular literature and film. It should be noted, however, that during the foreign occupation of Beijing (1900–1) considerable looting and pillaging occurred. Allied forces (now joined by British, French, German and Italian troops) also marched on surrounding cities and towns, ordering the execution of local officials and destroying city walls, gates and temples. Missionaries (mainly British and American) often supported such action, regarding it as divine punishment for the deaths of their colleagues and families during the uprising. This 'symbolic warfare', as it has been described (Hevia 1992), was a deliberate attempt to undermine the symbols of Chinese sovereignty and negate imputed indigenous beliefs; other examples of such 'symbolic warfare' included foreign troops marching through the hallowed precincts of the Forbidden City, the removal of imperial thrones, and the bivouacking of foreign troops at the Temples of Agriculture and Heaven (where emperors traditionally carried out important legitimizing rituals). In many ways, contemporary missionary accounts with their graphic portrayal of Boxer atrocities, Christian suffering and self-sacrifice, and ultimate retribution helped define in the minds of their Anglo-American audience what the Boxer uprising had represented and the nature of the West's 'noble enterprise' in China (ibid.: 325).

On the Chinese side, recent studies (Wasserstrom 1987; Cohen 1992, 1997) have shown that the symbolic and historiographical 'afterlives' of the Boxers in the twentieth century were to remain a 'contested terrain'; according to the political and cultural agenda of the time, they were either condemned or praised. Thus for radical intellectuals during the May Fourth Movement of the late 1910s, which critiqued traditional culture and promoted the benefits of 'rational' science and western notions of individualism (see chapter 2), the Boxers represented an irrational and superstitious anti-foreignism, a view adopted by the modernizing Guomindang (Nationalist Party) in the 1920s and 1930s. The Chinese Communist Party (CCP) in the 1920s, on the other hand, adopted a more positive view of the Boxers as dedicated patriots and anti-imperialists; such a heroic 'mythology' became dominant after the establishment of the communist-ruled People's Republic of China in 1949, and especially during the Cultural Revolution in the late 1960s and early 1970s. Only since the death of Mao Zedong in 1976, after which the CCP embarked on market reforms and more extensive interaction with the capitalist world, have the Boxers once again been derided as the symbols of backwardness and ignorance (Cohen 1997: 217–19, 224–34, 261–81).

Twilight Years of the Qing: State-building and Socio-cultural Change

With the signing of the Protocol, the allied forces finally evacuated Beijing in September 1901, although Russian troops that had entered the northeast (Manchuria) in the wake of the Boxer disturbances there did not leave until 1903. The court returned to Beijing from its internal exile in January 1902, and a chastened Cixi now decided to support a programme of political, educational and military reforms, many of which echoed the proposals of the 1898 reformers (although perhaps with different aims in mind). As noted earlier, an imperial edict in the names of both the Guangxu Emperor and Empress-Dowager Cixi had been issued in January 1901 bewailing the plight of the empire and promising to implement institutional reform (Bastid 1988: 3). During the course of the next few years new government ministries such as the *Waiwu bu* (Foreign Affairs Ministry) were created (Ichiko 1980: 375), the civil service examinations were abolished and replaced by a national system of modern schools, study overseas (especially in Japan) was encouraged, a nine-year constitutional programme was inaugurated with the eventual aim of establishing a national parliament, and the first steps were taken to build a unified and well-equipped national army; other, less well-known, reform measures during the last years of the dynasty included the first attempts to unify the currency and weights/measures, to bring about financial and budgetary centralization, and to begin drafting new civil, criminal and commercial legal codes (ibid.: 403–10). As will be discussed later, many of these reforms, known as *xinzheng* (new policies) and designed to strengthen dynastic rule and co-opt the support of the gentry elites, were to backfire on the dynasty and ultimately hasten its downfall.

Of equal significance, however, was the fact that the last decade of the Qing witnessed considerable socio-cultural change that transcended the disappearance of the imperial monarchy; some of these changes were the result of the institutional reforms, while others represented a progression of trends that had begun in the latter half of the nineteenth century (Bastid 1980). These long-term changes included the emergence of an industrial proletariat, growing cleavages amongst traditional elites, and the increasing importance of nationalism demonstrated by heightened sensitivity amongst a wider constituency to encroachments on, or slights to, national sovereignty.

Although China's first modern industrial workers were those employed by foreigners in repair workshops and dockyard maintenance in the treaty ports (and Hong Kong) after 1840, as well as those employed in the arsenals, dockyards and mines established by self-strengthening officials from the 1860s to 1880s, it was not until after the Sino-Japanese War of 1894–5 that a more substantial increase in the industrial workforce occurred. This was because the Treaty of Shimonoseki that concluded the war, in addition to granting Japan privileges already held by the other imperial powers, bestowed on Japan the right to establish manufacturing enterprises in the treaty ports (a right that was automatically extended to the other imperial powers on the basis of the Most Favoured Nation Clause). It was to be in these foreign-owned modern factories, as well as in later Chinese-run enterprises, in the treaty ports (especially in Shanghai) that the beginnings of an industrial proletariat can be detected. Overall, numbers grew from 100,000 in 1894 to 661,000 in 1912 (Bastid 1980: 572); mostly non-skilled, of recent rural origin and divided by native-place ties, this proletariat was still only a small proportion of the total working population (perhaps about 1 per cent). Nevertheless, 47 strikes (36 in Shanghai) occurred between 1900 and 1910, mostly in protest against low wages and the arbitrary nature of the contract system, whereby workers were recruited by, and beholden to, labour 'bosses' employed by the factories (ibid.: 574), and by the late 1910s and 1920s industrial workers were becoming increasingly involved in labour militance and political movements.

Just as changing economic conditions contributed to the emergence of a nascent proletariat, so they produced cleavages amongst the traditional gentry elite as some became increasingly urban-oriented, functionally differentiated and involved full-time in modern enterprises rather than seeking (or remaining in) bureaucratic posts (Rankin and Esherick 1990: 335–6). Some historians have referred to such a group as a new 'hybrid' class of gentry-merchants or 'commercial gentry' (Bastid 1980: 557; Bastid 1988: 15–17) and in fact the term *shenshang* (gentry-merchant) had become quite common by the end of the nineteenth century, although social and cultural fusion of merchant and gentry elites had occurred in some commercialized regions by the end of the eighteenth century (Rankin and Esherick 1990: 331). This commercial gentry not only invested in and managed modern enterprises, but also actively participated in the new chambers of commerce sanctioned by the court in 1904. At the same time, the reforms implemented by the dynasty had two long-term consequences. First, they eroded the status monopoly traditionally held by the Confucian educated scholar-official as commerce, the military and modern education became alternative channels for acquiring prestige and achieving social mobility. Second, they further stimulated public activism amongst gentry elites that had become especially evident during the latter half of the nineteenth century; during the last decade of the Qing such activist gentry were to expand their public roles at local, provincial and even national levels.

The incipient economic nationalism some historians have perceived as underpinning many self-strengthening projects and proposals during the latter half of the nineteenth century (see earlier) became more widespread in the last years of the dynasty as a wider constituency that included officials, gentry, merchants and students became increasingly sensitive to issues involving national sovereignty and assumed the right to pronounce on foreign affairs. This was manifested in several ways. Gentry and merchants, for example, campaigned for the return of railroad and mining concessions granted to foreign investors in what was known as the Rights Recovery Movement (Wright 1968; Chan 1977: 127–32). Between 1895 and 1913 549 Chinese-owned private and semi-official manufacturing and mining enterprises were founded (238 in the 1905–8 period) (Esherick 1976: 70–1). In this endeavour gentry and merchants had the support of provincial governors, whose administration now comprised bureaux of foreign affairs, mining and railways. One of the most powerful provincial officials in the early years of the twentieth century was Zhang Zhidong, a proponent of what one historian has described as 'bureaucratic nationalism' (Bays 1978: 3). A founder of modern enterprises (such as ironworks and textile mills) in the 1880s and 1890s, Zhang, as governor-general of Hunan and Hubei, mobilized gentry and merchant support in 1904–5 to recover the concession rights to build the Guangzhou–Hankou railroad originally granted to the American China Development Company but which had been taken over by Belgian interests and their French and Russian backers; since these same interests held the concession to build the rest of the railroad from Hankou to Beijing, Zhang feared a potential foreign monopoly of north–south communications (ibid.: 166). By June 1905 Zhang had secured a redemption of the concession (although only with the assistance of a loan from the Hong Kong government), an achievement that has been described as a victory for Chinese sovereignty (ibid.: 176–7). Although many of these 'rights recovery' enterprises later failed or fell under foreign control after 1910, it was the dynasty's attempt in May 1911 to take over (with the aid of a foreign loan) the remaining provincial railway companies founded in the wake of the Rights Recovery movement that sparked off the revolution.

In Shandong officials were able to blunt Germany's efforts to utilize its leasehold territory of Qingdao and railway–mining concessions granted in 1898 to expand its political and economic influence in the province (Schrecker 1971: 140–91). Thus Chinese control was retained over postal and telegraphic facilities along the Qingdao–Jinan railway and Germany's mining monopoly in the railway zone had been abolished by 1911. The Qing government also attempted, unsuccessfully, to reduce Japanese influence in Manchuria by inviting US participation in the region's economic development, a prospect that was not to be fulfilled once the US government reached an agreement with Japan in 1908 that recognized the latter's interests in the region (Hunt 1973); the Qing did, however, reorganize the region in 1907 as three regular provinces (Fengtian, Jilin and Heilongjiang) and encouraged Chinese settlement – the population of Jilin, for example, had grown to nearly four million by 1911, five times its level in 1897 (Bastid 1980: 583). The Qing was more successful in its last years in ending the opium trade (Wright 1968; Trocki 1999: 128–31). In 1906 an agreement with Britain pledged China to end domestic opium cultivation and use, and Britain to end its exports of Indian opium to China within ten years. Despite foreign scepticism considerable success was achieved in stamping out domestic opium cultivation; the Mongol bannerman, Xi Liang, for example, who was governor-general of Sichuan (1903–7) and Yunnan-Guizhou (1907–9), managed to eliminate opium cultivation altogether in these provinces (Des Forges 1973: 93–102). Such success compelled Britain in 1909 to uphold its part of the treaty and to phase out opium exports over the next seven years; the last shipment of Indian opium destined for China set sail in February 1913, although there was to be a resurgence of domestic opium cultivation with the advent of warlord rule in the late 1910s and 1920s.

Finally, the last years of the Qing witnessed greater public involvement in protest movements as a result of perceived foreign slights to Chinese sovereignty or prestige. Thus in 1905 gentry, merchants and students organized an anti-American boycott (mainly in Shanghai and Guangzhou) to protest against the ill-treatment and discrimination experienced by Chinese immigrants in the US (Hunt 1983: 237–9; Tsai 1983: 106–10). During the boycott Chinese doctors refused to buy American medicine and consumers smoked Chinese-manufactured cigarettes (Cochran 1980: 46–8); women, also, played a role when they refused to buy mooncakes (made with American flour) traditionally consumed at the mid-autumn Moon Festival and instead made their own ricecakes (Tsai 1983: 107). The anti-American boycott – eventually brought to an end by anxious officials after several months – was significant not only because it demonstrated the emergence of a 'public opinion' making its voice heard in foreign affairs (Iriye 1967), but also because it revealed a wider concern and identification with the plight of overseas Chinese (seen now as 'compatriots'). It might be noted here that the Qing government, in line with its changing perception of overseas Chinese, now actively courted overseas Chinese merchant communities (especially in Southeast Asia), encouraging wealthy entrepreneurs to invest in enterprises back home and awarding them honorific titles (Godley 1981). Another trade boycott occurred in 1908, this time targeted against Japan. When the Qing government acceded to Japan's demand for an apology and financial compensation following the seizure of a Japanese ship by Chinese officials on suspicion of gun-running, Hong Kong dockers refused to unload Japanese ships and a trade boycott was organized throughout the Pearl River Delta in southern Guangdong (Rhoads 1975: 136). The use of the trade boycott was to become a highly visible weapon in the armoury of a mass nationalism that developed in the 1910s and 1920s to denounce the actions and policies of the imperial powers in China.

Political, social and cultural change was also stimulated by the dynasty's reforms (Ichiko 1980). At the core of this reform programme was the attempt to create a constitutional form of government comprising provincial assemblies and a national parliament. By the end of the nineteenth century scholar-reformers had begun to identify constitutionalism as the source of national unity, wealth and strength in the West. Yan Fu (1854–1921), who studied naval seamanship in England during the late 1870s and later translated Adam Smith's *The Wealth of Nations* and John Stuart Mill's *On Liberty*, went even further and argued that individual liberty itself in the West had been the essential prerequisite for the achievement of *national* power and prosperity (Schwartz 1964). Some historians (Kuhn 1975; Min 1989) have also pointed out, however, that the debate over constitutionalism at this time also drew on an indigenous ideal which had in the past been contrasted with the practice of centralized bureaucratic rule. Referred to as *fengjian* (lit. 'enfeoffment') and originally describing feudal arrangements in China's early history, the term had increasingly been used by scholars after the seventeenth century to describe a system of rule in which local gentry would participate officially in the administration of their home districts and one of their number would be district magistrate (centrally appointed magistrates, according to the 'law of avoidance', were always non-natives so as to pre-empt the possibility that local interests might override loyalty to the centre). Just as *fengjian* proponents argued that such a system would enhance communication between the monarch and rank-and-file scholar gentry and thereby improve government efficiency, so Huang Zunxian (1848–1905), a diplomat and reformer who introduced the concept of *difang zizhi* (local self-government) from the Japanese in the 1890s, and Kang Youwei, who subsequently popularized the notion in his writings, argued that the activism and dynamism engendered by locally elected assemblies (although with a limited franchise) would contribute to the building of a powerful state (Kuhn 1975: 272–5; Strand 1995: 412).

The attraction of constitutionalism and its perceived link with national power was given a further boost with Japan's victory in the Russo-Japanese War of 1904–5. As the first defeat of a western power by an Asian nation, Japan's victory was a source of inspiration for Asian nationalists (such as in French Indochina). In another sense, however, it was perceived in China as the victory of constitutionalism over autocracy. In 1889 the Meiji Emperor in Japan had promulgated a constitution providing for a national Diet that complemented deliberative assemblies at prefectural, town and village levels already created in 1879–80. For Qing officials, therefore, Japan's victory clearly demonstrated the benefits of constitutional government in cementing unity between ruler and people and laying the foundation for the creation of a wealthy and militarily powerful state. It should be noted, however, that the concrete results of Japan's victory did not bode well as far as China was concerned. Japan had gone to war in 1904 in response to a perceived Russian threat to its dominant presence in Korea, but the Treaty of Portsmouth (1905) ending the war not only confirmed Japanese hegemony in Korea, but also sanctioned Japan's takeover of Russia's leasehold territory on the Liaodong peninsula in southern Manchuria (known in Japanese as the Kwantung leasehold), as well as the Russian-owned South Manchuria Railway – both of which had originally been granted to Russia by the Qing government in 1898. For the first time Japan had a military and political presence on the Chinese mainland, and in subsequent years sought actively to expand its interests and presence in the region (see chapter 4).

Not long after the Russo-Japanese War the Qing dynasty sent official missions abroad to investigate political conditions in Japan and the West (Ichiko 1980: 388–402), although it had already been decided to implement a constitution – the only questions being how and when (Meienberger 1980: 39–40). After the return of the missions in 1906, an imperial edict was issued proclaiming the need to establish constitutional government. At the same time the recently established boards of foreign affairs (1901), trade (1903) and police (1905) were transformed into western-style government ministries (unlike the traditional central government boards, such ministries were to have only one president and no differentiation was to be made between Manchu and Han Chinese). In 1908 plans for a nine-year 'preparation' programme were formulated (Fincher 1981: 80). Deliberative provincial assemblies were to be established in 1909 and a National Assembly to be convened in 1910 (with half its membership appointed by the throne, and the other half selected by the provincial assemblies). The crowning point of the programme would be the setting up of a national parliament in 1917 based on nationwide elections.

Provision was also made for the gradual implementation of local self-government in 1909, which would entail the establishment of elected councils (electors and those eligible to be elected could be any literate, tax-paying male over 24 who had resided in the area for at least three years) at district and township levels; 5,000 such councils had been elected by the time the dynasty fell in 1911, even though the official regulations had stated that the first councils were not to be elected until 1912–13 (Thompson 1995: 86, 110). The dynasty drew on measures already introduced by provincial officials. Thus as early as 1902 Zhao Erxun, the governor of Shanxi province, had proposed grouping villages or small towns under a chosen local headman to allow for more local participation by rural elites in administration (ibid.: 23–9), while in 1907 Yuan Shikai, governor-general of Zhili, sanctioned the creation of an elected municipal council in Tianjin (Fincher 1981: 41). Official sanction of local self-government was largely driven by the need to involve gentry and merchant elites in the management of new public facilities and institutions. Thus in Shanghai, municipal self-government first appeared in the form of the General Works Board (*zong'-gong ju*) in 1905 to oversee road maintenance, the supply of electricity and the direction of a police force. Combining executive and legislative roles, the Board comprised fifty degree-holding gentry and merchant members of the Shanghai Chamber of Commerce. In 1907 voting rights for the Board were extended to residents of five years' standing who paid a certain amount in local taxes (Elvin 1969).

For the Qing dynasty such a constitutional form of government was in no way meant to encroach on imperial sovereignty. Inspired by the Japanese example, the Qing constitutional blueprint accorded the emperor the power to convoke and dissolve parliament, approve laws and appoint ministers; furthermore, although parliament was to draft laws and advise the emperor, and could impeach ministers, it was not to have any role in military or foreign affairs, which remained the prerogative of the emperor (Ichiko 1980: 397; Meienberger 1980: 82–7). One historian, however, has pointed out that the 1908 programme marked a fundamental break in perceptions of the monarchy, as a constitutional definition of imperial authority now replaced more traditional beliefs concerning its religious and sacred nature (Bastid 1987). Such a break was the culmination of changing official attitudes that *predated* the early twentieth-century debate on the need to establish a constitution because of external pressures. A series of succession crises after 1861 had led to less emphasis being placed on the ritual aspects of monarchy and a growing acceptance that imperial authority was not one and indivisible – between 1861 and 1873, for example, there was collective rule by two empress-dowagers acting as regents for the young Tongzhi Emperor, while after 1889 imperial authority was virtually shared by the Guangxu Emperor and his aunt, Empress-Dowager Cixi, even though she had formally 'retired' as regent when the emperor attained his majority (Kwong 1984: 17–28). By the end of the nineteenth century imperial authority was increasingly perceived as an instrument of state and as a rational political institution, assumptions that were given a statutory basis in the 1908 constitutional programme (Bastid 1987: 180–3).

In the final analysis the Qing constitutional programme was aimed at co-opting the support of gentry elites – expressed in the oft-repeated rationale for a constitution that it would 'make ruler and people of one mind' (*shangxia yixin*) and shore up the foundations of dynastic rule; it was also anticipated that provincial assemblies would counter the influence of provincial governors. The dynasty's hopes notwithstanding, the experiment with the provincial assemblies was to have quite different consequences. Although the 1909 elections for these assemblies (the first in Chinese history, held in two phases with candidates elected from each district subsequently choosing assemblymen from among their own number) were based on a restricted franchise (with the vote limited to resident males over 25 years of age with educational qualifications and/or possessing a certain amount of capital or property), it has been estimated that about one million out of an eligible electorate of 1.7 million (i.e. 0.4 per cent of the total population) voted (Ichiko 1980: 398–400; Fincher 1981: 112–15). Most of those elected were members of the traditional degree-holding elite and the majority of assembly chairmen were holders of the *jinshi*, the highest degree in the traditional civil service examinations. These men viewed the assemblies (designed principally as advisory bodies) as a platform to widen and legitimize their involvement in public affairs; almost immediately the assemblies clashed with provincial governors over budgetary matters and asserted the right to pronounce on Qing foreign policy, criticizing the court's inability to stem the tide of foreign economic encroachment in China (Esherick 1976: 99–100). The Fujian provincial assembly passed resolutions restricting foreigners' rights to own property outside the treaty ports, while the assemblies in Hunan and Hubei condemned the use of foreign loans to build railways (Fincher 1981: 133–6). A study of Hunan and Hubei provinces during this period has argued that the assemblies were the institutional expression of the political power of an 'urban reformist elite' – although progressive and nationalist in championing social reform and indigenous economic development, they were also thoroughly elitist, fearful of popular disruptions to law and order and increasingly alienated from the rural hinterlands (Esherick 1976: 91, 104–5). The assemblies also coordinated a petitioning campaign in 1910 to demand the early establishment of a national parliament, a demand only reluctantly agreed to by the court when it announced in early 1911 that the planned parliament would open in 1913 (Fincher 1981: 149). As gentry members of the provincial assemblies increasingly viewed the court as an obstacle to their political and economic ambitions, so they became progressively alienated from the dynasty.

Educational reforms also had unintended consequences for the dynasty. After several years' petitioning by reforming officials such as Yuan Shikai and Zhang Zhidong, the traditional civil service examinations – deemed ill-suited to prepare the country for current challenges with their emphasis on the rote memorization of Confucian texts – were abolished in 1905; since the civil service examinations had been used to recruit directly for the bureaucracy the intimate link between scholarship and state service was now broken, thus allowing for the emergence of a more independent intelligentsia (although throughout the twentieth century intellectuals, like their Confucian scholar-gentry predecessors, continued to perceive themselves as the moral guardians of society). Henceforth, attention was to be focused on the creation of a three-tier system of higher, secondary and primary schools overseen by a Board of Education (*xuebu*) which had been established the year before. Modern schools, in fact, had begun to be sponsored by gentry activists several years previously, and the system that developed after 1905 was to comprise 'official', 'public' (i.e. gentry-sponsored) and 'private' schools. The number of modern schools increased from nearly 36,000 in 1907 (with an enrollment of one million) to nearly 87,000 (with an enrollment of three million) in 1912 (Bastid 1980: 560; Bastid 1988: 68). A number of private girls' schools had also been created before 1905, although it was not until 1907 that the court officially sanctioned women's education (only for separate primary and teacher-training schools); conservative unease about the benefits of women's public education – traditionally, the daughters of elite families had been educated within the family household – was to persist through-out the last years of the dynasty and on into the early years of the Republic (Bailey 2001). Nevertheless, the number of female students in modern schools increased from nearly 2,000 in 1907 to just over 141,000 in 1912–13 (ibid.). Secondary education and higher education for women were to be formally sanctioned in 1912 and 1919, respectively.

As indicated by the educational aims issued by the Board of Education in 1906, the dynasty anticipated that modern schools would encourage loyalty, discipline and unity (Borthwick 1983: 129; Bailey 1990: 36–41). Gentry elites participated enthusiasti-cally in the founding of new schools (which included a wide variety of part-time, vocational and literacy schools), emphasiz-ing their function as the training of a hard-working and economically productive populace shorn of its 'backward' and 'superstitious' beliefs (Bailey 1990: 72–9). As with constitutional reforms, however, such activities also provided gentry elites with further opportunities to expand their public roles. They estab-lished education associations of their own (of which there were 723 by 1909 with a membership of 48,432) (Bastid 1980: 562) to promote and co-ordinate a wide range of initiatives that included the publishing of textbooks and drawing up of school curricula, as well as the founding of new schools. A prominent example of the new gentry–merchant class involved in consti-tutional and educational reform was Zhang Jian (1853–1926). A metropolitan degree-holder who had abandoned a potential official career, Zhang invested in modern enterprises (such as a cotton-spinning mill) and established primary and normal schools in his home district of Nantong (Jiangsu province). He also presided over the provincial education association, and as chairman of the Jiangsu provincial assembly invited repre-sentatives from the other provincial assemblies in 1909 to meet in Shanghai and establish the Association of Comrades Peti-tioning for a National Parliament (*guohui qingyuan tongzhi hui*), which was to spearhead the campaign for an early con-vening of parliament. Although gentry activists like Zhang were willing to collaborate with officials during the early years of reform, when it became evident that the court wished to control and restrict their activities such co-operation had evaporated by the last years of the dynasty, to be replaced by mutual mistrust and suspicion (Bastid 1988: 19–28, 33–43, 50–73).

To the consternation of the dynasty, also, the modern schools themselves became sites of disruption and unrest (Borthwick 1983: 141–50; Bailey 1990: 164–5). The last years of the dynasty witnessed a series of student strikes and protests, referred to in the contemporary press as a 'student tide' (*xuechao*). Some were due to dissatisfaction with the quality of the teaching personnel or poor working conditions in the schools, while others were more political in nature, expressing criticism of the dynasty's foreign policy. Students returning from Japan to take up teaching posts in the new schools were also conduits for anti-Manchu and republican propaganda. Although in the past the periodic gathering of candidates to take the civil service examinations had sometimes been the occasion for protests of various kinds (the most recent example of which had been in 1895 when Kang Youwei and others taking the metropolitan examinations expressed dismay over the terms of the Treaty of Shimonoseki), student protest emanating from the modern schools was to become in the twentieth century a far more pervasive and frequent phenomenon, which, in the words of a recent study, 'helped change the course of Chinese history' (Wasserstrom 1991: 293).

Ironically, the encouragement of study overseas in Japan had been another important feature of the dynasty's educational reforms. Originating as a government-sponsored initiative in 1896, when thirteen students travelled to Japan and enrolled at the Tokyo Normal School, overseas study in Japan quickly attracted increasing numbers from amongst the scholar–official class. In what has been described as the first large-scale (mostly unregulated) migration of students abroad anywhere in the world (Harrell 1992: 2), up to 9,000 Chinese students were enrolled in various Japanese educational institutions by 1905–6 (after which numbers gradually declined). Some went on government stipends, but the majority were self-financed (Jansen 1980: 348–53). For Japanese officials such a phenomenon repre sented an opportunity to enhance Japan's influence on a future Chinese elite; this was also a time of increasing Japanese interest in forging more extensive cultural links with China in line with both pan-Asianist ideals and the perceived necessity for Japan to exert a greater role in China (Harrell 1992: 20–30). In a sense Japan's example was later followed by the United States (see earlier) and France (see chapter 2), which likewise perceived a direct link between increasing educational interaction and the overall enhancement of their political and economic influence in China. Recent studies (e.g. Reynolds 1993) have, in fact, highlighted the important role Japan played in the late Qing reforms. Japanese teachers and educational advisers were employed in the modern schools and educational administration (up to 424 in 1909), while the Qing government made use of Japanese experts in its legal and police reforms (ibid.: 68–102; 162–9). For the Qing dynasty overseas study in Japan represented the most effective and economical way to acquire western learning (by making use of extensive Japanese translations of western works, which introduced new political concepts and technological terms) and to cultivate a future corps of dedicated and competent administrators; Japan was also perceived as a positive example of an Asian country that had successfully learnt the secrets of western power without abandoning its own identity (Harrell 1992: 47).

Ultimately, the initial hopes of the dynasty (and of Japan) were to be unfulfilled. Many of the Chinese students who went to Japan became alienated from the dynasty while at the same time acquiring ambivalent attitudes towards Japan; very few returned as enthusiasts for Japanese-inspired pan-Asianist ideals (ibid.: 58). They came from all provinces in China (except for the remote western province of Gansu) and were mostly the male scions of scholar–official families, although up to a hundred female students also went to Japan at this time (ibid.: 72–3). For the first time large numbers of young people from different regions in China were able to form closely knit groups, thereby contributing to the development of a national consciousness. Feelings of solidarity were also stimulated by the lack of interaction with the host society; many students were later to recall the humiliating taunts they suffered at the hands of their Japanese hosts – in particular their traditional long gowns and queues were targets of condescending mockery. Exposed to western ideas of democracy and republicanism through their reading of Japanese translations, Chinese students became politicized, producing their own journals and creating associations that gave them their first taste of public speaking, political debate and organization-building (ibid.: 89). In a highly symbolic gesture many students cut off their queues. They also participated in strikes and protests, reflecting their increasingly

critical stance towards the Qing dynasty for its appeasement of
the foreign powers, as well as towards the Japanese government
for its attempts to restrict their activities and movements. It was
these students who on their return helped spread radical ideas
via the modern schools or new army units; some also participated in more overt anti-Qing activity.

One of the most celebrated of the latter was Qiu Jin
(1875–1907), later eulogized as China's first revolutionary
female martyr. Qiu Jin had been one of the hundred or so
Chinese women who went to Japan in the early years of the
century and while there became an active supporter of the anti-
Qing cause, as well as founding several women's journals. These
journals were part of an emerging Chinese women's press in
Japan and Shanghai – itself a significant development since
for the first time journals were now being founded and edited
by women – that often rationalized its demands for gender
equality in instrumentalist terms of strengthening the country
(Beahan 1975). Qiu Jin herself, in the journals she edited, called
on women to participate in the national revolution against the
Manchus as a means of achieving emancipation (Rankin 1975).
On her return to China she continued with her radical activities
while directing a local girls' school in Shaoxing (Zhejiang
province); she was arrested and executed in 1907 after being
implicated in an abortive anti-Qing uprising (Spence 1982:
50–60; Wills 1994: 306–10).

The third feature of the late Qing reforms was the creation of
new army units. The first 'modern armies' (making use of
western-style weapons, drill and organization) had been organized in 1895–6 in the wake of the Sino-Japanese War (McCord
1993: 33). One of them, the Newly Created Army (*xinjian lujun*)
under the command of Yuan Shikai (1859–1916), was to become
the nucleus of the largest and most powerful modern army unit
in the country, the Beiyang (Northern) army, formally created in
1904. Yuan's military and administrative expertise (he had failed
to pass the lower-level civil service degree examinations) earned
him promotion as governor of Shandong in 1899 and, after 1901,
governor-general of Zhili, but it is important to note that
although Yuan was the principal commander of the Beiyang
army, it was not a regionally based army under his personal
control – and therefore not, strictly speaking, the forerunner of
the warlord forces in the 1920s (ibid.: 36–7). As a study of Yuan's

administration in Zhili has shown, the court not only sanctioned the creation of the Beiyang army but also retained financial and administrative control over it (Mackinnon 1980: 56–9, 72, 90–107). Division commanders were frequently transferred and middle-ranking officers often recruited (on the basis of professional qualifications rather than personal connections) from outside the officers' training academy Yuan established in Baoding in 1902. In the final analysis, Yuan's power (and his ability to receive funds) was based on his position in the capital, where he held concurrent posts in two new central-government institutions – the Government Affairs Bureau (established in 1901 to plan for institutional reform) and the Military Reorganization Bureau (established in 1903 to oversee military forces in the provinces and plan for the creation of new army units).

In 1906 the Military Reorganization Bureau became the Ministry of War, which ordered the formation of thirty-six new army divisions (two for each province) over the next ten years. The court's attempt to centralize military control (especially as the Ministry of War was headed by Manchus) aroused the suspicion of an increasingly alienated provincial gentry as well as giving a boost to anti-Manchu propaganda amongst Chinese republican revolutionaries in Japan (see later). Ultimately, however, the court failed to create a unified military system (McCord 1993: 45). On the eve of the 1911 Revolution the seventeen New Army divisions (and a number of brigades) that had been created were concentrated in provincial capitals and generally enjoyed better working conditions than the more traditional forces that were scattered beyond the major urban centres (Fung 1980: 23–32).

Accompanying the formation of New Army divisions was an attempt to foster a more positive image for the military, traditionally held in low esteem when compared with the more prestigious civil bureaucracy. One of the educational aims for the new schools announced in 1906 was the promotion of a martial spirit (*shangwu zhuyi*) that exalted military ideals of courage and discipline (ibid.: 92–9), and military-style drill was to become an important aspect of school life. As the army was increasingly portrayed as a key institution contributing to national self-strengthening, a military career was now seen as a respectable alternative to that of civil official, as well as one in which upward mobility was possible. Many degree-holders and the scions of scholar–official families enlisted in the New Army units; more significantly, many of those who rose through the ranks (and who were to become prominent militarists during the 1920s) came from lowly social origins. Military students were also sent to Japan, the first ones going in 1898. In 1903 the Shinbu Gakkō (Military School) was established in Japan exclusively for Chinese military students – up to 1,000 trained there until the school was closed in 1914. Also, between 1900 and 1911 nearly 700 Chinese students entered the more prestigious Shikan Gakkō, a Japanese training academy for middle-grade officers (Reynolds 1993: 153). Like their civilian counterparts many of these military students became influenced by anti-Qing republicanism during their sojourn in Japan (Sutton 1980: 45–51) and on their return formed quasi-political associations and established contacts with republican revolutionaries. Although by the end of the dynasty the original aim of creating full divisions in every province had not been achieved, it was no coincidence that the military mutiny that ignited the 1911 Revolution occurred within such a politicized New Army unit. This New Army unit was the Hubei New Army (comprising the 8th Division and the 21st Mixed Brigade), one of the largest in south-central China and in which politicization amongst the rank and file was common after 1904. By 1911 up to one-third of Hubei's New Army had been recruited into revolutionary organizations that had begun to appear after 1908 (Fung 1980: 121–31; McCord 1993: 63). Increasing politicization was fuelled by growing discontent as a result of cutbacks in pay and poor career prospects (Esherick 1976: 149–53; Fung 1980: 142–3).

As has been noted by several historians (e.g. Duara 1988; Thompson 1995), the late Qing reforms contributed to the modern state-building process. Government initiatives in self-government, education, police organization and public health (Benedict 1996: 150–64) resulted in the creation of numerous official and semi official institutions and offices that represented an ever more intrusive state penetration of society. In order to pay for these institutions, however, new miscellaneous taxes were imposed and land tax surcharges increased. Since the burden of these increased taxes fell on the poorer groups of society (principally the peasantry) and those less likely to benefit from the reforms (Esherick 1976: 106–7; Mackinnon 1980: 150–9), the last years of the dynasty witnessed a series of local tax revolts (Bernhardt 1992: 147–8, 156–9) in which the new institutions themselves were physically attacked; local self-government offices and modern schools, for example, often became the target of mob wrath. As a recent study has demonstrated (Prazniak 1999), such opposition to the late Qing reforms (and accompanying tax increases) was motivated by genuine popular concerns that they posed a threat to local livelihoods. A study of Hunan and Hubei provinces has argued that such popular outbursts against the reforms produced a concern for law and order amongst the gentry elites, inducing them to support the 1911 Revolution in order to control it (Esherick 1976: 7–8). Popular discontent during the last years of the dynasty was exacerbated by poor harvests and natural disasters, which led to high food prices and near famine conditions in some parts of the country in 1910–11.

The Republican Revolutionary Movement

Against the background of growing gentry and merchant alienation from the dynasty and popular discontent with intrusive government reforms, an anti-Qing republican movement amongst Chinese exiles, émigrés, and overseas students emerged. The principal figure associated with this movement was Sun Yatsen (1866–1925) (Wills 1994: 310–21). Unlike the leaders of the 1898 reform movement such as Kang Youwei and Liang Qichao, Sun was not a member of the Confucian scholar class; he came from a peasant family in Guangdong province and received a western missionary education in Honolulu (to where his elder brother had earlier emigrated). In 1884 he was baptized a Christian and later studied western medicine in Hong Kong in 1886–92 (Schiffrin 1968: 10–30). Sun founded his first anti-Manchu organization – the *Xingzhonghui* (Revive China Society) – in Honolulu in late 1894; a branch organization was created in 1895 in Hong Kong, by which time a secret oath binding its members may have called for the creation of a republic (Bergère 1998: 50). After an unsuccessful attempt in 1895 to foment an uprising in Guangzhou from his base in nearby Hong Kong (Schiffrin 1968: 61–97), Sun spent the next sixteen years in exile. The failed Guangzhou uprising had brought Sun to the attention of the Qing authorities; one year later, while in London, Sun gained both national and international notoriety when the Qing embassy there kidnapped him with the aim of transporting him back to China for certain execution. His plight was made known in the domestic press by British friends he had earlier cultivated in Hong Kong, and the ensuing outcry compelled the Qing embassy to release him. Sun skilfully exploited the incident by writing of his experience (in a book entitled *Kidnapped in London* and published in 1897) and portraying himself as a bold and fearless revolutionary (Schiffrin 1968: 105–29; Bergère 1998: 68).

At first Sun concentrated on seeking support from overseas Chinese merchant communities in North America and Southeast Asia (in competition with the exiled leaders of the 1898 reform movement, who favoured a constitutional monarchy under Guangxu), as well as making contacts with traditional secret societies within China. Most of these secret societies operated in central and southern China and were known by a variety of generic names such as the Triads or the Heaven and Earth Society. Originating in the early years of the Qing dynasty they were associations cemented by oaths of sworn brotherhood dedicated to opposing the Manchus and restoring the Chinese Ming dynasty. Over time they also became involved in banditry, salt smuggling and gambling rackets, although a recent study (Ownby 1996) has also emphasized their important role during the course of the eighteenth century as mutual aid organizations for the marginalized and insecure members of society at a time of economic, demographic and social change. Sun hoped to infiltrate these societies and use them for his republican revolution; the Triads were enlisted for the unsuccessful Guangzhou uprising in 1895, and they were to be recruited again for another abortive uprising in 1900 in eastern Guangdong, after a quixotic and fruitless attempt in the summer of 1900 to persuade Governor-General Li Hongzhang (through intermediaries) to declare Guangdong's independence (Schiffrin 1968: 181–200). The idea of making provincial autonomy or independence the route to eventual national unity and strength had first been raised by Liang Qichao in 1897 (see earlier) and was to become an important plank in Sun's early revolutionary strategy. It was also to resurface during the early 1920s in proposals for a federalist solution to China's increasing fragmentation amidst the breakdown of centralized government control (Chesneaux 1969). Sun's use of mercenaries (i.e. secret societies) and his search for foreign aid (in 1895 he had sought the assistance of the British colonial administration of Hong Kong, and in 1900 had looked to Japan for assistance) were other features of Sun's revolutionary strategy (Bergère 1998: 58).

By 1905, however, Sun was attracting the support of Chinese students in Japan (previously they had viewed him as a rustic gadfly), and many joined his new revolutionary organization, the *Tongmenghui* (Alliance League), when it was formed in Tokyo in 1905. Sun's revolutionary platform, known later as the Three Principles of the People (*sanmin zhuyi*), advocated nationalism (i.e. anti-Manchuism), democracy (i.e. the creation of a republic) and the improvement of the people's livelihood. Sun equated this last principle with socialism (specifically referring to the 'equalization of land rights', which involved taxing unearned increments from the sale of non-agricultural land), and claimed that by carrying out political and social revolution simultaneously China could prevent the glaring class differences prevalent in the contemporary industrialized West. With the support of Chinese students after 1905 Sun could now claim to head a national revolutionary movement, the first non-gentry leader of a political movement comprised mainly of intellectuals (Schiffrin 1968: 8–9; Bergère 1998: 128–9).

Between 1905 and 1908 a furious debate broke out between Sun and his followers on the one hand, and constitutional monarchists like Liang Qichao on the other in the various journals each side published in Japan (Gasster 1980: 495–9). For a brief period after the failure of the 1898 reforms Liang had fiercely denounced the Qing monarchy and seemed to favour a republic. After a visit to North America in 1903, when he had condemned the moral 'backwardness' of the Chinese communities there, and also deferring to the staunchly monarchist views of his mentor, Kang Youwei, Liang returned to the reformist camp. He derided the revolutionaries' anti-Manchuism, arguing that the Manchus were already assimilated, and warned of the anarchy and chaos that would ensue if a republic was established. For Liang a constitutional monarchy (at other times he referred positively to 'enlightened despotism') was the ideal solution to guarantee stability and order; his priority was the improvement and expansion of education, which would train a 'new citizen' (*xinmin*) whose commitment to the public good would override all parochial and selfish concerns. Interestingly, in contrast to the revolutionaries' assumption that a republic would automatically gain foreign support, Liang warned that it would only further invite foreign encroachment. As hostility to the Qing dynasty grew, however, Liang's call for restraint became increasingly unpopular amongst the radical Chinese students in Japan.

Sun was involved in eight further abortive uprisings between 1905 and 1911, but by the time of the last two (both in Guangzhou, in February 1910 and April 1911) his revolutionary tactics had changed. Earlier lack of success with the secret societies prompted him to turn to the New Army units as potential support for his republican cause. This strategy was particularly effective in the central provinces of Hunan and Hubei, where revolutionaries made contact with politicized army officers and established front associations to spread republican propaganda.

Although Sun's revolutionary movement played an important propaganda role in spreading anti-Qing feeling, it should be noted that the *Tongmenghui* was never a united organization under Sun's undisputed leadership. Despite later nationalist historiography that attributed to Sun and his organization the predominant role in the overthrow of the Qing, the *Tongmenghui* was more of an umbrella organization that brought together already existing groups in which there existed a wide variety of views and outlook. By the time of the 1911 Revolution, in fact, a separate and virtually independent branch had been set up in central China; furthermore, Sun's leadership, virtually from the beginning, had been vigorously contested. At times it seemed only a crude anti-Manchuism united these different groups. In many ways, as Liang Qichao pointed out, the Manchus had been assimilated by the early years of the twentieth century. The Manchu language was defunct, while the dynasty's proscription of intermarriage between Manchu and Chinese had been abolished in 1902 and all legal differences between Manchu and Han Chinese removed in 1907; also the ban imposed on the residents of the Manchu Banner garrisons to participate in local commerce and trade had fallen into disuse. In blaming the 'barbaric' Manchus for China's weakness and problems, however, revolutionaries also engaged in the 'construction' of a Han Chinese ethnic identity. Although a recent study has pointed out that a sense of Han Chinese 'racial' identity had existed since early times (coexisting with 'cultural-ism', which explained differences among people according to their cultural attributes) (Dikotter 1992), revolutionary propa-ganda in the early twentieth century went much further in stressing a unique, timeless and homogeneous Han Chinese ethnic identity – often described in terms of a common 'lineage' (*zu*) (Dikotter 1997: 9; Chow 1997: 40).

The 1911 Revolution

Qing government policy itself fuelled anti-Manchu phobia. Thus suspicion that the dynasty was exploiting the reforms to create a governing Manchu oligarchy seemed to be confirmed in 1909, when Manchu princes were appointed to head a General Staff Council overseeing the New Army units, and in May 1911, when a Manchu-dominated cabinet was announced. Violent gentry-led protests broke out in Sichuan province in May 1911 when the court announced its policy of using a foreign loan to take over responsibility for the construction of a number of railway lines (including a projected Hankou–Sichuan line) from pro-vincial railway companies in which gentry elites had invested. This in turn sparked off an army mutiny at Wuchang (Hubei province) in October. The Wuchang mutiny was soon followed by anti-dynastic uprisings in the central and southern provinces, where the provincial assemblies, in alliance with New Army commanders (many of whom declared themselves as military governors), declared their independence from Beijing (Spence 1999a: 258–63). The court called upon Yuan Shikai to quell the uprising. Meanwhile representatives of the southern provinces met in Nanjing and declared their intention to establish a repub-lic. Sun Yatsen, who was in the United States seeking funds at the time of the Wuchang mutiny, was elected provisional presi-dent and was given a rapturous welcome when he returned to China in December 1911.

As Yuan's government troops besieged Wuchang and a stale-mate ensued between the two opposing forces, the revolution-aries sought to negotiate a deal. Sun Yatsen offered to hand over the presidency to Yuan Shikai if he openly declared support for the republic and promised to abide by a new constitution. The revolutionaries also assumed Yuan would be able to use his power and influence to persuade the dynasty to abdicate

(Young 1968). Some misgivings were raised about this compromise. After all, Yuan Shikai had risen to prominence as an important military and civilian official of the Qing dynasty. It was also widely believed that Yuan had broken a promise of support for the 1898 reformers in backing Empress-Dowager Cixi's coup against the Guangxu Emperor and his advisers (Kwong 1984: 213–14). Following Cixi's death in 1908, court intrigue had resulted in his forced retirement. After the Wuchang uprising Yuan was recalled to command the government forces and appointed prime minister of the newly formed cabinet.

Recognition of the fact that Yuan commanded the most modern and well-equipped military force available, and the real fear held by revolutionaries that continued civil war might prompt the intervention of the powers to protect their economic stake in China, convinced them, however, that a compromise was necessary. Yuan, for his part, was well aware that support for the dynasty was crumbling, as some northern provinces in November 1911 joined the south in declaring independence from Beijing. In February 1912 Yuan secured the dynasty's abdication and the following month Sun Yatsen handed over the provisional presidency to Yuan Shikai. Although the revolutionaries had hoped the capital would be located in Nanjing, Yuan was able to get his own way and have the capital located in Beijing, the centre of his military power.

In assessing the nature of the 1911 Revolution, it is important to note that it had been spearheaded by the provincial assemblies (dominated by the scholar–gentry elite that had progressively become alienated from the dynasty) in alliance with New Army commanders (many of whom declared themselves provincial military governors). In some provinces like Hunan the anti-Qing movement was given a more populist flavour with the participation of secret societies, but in general there was little direct mass involvement, in the aftermath of the dynasty's overthrow local power was firmly in the hands of established elites. One study has characterized the revolution as a victory for an 'urban reformist elite' that supported the new order to preserve its interests and maintain law and order (Esherick 1976: 259). On the other hand, it might be noted that the revolution did not simply represent the triumph of local elites over the state, since during the last years of the dynasty *both* the state and local elites were organizing in new ways and increasing their resources. This state-building process was to continue after 1911 (Rankin and Esherick 1990: 343). Neither did the revolution represent the beginnings of a 'nascent warlordism'. Although the military played a key role (and by so doing legitimized the use of military power for political purposes), it was not an autonomous force, but rather a component of a broader elite coalition; military commanders in the aftermath of the revolution did not exercise personal power and civil administration remained in place (McCord 1993: 77, 79, 82–3).

Furthermore, although Chinese Marxist historians have conventionally described the events of 1911–12 as a 'national bourgeois-democratic revolution' (Hsieh 1975: 42–3), western historians (e.g. Bergère 1968) have argued that the Chinese bourgeoisie at this time was too politically weak and numerically insignificant to have played a substantial role in the revolution (although overseas Chinese merchant communities had donated funds to Sun Yatsen's revolutionary movement, and Shanghai merchants had financially supported the provisional revolutionary government in Nanjing). Even the *Tongmenghui* itself played only a minor role in the events of 1911–12, although some of the civil governors in the south who emerged in the wake of the revolution, such as Hu Hanmin in Guangdong, were *Tongmenghui* members. In some ways the 1911 Revolution might be characterized as a nationalist one (of the ethnic variety) in the sense that republican revolutionaries justified their movement in terms of a 'racial' struggle waged by a subjugated Han Chinese population against its oppressive 'alien' rulers, the Manchus (during the course of the revolution Manchus were sometimes specifically targeted for attack and in Xian large numbers were massacred) (Spence 1999a: 261). However, all governments after 1912 were to lay claim to the boundaries of the former Qing empire (which included Tibet and Mongolia) on the basis of western principles of state nationalism; ethnic minorities were either held to be insignificant or assumed to be 'assimilable' to the majority Han Chinese culture. In other words, non-Chineseness was not considered a barrier to incorporation within a Chinese state (Townsend 1996: 16).

Finally, the compromise of 1912 had brought to power someone very much associated with the *ancien régime* whose commitment to a republic was uncertain. Nevertheless, hopes were high that the creation of a republic would usher in a new era for China, one in which it would gain the respect of the foreign powers and lay the foundations for a democratic and prosperous nation. The events of the following decade would result in the crushing of those hopes and the emergence of radical new solutions to deal with the political instability that continued to plague the country.

2

The Early Republic

The failure of the early republic and its descent into corruption and disunity has conventionally been attributed to the unprincipled opportunism of its first president, Yuan Shikai, who demonstrated little understanding of, or commitment to, republican government (e.g. Ch'en 1961). Yuan was ultimately to betray the republic by attempting to restore the monarchy in 1915 with himself as the emperor of a new dynasty. Later studies of Yuan (Young 1976, 1977, 1983) modify this view by portraying him as a 'modernizing conservative' who made an unsuccessful bid to reassert centralized control and thus reverse the trend towards regionalism that had emerged during the last years of the Qing. On the one hand, Yuan's freedom of manoeuvre was restricted by increasing foreign influence over the economy – China at this time has been compared with a 'Third World' nation struggling for autonomy (Young 1977: 4) – while on the other, his centralizing policies aroused the opposition of both provincial military governors and local gentry/merchant elites. Other studies of the period have also highlighted the activities of the political parties that emerged after 1911, arguing that their factionalism and lack of understanding of the principles of parliamentary government did as much as Yuan's policies to bring the republic into disrepute (Yu 1966).

Yuan Shika's failure to reassert centralized control led to a period of instability and disunity in which political power gravitated into the hands of provincial militarists (or warlords). At the same time disillusionment with the baneful political consequences of the revolution stimulated an intellectual movement that sought deeper causes for the republic's failure. In what is known as the May Fourth (or New Culture) Movement, a number of radical intellectuals condemned the continuing influence of 'traditional' cultural values, which for them explained the absence of any substantial and progressive social change after 1911. Representing more of a continuity with trends already apparent during the last years of the Qing dynasty than a novel phenomenon, this cultural critique was accompanied by a wide-ranging exploration of western-inspired ideologies, experimentation with new forms of literature and language, and a dramatic increase in the number of journals and newspapers published in the urban centres. Out of this cultural and ideological ferment emerged the Chinese Communist Party in 1921, although recent studies have emphasized that its ideological uniformity and organizational identity were not achieved until several years later (Dirlik 1989; Van de Ven 1991).

Politics in the Early Republic

Most observers, including Sun Yatsen (who was appointed director of railways in September 1912), assumed that Yuan Shikai would abide by constitutional procedures. Under the provisional constitution approved in early 1912 Yuan, as president, had considerable executive power, but he was also to share responsibility with a prime minister (whom the president was to appoint with the concurrence of parliament) and his cabinet. Elections were also to be held at the end of 1912 and early 1913 for a bicameral parliament and new provincial assemblies, to replace the old National Assembly and provincial assemblies that had been convened in the last years of the Qing.

Sun Yatsen's pre-1911 revolutionary organization, the *Tongmenghui*, was now reorganized into a parliamentary political party, the Guomindang (Nationalist Party), to contest the elections promised for the end of the year. Other political parties were formed, whose membership included ex-officials and bureaucrats associated with the former regime as well as former revolutionaries. Alliances among them were made and unmade with bewildering frequency, and their factionalism and susceptibility to government bribes were severely to damage the credibility of parliamentary politics.

With the effective organizational skills of Song Jiaoren (1882–1913), who had established the central China branch of the *Tongmenghui* before 1911, the Guomindang, in contrast to the other parties, embarked on a well-planned and co-ordinated electoral campaign (Liew 1971). The party platform championed the cause of local self-government and called for limited presidential power and cabinet responsibility to parliament (Scalapino and Yu 1985: 347). The elections, in which over 300 political parties participated and 40 million were entitled to vote (Fincher 1981: 222–3), were a victory for the Guomindang, which emerged as the largest single party in both houses of parliament (Young 1977: 114). The military governors of Anhui, Jiangxi and Guangdong provinces were also adherents of the Guomindang. Yuan Shikai regarded the election results as a threat to his own position; it was no coincidence that in March 1913, a month before parliament was due to convene, Song Jiaoren, who more than anyone had demanded ministerial responsibility to parliament, was assassinated in Shanghai. It was widely believed that Song's murder had been carried out on Yuan's orders.

Yuan's already strained relations with the Guomindang reached a crisis point in April 1913 over the question of foreign loans. From the beginning of his presidency Yuan had been hampered by a lack of funds. By 1911 the central government derived most of its revenue from the maritime customs duties, since a large proportion of the land tax and other internal taxes had been appropriated by the provinces – receipts from the land tax as a proportion of total central revenue had in fact steadily fallen throughout the Qing dynasty (Wang 1973). During the course of the revolution the foreign powers tightened their control over the maritime customs by taking over the collection, banking and remittance of customs revenue (before 1911 the foreign-controlled Maritime Customs Service had simply assessed the correct duties and reported to the Qing government). Such revenue was to be deposited in foreign banks (in the treaty ports) and then remitted to the Chinese government specifically for repayment of foreign loans contracted by the Qing before 1911 (Feuerwerker 1983b).

The customs revenue was also to be pledged for any foreign loans contracted after 1912; such loans, however, had to be negotiated through a six-power Banking Consortium representing

Britain, the United States, France, Germany, Russia and Japan. This consortium, originally created in 1910, effectively blocked any attempt by Yuan's government to negotiate with individual foreign banks. Yuan, anxious to secure funds and formal recognition of his regime by the powers, obtained a Reorganization Loan of £25 million from the consortium in April 1913. Of this sum Yuan was actually to receive £21 million, since the loan was to comprise bonds sold at only 90 per cent of their face value, with a further 6 per cent of the total deducted for commission. Nevertheless, the original principal, at 5 per cent interest, still had to be repaid (Mancall 1984: 200). The salt tax revenue was pledged as security for the loan, and in order to ensure its efficient collection foreigners were to assist in the salt tax administration (Feuerwerker 1983b). Foreign influence over the economy was thus further expanded. (The US, under the presidency of Woodrow Wilson, withdrew from the consortium in protest against this infringement on Chinese sovereignty, although Chinese hopes that the US might henceforth champion China's cause were to remain largely unfulfilled.) As further testimony to the weakness of the new republic, Yuan was compelled in 1913 formally to recognize the autonomy of Outer Mongolia (confirmed by the Treaty of Kiakhta in 1915) and Tibet – originally part of the Qing empire but still claimed as part of China by the new republic – before Russia and Britain, which had strategic interests in those regions, would formally recognize Yuan's regime (although it should be noted that China's formal control over Tibet was never renounced).

Since Yuan had signed the Reorganization Loan without consulting parliament, the Guomindang attempted to impeach the president. Yuan averted this threat, primarily through manipulation of the other political parties, and then went on the offensive. He dismissed the Guomindang governors of Jiangxi, Anhui and Guangdong in June 1913 and replaced them with his own nominees. Armed conflict broke out in the south (known as the Second Revolution), as the dismissed governors and their Guomindang followers sought to launch a nationwide campaign against Yuan.

The Second Revolution barely lasted three months (July–September 1913) and ended in a complete rout of the anti-Yuan forces. Yuan's ability to buy the support of important provincial military governors, in addition to the general antipathy felt by gentry and merchant elites for the disruptive influence of the Guomindang, ensured the defeat of the uprising. Sun Yatsen, bitterly disillusioned, was forced once more to go into exile. In Japan he founded a new party in 1914, the Chinese Revolutionary Party (*Zhonghua gemingdang*), which represented a reaction against the broad-based and open parliamentary party that had been the Guomindang in 1912. Sun now emphasized the importance of a tightly knit secret party organization whose members would swear an oath of loyalty to him personally. Also, whereas before 1911 Sun had referred to the need for a period of temporary military rule to pave the way for democratic government, he now insisted that military rule had to be followed by an unlimited period of party tutelage to prepare the people for constitutional government (Bergère 1998: 257).

Yuan's victory enabled him to expand his control in the provinces, as well as to launch a frontal assault on all self-government institutions. He first succeeded in coercing parliament to elect him permanent president in October 1913; by the beginning of 1914 he had banned the Guomindang and dissolved parliament. Provincial and district assemblies were also abolished. Yuan also attempted to increase Beijing's control over the provinces by appointing civilian governors to balance the power of the military governors. After 1913 he succeeded in appropriating for the central government a larger proportion of the land tax. As part of his campaign to ensure public order through a reassertion of traditional moral values such as deference and loyalty, Yuan at this time ordered that primary schools restore the Confucian Classics to the curriculum (they had been eliminated from the curriculum under the new school system promulgated in 1912).

Yuan's regime after 1913 has been described as a 'republican dictatorship . . . constructed around the principles of administrative centralization and bureaucratic order' (Young 1983: 238). Apart from a certain 'reign of terror' designed to intimidate (and worse) opponents and critics of the regime, Yuan's policies themselves met with increasing opposition, not only from provincial military governors, but also from gentry and merchant groups (the very people, ironically, who had supported him in 1913); the abolition of local assemblies, restrictions placed on chambers of commerce, and plans to impose a government income tax all fuelled resentment. In a desperate attempt to divert opposition to his regime Yuan Shikai played his last trump card. In 1915 he encouraged a campaign calling for the restoration of the monarchy (Scalapino and Yu 1985: 415). The campaign, orchestrated by Yuan's followers, led to 'pleas' by 'concerned citizens' for Yuan to assume the Dragon Throne. Yuan, however, had committed a fatal blunder. He had assumed that the very symbols of monarchical power would be sufficient to cement national unity and enhance his personal power. Yet the clock could not be turned back. The monarchy had been totally discredited in 1911 (at least amongst elites), while the military governors were too jealous of their recently acquired power to accept the claims of a new emperor. A classic study of Confucianism and its fate in the twentieth century also argues that Yuan's monarchical attempt was a 'parody', in that his artificial use of Confucian symbols and procedures during his enthronement in 1916 jarred with changing political and intellectual trends that had already drained traditional monarchy (and Confucianism) of its universal value; the result was that Yuan's cynical ploy to exploit tradition made him 'traditionalistic' rather than an 'authentic, traditional emperor' (Levenson 1964: 4–20).

As Yuan prepared to install himself as emperor at the end of 1915 (under the reign name of Hongxian), military governors in the south rose up in revolt, declaring their provinces independent of Beijing. At the same time Sun Yatsen, financed by the Japanese, attempted to stage uprisings in the province of Shandong. His close association with the Japanese (and reports that he had offered Japan future economic concessions in return for assistance) at a time when there was much anti-Japanese feeling in the country due to Japan's increasingly aggressive activity in China (see next section) laid Sun open to the charge of being a traitor in the pay of a foreign enemy. Sun's campaign quickly fizzled out. As in 1911–12 it was to be the provincial military governors, and not Sun Yatsen, who would reap the benefits of successful revolt.

Fearing the consequences of civil war, the powers were decidedly lukewarm to Yuan's scheme. Japan, in particular, was hostile and even managed to persuade Britain and the US to submit a joint note advising postponement of the restoration.

Even after Yuan abandoned his scheme in March 1916, provinces continued to declare their independence. It was only his death in June of that year which saved Yuan from the ignominy of being overthrown. Yuan's innate conservatism, his lack of sympathy for the principles of constitutional government, his ruthless treatment of political opponents, and his cynical manipulation of parliament had dealt a blow to the republic from which it was never really to recover. In the words of one historian, Yuan's failure to mobilize social support for 'orderly reform and modernization' under the aegis of a centralizing bureaucratic state opened the way for the use of military power to solve political issues (Rankin 1997: 267–8). After 1916 a powerless parliament and a weak civilian government were increasingly to become the mere playthings of a succession of warlord cliques.

China and the First World War

Before discussing the intellectual ferment known as the May Fourth Movement and the emergence of warlordism following the death of Yuan Shikai, it is necessary first of all to assess the impact of the First World War on China. This was a crucial phase in China's twentieth-century history, since the actions taken by Japan, Britain, the US and France were to confirm China's weakness and demonstrate that the interests and ambitions of the powers themselves took priority over China's territorial sovereignty. The anger and disillustionment that ensued helped fuel a more intense anti-imperialist nationalism that dated from the last years of the Qing dynasty.

When war broke out in Europe in August 1914 Japan immediately expressed willingness to come to the aid of its ally, Britain. Under the terms of the 1902 Anglo-Japanese alliance (renewed in 1905) the Japanese government offered to declare war on Germany, which would have given Japan the justification to attack Germany's leased territory centred on the port of Qingdao in Shandong province. While the British government was amenable to the idea of the Japanese navy patrolling East Asian waters to protect British shipping and trade against possible German attack, it was more ambivalent about seeing a greater Japanese presence in China (Chi 1970). Japan's victory over Russia in 1905 had already led to an enhancement of the country's economic influence in Manchuria, and Britain, as the power still with the greatest economic stake in China, was beginning to view Japan as a potential rival.

Japan, however, went ahead with its offensive against the German leased territory. Ignoring China's declaration of neutrality, Japanese troops landed in north Shandong and took Qingdao overland. In addition to Qingdao, Germany had also in 1898 obtained the right to build a railroad from Qingdao to the provincial capital of Jinan, as well as acquiring mining concessions along the route of the railroad. Despite China's attempts to limit Japan's actions Japanese troops soon advanced inland from Qingdao and took control of the completed railroad.

It was at this point that Tokyo decided to consolidate and strengthen Japan's position in China by imposing on Yuan Shikai the infamous 'Twenty-One Demands'. In January 1915 the Japanese minister to China handed over to Yuan a series of demands which, if accepted in their entirety, would have virtually transformed China into a Japanese protectorate. These demands included not only an extension of Japan's lease on Port Arthur (on the Liaodong peninsula in southern Manchuria) and the South Manchuria Railway, but also the granting of mining, trading and residential privileges in south Manchuria and Inner Mongolia, recognition of Japan's dominant presence in Shandong, and a promise by the Chinese government not to allow any part of China's coast to fall under the influence of another power. The last series of demands, however, were especially ambitious. The Chinese government was to employ Japanese political and military advisers; a joint Sino-Japanese police force was to be created; and China was to purchase a fixed amount of weapons from Japan (Chi 1970: 32). Yuan Shikai prevaricated, hoping for support from Britain and the United States. Although the two countries protested against the last series of demands, prompting Japan to agree to their 'postponement', neither was willing to antagonize Japan. Moreover, the American Secretary of State, William Jennings Bryan, publicly stated in March 1915 that 'territorial contiguity' created special relations between Japan and the Chinese territories of Shandong and southern Manchuria.

On 25 May 1915, a day later to be called 'National Humiliation Day' by Chinese students, Yuan signed Japan's demands.

Widespread anti-Japanese demonstrations, which often took the form of boycotts against Japanese goods, occurred in all the main cities. Despite an ineffective warning by the US that it would not recognize any Sino-Japanese agreement that impaired China's political and territorial integrity, Japan was able to gain approval from Britain and France in 1917 concerning its claims in Shandong; in the same year the US again recognized that Japan had special interests in China due to the geographical closeness of the two countries (Chi 1970: 110).

Confident now that its claims in Shandong would be recognized in any future peace conference, Japan agreed to go along with Britain's attempt to persuade China to declare war on Germany. In fact, Yuan Shikai had offered in 1914 and 1915 to participate militarily in the war on the allied side (even proposing a Chinese expedition to the Dardanelles) in the hope of pre-empting Japanese military action against Germany in Shandong (Chi 1970; Bailey 2000: 181–2). For this very reason Japan had opposed the idea. Britain, for its part, desired China to declare war on Germany simply to ensure that German property and shipping in China could be requisitioned. Neither Britain nor the US were enthusiastic about Chinese military participation (another offer was mooted in 1917), principally because Chinese fighting abilities were not highly rated and there was a shortage of convoy ships.

Nevertheless, Duan Qirui, who had been one of Yuan Shikai's generals and now dominated the civilian government in Beijing, was a keen supporter of the allied proposal. Others feared, however, that if China declared war Duan would secure allied funds which he could then use to strengthen his position *vis-à-vis* internal opponents. Duan intimidated the parliament (restored after Yuan's death) with a show of military force and war was declared on Germany in August 1917. The Guomindang, under Sun Yatsen's leadership, left Beijing in protest and, along with other former members of the pre-1915 parliament, set up a rival southern parliament in Guangzhou (Guangdong province) (Bergère 1998: 271–2). Henceforth Sun disputed the legitimacy of the Beijing government and aimed to create his own government in the south associated with the protection of the constitution and defence of the republic (Rankin 1997: 269). Those who supported China's declaration of war hoped that this would not only ensure China's participation in the future peace conference but would also lend weight to China's demands that the unequal treaty system be ended. Such hopes were buttressed by the fact that although no Chinese troops were sent to the Western Front, from 1916 the French and British governments were able to recruit Chinese labour for war-related work in France. Ultimately, approximately 150,000 labourers were enlisted; the majority came from northern China (especially Shandong province) and while in France were engaged in a wide variety of tasks, ranging from the repair of trenches and roads, burying war dead and building aerodromes, to working in armaments and machinery plants (Bailey 2000: 182–4).

Chinese hopes of an end to the unequal treaty system were also given a boost by the inspiring rhetoric of US President Woodrow Wilson, who in 1918 referred to the need for a new international system after the war based on open diplomacy, equality amongst nations and self-determination for peoples. The Versailles Peace Conference in 1919 was to prove a bitter disappointment as Wilson's lofty ideals collided with the concrete reality of power interests. If Chinese representatives had to accept that the powers would not end extra-territoriality in China or restore tariff autonomy, they at least expected that the leased territory of Qingdao and the Jinan–Qingdao railroad would be returned to Chinese control.

Japan, however, was able to bolster its claims in Shandong by citing not only the approval given by Britain and France in 1917, but also secret joint-defence treaties signed by Tokyo and Duan Qirui's government in 1918 which had implicitly recognized the Japanese presence in Shandong. More importantly, Britain and the US, as in 1915, were not willing to commit themselves fully to China's cause and thus risk incurring the hostility of Japan, now a major military and naval power in East Asia. Furthermore, President Wilson was anxious that all allied powers participate in the proposed League of Nations and when Japan hinted that it might not join if the Shandong concessions were returned to China he bowed to the inevitable (ironically, of course, isolationist sentiment in the US Congress later ensured that it was to be the US that rejected participation in the League of Nations).

When news was received in China on 4 May 1919 that the allies had decided to award Germany's rights in Shandong to Japan, there were massive student demonstrations in Beijing that quickly spread to other major cities (Chow 1960). Pro-Japanese ministers were attacked and a boycott of Japanese goods organized in which merchants and urban workers, especially in Shanghai, participated (Chen 1971). Chinese representatives at Versailles, bombarded by telegrams denouncing the peace settlement, did not sign the treaty. Although the political demonstrations of May 1919 have conventionally been described as marking the beginnings of modern Chinese nationalism (Chow 1960), it should be noted that they represented more a continuity of trends that had begun during the last years of the Qing dynasty (see chapter 1). What *was* novel was the large number of students, merchants and urban workers who had been galvanized into political action. A study of student protest in the twentieth century has also highlighted the May Fourth demonstrations as the beginning of a highly effective 'political theatre of the street' that students were to employ and develop during the rest of the century (Wasserstrom 1991: 5). Such 'political theatre' mimicked, appropriated and subverted official rhetoric, rituals and ceremonies to challenge the legitimacy of governing authorities. During the demonstrations in Shanghai in May and June 1919, for example, students formed their own 'protest bureaucracies' (through elaborately organized unions), modelled their own written propaganda on official proclamations, organized their own patriotic parades (replete with oath-swearing, raising of the national flag and musical interludes) and even 'policed' their own boycott of Japanese goods (ibid.: 57–70, 74–81, 85–9). Furthermore, the demonstrations of May 1919 were part of a wider process which came to be known as the May Fourth Movement.

The May Fourth Movement

In 1915 a new journal began publication in Shanghai. Entitled *Xin Qingnian* (New Youth) and edited by Chen Duxiu (1880–1942), who had studied in Japan before 1911 and participated in the 1911 Revolution, the journal over the next few years denounced traditional morality and practices and advocated wholesale cultural and intellectual change (referring to western democracy and science as inspiration). For many Chinese intellectuals the corruption of republican politics had shown that changes in attitudes had to precede political change

(Grieder 1981). Chen, in particular, launched a fierce attack on Chinese tradition, arguing that the persistence of Confucian beliefs blocked the emergence of a dynamic and youthful citizenry. He especially criticized the traditional family system with its emphasis on deference to the elderly and relegation of women to an inferior status.

Such an onslaught on tradition, captured by the slogan 'Overthrow Confucius and Sons', also reflected radicals' dismay with what they perceived as reactionary currents in the early republic. Kang Youwei, for example, whose attitude towards the new republic was lukewarm at best, orchestrated a campaign to promote Confucianism as a state religion, an idea he had first formulated during the 1890s (Kwong 1984: 93–107). Conservative educators, alarmed that the growing number of girls' schools were not inculcating the 'appropriate' attitudes and behavior befitting women, demanded that such schools both exalt traditional female virtues of deference, loyalty and passivity and devote more of their time teaching 'useful' subjects such as domestic science and household management (Bailey 2001). Finally, there had been Yuan Shikai's 1915 decision to reintroduce Confucian learning in the primary schools (overturned after his death) and an abortive attempt in Beijing (lasting several days) to restore the Qing monarchy in 1917, when a northern warlord, Zhang Xun (known as the 'pig-tailed General' because he continued to sport the Manchu-style queue), brought Puyi out of his secluded 'retirement' in the Forbidden City.

Chen Duxiu's uncompromising critique of Chinese tradition *in toto* has been described as 'totalistic iconoclasm' (Lin 1979). Since Confucian norms, it is argued, underpinned all aspects of traditional government, society and culture (all of which were perceived as organically linked by Confucian scholars), radical intellectuals like Chen likewise adopted a 'holistic' approach in promoting a root and branch denunciation of tradition. Another study (Feigon 1983), however, has noted that Chen was able to draw on an *indigenous tradition* of dissent and that his radical criticisms of Chinese culture were consistently prompted by a deeply felt nationalism in evidence since his student days during the last years of the Qing. In any event, such a blanket condemnation of a homogeneous past was a temporary phenomenon as more nuanced and discriminating views came to prevail amongst May Fourth intellectuals. It should also be noted that 'tradition' in its various guises has continued to be appropriated, manipulated and exploited throughout the twentieth century.

Another contributor to *Xin Qingnian* was Hu Shi (1891–1962). Hu had received a government scholarship to study in the US in 1910 (made possible by the Boxer indemnity funds remitted to China by the US), and while at Cornell University he had written articles condemning the rigidity and formalism of the Chinese classical language (*wenyan*). On his return in 1917 he contributed an article to *Xin Qingnian* promoting a literature based on vernacular speech (*baihua*); such a literature, he argued, would not only be more lively and practical, but would also enable China to escape the stultifying effects of Confucian culture so much associated with the classical language (Grieder 1970). Hu subsequently pioneered scholarship on, and promoted the virtues of, traditional popular novels that had been written in the vernacular. Two of the most well known were *Shuihu Zhuan* (known in English translation as either *The Water Margin* or *All men Are Brothers*, and probably written in the fourteenth century), which relates the boisterous and outrageous exploits of a bandit fraternity, and *Xiyou Ji* (known in English as either *Journey to the West* or *Monkey*, and written in the sixteenth century), which recounts the adventures of the mischievous and daring monkey king, Sun Wukong, as he protects a Buddhist monk against demons on his epic journey to collect holy scriptures from India; both novels were avidly read by the young Mao Zedong.

Literature was also seen as a vehicle for change by Lu Xun (1881–1936), one of China's foremost writers of the twentieth century. He had originally gone to Japan in the early years of the century to study medicine, but had given up in despair (like many of his compatriots in Japan at this time, he had experienced personal humiliation during his stay and was aghast at the derisory way in which Chinese people were regarded), concluding that until a fundamental change in mentality occurred amongst the people science would not of itself 'save' China. Through the medium of literature Lu Xun hoped to draw attention to the evils of traditional society and thereby encourage a questioning of the attitudes that underlay them (Lyell 1976; Spence 1982: 61–71, 85–8, 107–13; Lee 1987; Lyell 1990: iv–xxiv).

He pioneered a new literary form, the vernacular short story, in 1918, when he published in *Xin Qingnian* a biting satire entitled 'Diary of a Madman' (*Kuangren riji*), which described Chinese tradition in terms of a voracious cannibalism. Thus the hero, deemed 'mad' by his family and neighbours for having 'trampled the account books of Mr Antiquity' and convinced that people are about to devour him, notes in his diary:

> You have to *really* go into something before you can understand it. I seemed to remember, though not too clearly, that from ancient times on people have often been eaten, and so I started leafing through a history book to look it up. There were no dates in this history, but scrawled this way and that across every page were the words BENOVOLENCE, RIGHTEOUSNESS, and MORALITY. Since I could not get any sleep anyway, I read that history very carefully for most of the night, and finally I began to make out what was written *between* the lines; the whole volume was filled with a single phrase: EAT PEOPLE! (Lyell 1990: 32)

As in the case of Hu Shi, however, Lu Xun's 'iconoclasm' did not preclude him from admiring certain aspects of traditional culture; in particular, he later championed the aesthetic qualities of traditional woodcut prints.

By 1918 Chen Duxiu, Hu Shi and Lu Xun were all teaching at Beijing University, which, under the chancellorship of Cai Yuanpei (1868–1940), had become a dynamic centre of intellectual debate. Cai, holder of the metropolitan degree (*jinshi*) under the traditional civil service examination system, had joined Sun Yatsen's *Tongmenghui* during the last years of the dynasty. In 1912 he became the first republican minister of education, but had soon resigned in protest against Yuan Shikai's policies. In 1916 he was appointed chancellor of Beijing University and set about transforming its woeful reputation as the safe and undemanding haven for the idle sons of burcaucrats. Cai succeeded in transforming the university into a reputable academic institution, insisting that it be a place where a wide variety of differing ideas and opinions could be expressed (Duiker 1977). While teaching at the university Chen Duxiu and the others had an enormous impact on the students.

The intellectual ferment of this time produced a host of journals (some published by the students themselves) and stimulated a keen fascination with western literature and political thought among radical youth. Writers such as Turgenev and Shaw were translated, while public performances of Henrik Ibsen's play, *A Doll's House*, enlivened current debates about the status of women in society and elevated Nora (the heroine of the play) as a symbol of the courageous assertion of autonomy and rejection of traditional roles (Ono 1989: 99–100; Wang 1999: 50). In 1919–20 prominent western philosophers and educators like Bertrand Russell and John Dewey were invited to China, where they lectured to rapt audiences of university students. Increasing interest (dating from the early years of the century) was also shown in the western political ideologies of socialism and anarchism.

Although the introduction of socialist theories in China at the turn of the century, and how socialism was subsequently interpreted by Chinese intellectuals such as Liang Qichao and those associated with Sun Yatsen's *Tongmenghui* during the last years of the Qing dynasty, have been well documented by historians (e.g. Gasster 1969; Bernal 1976), the significance and impact of anarchist ideas have only recently been accorded substantial discussion (Zarrow 1990; Dirlik 1991). In the opinion of one historian (Dirlik 1991), the assumption that the most important political result of the May Fourth Movement was the founding of the Chinese Communist Party in 1921 has tended to obscure the pervasive, if somewhat diffuse, influence anarchism exerted on May Fourth discourse (needless to say, anarchism's role at this time was virtually ignored by later Chinese Marxist historiography, at least until fairly recently).

The inspiration for many of the ideas and practices of the May Fourth period can be traced to the influence of pre-1911 Chinese anarchists, who had gone to Japan and France to study. It was these anarchists, especially those in Paris, who had condemned the tyranny of the family system, advocated new forms of social interaction based on mutual aid, and extolled the benefits of education and science in bringing about a more humane and equal society (Bailey 1988; 1990: 227–33). They also pioneered the concept of work-study as a means of bridging the gap between intellectuals and workers which they felt had always characterized Chinese society. Anarchist organizations and publications continued to proliferate during the early years of the republic, while Beijing University students in the late 1910s attempted to put anarchist ideas into practice by experimenting with communal living arrangements, creating work-study schemes, and organizing popular lecture teams that toured the suburbs and surrounding countryside to spread 'modern' knowledge amongst ordinary folk (although such efforts were often rationalized in elitist terms as the natural duty of an intellectual vanguard to eliminate the ingrained 'superstitions' and 'ignorance' of the people).

One of the most ambitious anarchist-inspired projects was a work-study scheme that sent over 1,500 Chinese students to France between 1919 and 1921 (Bailey 1988). Organized by prominent anarchists who had been active in Paris before 1911 such as Li Shizeng, the scheme aimed to provide less well-off students the opportunity to work in French factories and earn money to pay for their later tuition in French schools and colleges. Li Shizeng also hoped that by engaging in manual work Chinese students would divest themselves of elitist attitudes, while their interaction with the remaining Chinese workers in France recruited during the war (most of whom were repatriated by 1921) through the teaching of literacy classes would help raise the workers' cultural level. Interestingly, the scheme was also initially welcomed by French officials and educators, who underlined its long-term benefits for the enhancement of their country's political, cultural and economic influence in China – in much the same way as their American and Japanese counterparts had welcomed Chinese students to their countries earlier on in the century (ibid.: 453; Bailey 1992: 826–8). Although the scheme eventually foundered on the rocks of the postwar economic depression in France (leaving many Chinese students unemployed) and was wound down by 1921, the ideal of work-study as a means of abolishing rigid distinctions between mental and manual work was to have a continuing influence on later communist leaders such as Mao Zedong (see chapter 5). Also, during their sojourn in France many work-study students became highly politicized; they included some of the most important future communist leaders, such as Zhou Enlai (1898–1976), premier and foreign minister of the People's Republic after 1949, Deng Xiaoping (1904–97), the party's general secretary in the 1950s and 'paramount leader' in the

1980s and 1990s, Nie Rongzhen, a marshal of the People's Liberation Army after 1949, and Li Fuchun, minister of state planning in the 1950s.

The May Fourth (or New Culture) Movement thus embraced an extraordinary range and diversity of ideas, and for this reason has often been referred to as a unique period in modern Chinese history. Such a view was first propounded by participants such as Hu Shi, who subsequently wrote of the movement's path-breaking impact (and especially his own pioneering role in championing the use of the vernacular in literature and schools) in a book entitled *The Chinese Renaissance* (published in 1934). A later classic study of the origins of the Chinese communist revolution (Bianco 1971: 27–8) compared the May Fourth intellectuals with the thinkers of the European Enlightenment; just as the latter paved the way for the French Revolution, so the former, with their critique of tradition and promotion of democracy and science, prepared the path for the communist revolution of 1949. A more recent study has repeated this comparison between the May Fourth Movement and the European Enlightenment (Schwarcz 1986).

It is important to remember, however, that just as the nationalism of the May Fourth period and exploration of radical ideologies had their roots in the earlier years of the century, so the iconoclastic critique of tradition, promotion of the vernacular, the emergence of 'modern' literature, and emphasis on the importance of popular education – all of which are closely associated with the May Fourth period – represented continuity with trends already apparent during the last years of the Qing. The pre-1911 anarchists, for example, were among the first to construct a systematic critique of the traditional family system (Zarrow 1990; Dirlik 1991). Chinese educators and reformers began to compile school textbooks and publish journals in the vernacular from the late 1890s onwards (Bailey 1990: 73–5). Discussion of literary reform was pioneered by reformers such as Liang Qichao in the early years of the century (Dolezelova-Velingerova 1977; Hsia 1978; Lee and Nathan 1985); furthermore, a recent study (Wang 1997) has underlined the innovative nature of late Qing fiction (which May Fourth intellectuals and later literary historians tended to ignore or denounce as frivolous and reactionary) and its contribution to the emergence of a literary 'modern' because its themes and subject-matter were no longer indigenously bound but now affected by the 'multilingual, cross-cultural trafficking of ideas, technologies and powers in the wake of nineteenth-century western expansionism' (ibid.: 5). Finally, as mentioned in chapter 1, the need to implement widespread popular education was a constant refrain in educational debates after 1900, and led to the creation of literacy, half-day and vocational schools by gentry and merchant elites during the last years of the Qing (Bailey 1990: 64–133).

Recent studies have further noted the continuing significance and effectiveness of so-called 'traditional' institutions during the May Fourth Movement and after. Thus native-place associations (*huiguan* or *tongxianghui*) comprising migrants and sojourners in cities such as Shanghai originally hailing from the same locality or region (and which played an important role in providing charity and security for their members), far from representing an unchanging and 'backward' parochialism, could transcend urban boundaries as well as facilitate mobilization for nationalist movements – especially during the anti-Japanese boycott of May–June 1919 (Goodman 1995: 262–70). Also, a study of student radicals who originally came from undeveloped rural regions of Zhejiang province (hence diverting attention from the usual focus on Beijing or Shanghai during the May Fourth Movement) argues that their espousal of anarcho-communism at this time was prompted by a desire to salvage the ethical content of Confucianism thay had imbibed in family and village schools (Yeh 1996: 5). Perhaps most significantly, however, new research on the meaning of Chinese modernity during the first three decades of the twentieth century is now exploring the long-term transformations and mutations in the material culture of everyday life (which did not necessarily represent sudden ruptures with the past), rather than equating modernity simply with the iconoclastic discourse of intellectuals and the political mobilization of students (Lee 1999; 2000)

The Founding of the Chinese Communist Party

One of the first Chinese intellectuals to write about the significance of the Bolshevik Revolution was another key member of the May Fourth radical intelligentsia and teacher at Beijing University – Li Dazhao (1888–1927). In an article published in

Xin Qingnian in 1918 Li underlined its messianic message, claiming that it was the most important event in world history, which gave China hope that it, too, might emerge from a period of decay and achieve a spiritual rebirth (Meisner 1967: 63–5). It has also been pointed out that Li described the Bolshevik Revolution very much in anarchist terms, evidence of the pervasive influence of anarchism at this time (Dirlik 1989: 23–7). In the same year Li established the Society for the Study of Marxism at Beijing University and began to probe deeper into the doctrinal aspects of the Bolshevik Revolution. A special issue of *Xin Qingnian* in May 1919 was devoted to Marxism, although it was not until *after* 1919 that a more substantial number of Marxist works became available in Chinese (extracts from the Communist Manifesto, however, had been translated as early as 1906).

In addition to teaching political science at Beijing University, Li Dazhao was also in charge of the university library. One of his assistants was Mao Zedong (1893–1976), the son of a well-to-do peasant (who owned about three acres) who had come to Beijing in 1918 after graduating from a teachers' training school in his home province of Hunan. One year earlier, Mao had contributed an article to *Xin Qingnian* (his first publication) on the benefits of physical exercise for the Chinese people (Spence 1999b: 2–35). Like many students of the time, Mao was attracted to a wide variety of ideas and political thought, later admitting that on the eve of his departure for Beijing his ideas comprised a 'curious mixture of liberalism, democratic reformism and utopian socialism' (Schram 1966: 44); while in Beijing, under the influence of Li Dazhao, he was introduced to Marxism.

Chen Duxiu was also to devote more attention to Marxism after 1919. Increasingly disappointed with republican politics, Chen, who had previously pinned his hopes on cultural and educational change and the gradual implementation of democracy on the Anglo-American model, argued that thorough-going social and economic transformation was needed. By 1920 he had formally announced his conversion to Marxism. The stance taken by Li and Chen signified a breakdown in the consensus amongst May Fourth radical intellectuals, which was illustrated in the exchange of views between Li Dazhao and Hu Shi in 1919 (known as the 'problems and isms' debate). Hu, influenced by the pragmatism of the American educator and philosopher,

John Dewey, advocated incremental and piecemeal social change and warned against the foolhardy and wholesale adoption of any particular ideology (Keenan 1977: 46–8). In 1920 Hu Shi left the editorial board of *Xin Qingnian*, and the journal henceforth became the sounding board for the Marxist views of Li and Chen.

Disillusionment with the West as a result of the Versailles decision in 1919 and the declarations by the new Soviet government in Russia in 1918 and 1919 that it would renounce the unequal treaties signed by the former csarist regime and the Qing dynasty also stimulated a growing interest in Marxism amongst Chines students and intellectuals. While representing to many the very latest in western thought, Marxism at the same time provided a powerful critique of western society and seemed to spell out a programme of action to deal with China's predicament. Of course, it should be noted that even at the height of the New Culture Movement, when radicals such as Chen Duxiu and Hu Shi at times advocated wholesale westernization, there were always others (including members of Beijing University staff) who adopted a more ambivalent view – a view confirmed by the horrors of the First World War in Europe. After 1919 Liang Shuming (1893–1988), who had been appointed professor of Indian philosophy at Beijing University in 1916, argued that while China might absorb western material culture it should not abandon the ethical values of traditional Confucian culture; for Liang such values prized harmony, cooperation and contentment with life in contrast to the selfish individualism, greed and the ceaseless (and ultimately fruitless) struggle to attain satisfaction that underpinned western values (Alitto 1979). Another prominent intellectual, Liang Qichao, who toured Europe in 1918–20 and attended the Versailles Peace Conference, likewise experienced disillustionment with the West and was prompted to advocate a more creative synthesis of Chinese and western values. A recent study has argued that Liang's vision of modernity now encompassed a 'global imaginary of difference' in which cultural differentiation rather than political uniformity was the source of meaning (Tang 1996: 180–3, 195–222). Such views were not restricted to Chinese intellectuals; a questioning of the supposedly civilized agenda of western material civilization in the wake of the First World War was also a phenomenon in the West at this time, and was forcefully expressed by some of the foreign visitors who were invited to China during the May Fourth period, such as Rabindranath Tagore (1861–1941), the Bengali writer and educator, and Bertrand Russell (1872–1970), the British philosopher and mathematician.

Although Marxist study groups were formed in Beijing and other cities in 1919–20 they tended to be rather loose organizations of students and intellectuals with a general interest in political and social change. The fluidity of their views was illustrated by the fact that many of them professed interest in anarchism and other forms of non-Marxist socialisms. While earlier studies (Schwartz 1951; Meisner 1967) emphasized the indigenous roots of Chinese communism, and in particular the importance of nationalism (engendered by opposition to western imperialism) as a factor in the conversion of Li Dazhao and Chen Duxiu to Marxism, a recent study (Dirlik 1989) argues that the role of Comintern (i.e. the Communist International, established in Moscow under the auspices of the Soviet Communist Party in 1919 to promote worldwide revolution) advisers such as Voitinsky – who met with Li and Chen in 1920 – was crucial in convincing them and other radicals that the loosely organized and open study societies had to be transformed into a tightly organized, disciplined and secret Bolshevik-style party committed to class revolution.

The receptiveness to the Comintern message was enhanced by three contingent factors: the growing political importance of urban labour (demonstrated by increased strike activity), the failure of experiments in anarchist-inspired cultural change such as the various work-study and communal living schemes, and increasing government repression of radical activity in the wake of the May Fourth political demonstrations. By early 1921 Communist Party branches had been set up in six cities, including Beijing, Guangzhou, Shanghai and Changsha (where Mao Zedong was particularly active). The first congress of what was to become the Chinese Communist Party (CCP) met in Shanghai's French Concession in the summer of 1921. Twelve delegates attended (including Mao), representing perhaps no more than fifty committed communists (Harrison 1972: 31–2). Chen Duxiu, who was in Guangzhou at the time, was elected secretary-general of the new party. It would take several more years, however, before the CCP fully became a unified and disciplined organization characterized by ideological uniformity (Luk 1990; Van de Ven 1991).

The Warlord Period 1916–1928

Although an appearance of normality was restored after Yuan Shikai's death in 1916 with the reconvening of parliament and the succession to the presidency of the former vice-president Li Yuanhong, centralized control from Beijing – already weakened during the last year of Yuan's rule – rapidly disintegrated as provincial and local militarists strengthened their grip over their respective domains (Sheridan 1983). These militarists, or warlords as historians have come to call them (McCord 1993: 4), exercised direct political power, retaining control over civil administration (as well as issuing their own currency) and imposing their own taxes to pay for their armies, which were the sole basis of their power. It should be noted, however, that provincial warlords did not always have complete control over their own domains or all the military forces within any one province (ibid.: 267–8). The fiction of a civilian government in Beijing was preserved by whichever warlord faction or clique held sway in the north, since the powers continued to recognize the Beijing government as the sole legitimate government of China. In this way the warlord faction in control of Beijing could hope to acquire legitimacy as well as the customs revenue remitted to the central government by the powers.

China was not to experience a semblance of unity until 1928 when the Guomindang established a new national government at Nanjing, but even then its control over large areas of China remained severely limited by the continued existence of former warlords who, while acknowledging the Nanjing government, retained control of their armies. This has led one historian (Sheridan 1966, 1977, 1983) to describe the entire republican period from 1912 to 1949 as one in which China as a national entity became progressively fragmented, although he does make a distinction between the 1916–28 period, as one of 'pure warlordism', and that after 1928, which was one of 'residual warlordism'. A case study of the evolution of one particular army unit from the late Qing to the mid-1920s seeks to demonstrate this larger process of fragmentation and argues that warlordism should be seen as 'militarism in disintegration' or 'fragmented militarism' (Sutton 1980: 7). Focusing on the Yunnan provincial army (19th Division), it charts the army's transformation as a united and cohesive force underpinned by nationalist ideals when it was established in 1905, to one that by 1920 had broken up into loosely affiliated factional forces cemented exclusively by personal ties. Recent studies, however, have given more credit to the continuing modernization of the urban sphere throughout the republican period, rather than simply viewing it as a chaotic interregnum between empire and communist state (Bergère 1997: 309); a study of Beijing during this period, for example, highlights the development of professional associations, urban institutions (such as the police) and labour unions that contributed both to state-building and an enlargement of political space (Strand 1989).

Although several conferences were held in the years immediately following Yuan's death to work out some form of unity amongst warlords, the creation of various factions or cliques bred mutual suspicion, which after 1920 led to a series of wars that affected large areas of the country. Such cliques were held together by self-interest, so that betrayals and defections were common. No one clique was able to dominate, as alliances would be formed against any that threatened the status quo. This has led one historian (Ch'i 1976) to describe the warlord period in terms of an 'international system' in which a balance of power was the operative principle; the period has also been likened to Renaissance Europe, when individual states shared a common upper-class culture and the ideal of a 'universal ruler' was preserved (Mancall 1984: 202–3). Another study, perhaps overlooking the chaos and destruction of the period in its obsession with applying a coherent political-science 'model', describes it as a time when a more openly competitive and pluralist system prevailed, in contrast to the imperial monarchy before 1911 and the 'totalitarian' communist regime after 1949 (Pye 1971).

While warlords frequently announced their commitment to national unity, none was willing to abandon control over his own army. The number of men under arms increased from 500,000 in 1916 to 2 million in 1928 (Ch'i 1976: 78), and the funds required by warlords to retain the loyalty of their troops led them to impose a bewildering array of taxes on a hapless peasantry. Regular taxes, such as the land tax, were constantly increased and in many cases collected years in advance. Warlord armies themselves, recruited from among ex-bandits, the unemployed and landless peasants, wreaked havoc on local communities by engaging in systematic looting, with the result that in the popular mind there was little to distinguish regular soldiers from bandits (Lary 1985: 59–62). The growth of warlord armies was also accompanied by a dramatic increase in bandit activity in the republican period; by 1930 the total bandit population was estimated to be 20 million, prompting newspapers to describe China as a *feiguo* (bandit nation) rather than a *minguo* (republic) (Billingsley 1988: 1, 5).

While it is recognized that generally the warlord period brought misery and chaos, individual studies of warlords have attempted to provide a more in-depth analysis of their backgrounds and aims (Sheridan 1966; Gillin 1967; McCormack 1977; Wou 1978). Many of them came from modest backgrounds with little or no traditional education. Zhang Zuolin, the warlord of Manchuria, had been a bandit during the last years of the Qing dynasty; some, like Yan Xishan, the warlord of Shanxi, had received training in military academies in China and Japan, while others, like Feng Yuxiang, had risen through the ranks in one of the New Army divisions created by the Qing after 1904. Some warlords, like Wu Peifu (who was a lower-degree holder under the old civil service examination system), propagated traditional Confucian values, hoping thereby to supplement military control with moral control (Wou 1978). Feng Yuxiang even converted to Christiantiy in 1914 and was one of the few who attempted systematically to implement some form of ideological indoctrination amongst his troops – in this case a blend of Christian maxims and Confucian homilies (Sheridan 1966).

Very few warlords either had the inclination or the time to concentrate on political reform and economic development. Feng Yuxiang, for example, although at times evincing an interest in tackling social problems such as opium addiction, was never in one place long enough to see through any concrete measures. One exception was Yan Xishan, who became military governor of Shanxi in 1912 and remained in control of the province virtually until the communist victory in 1949. Yan attempted to promote both heavy and light industry, cracked down on opium-smoking, sponsored vocational education, and began to overhaul local administration by providing for village deliberative assemblies and the training of a more efficient and suitably indoctrinated district magistracy to combat the informal influence of powerful local gentry. One study argues that Yan's schemes 'constitute one of the last systematic attempts made in China to bring about reform along conservative lines' (Gillin 1967: 295). Be that as it may, the results of his economic schemes were meagre at best, while his attempts at local government reform were consistently sabotaged by local gentry. Yan's failure to extend his control to the grassroots level anticipated that of the Nationalist regime after 1928.

Before the rise of the Guomindang government in Guangzhou (see chapter 3), only Feng Yuxiang (who received a certain amount of aid from the Soviet Union when he was based in the northwest) openly attacked foreign imperialism in China, although a study of Zhang Zuolin has shown that he attempted to halt Japanese economic penetration of Manchuria by encouraging Chinese development in the region (McCormack 1977). In the confusing and unpredictable situation that prevailed in China from 1916 onwards foreign governments were reluctant to pin all their hopes on any one warlord, although most warlords were able to obtain their arms from a variety of foreign sources. Thus despite an Arms Embargo Agreement drawn up by the powers in May 1919 (and which lasted until 1929), warlords could still obtain arms from a variety of independent foreign salesmen without formal affiliation to their home governments. A warlord such as Zhang Zuolin dealt with Japanese, French, German, Italian, Czech and British arms traders, while British and American companies continued to sell aircraft (ostensibly for 'commercial use' only) to a number of warlords (Chan 1982: 50–65).

By 1926 a relatively stable balance of power had been created between Zhang Zuolin, who controlled the Beijing area and the northeast, and Wu Peifu, who controlled much of central China. This balance was to be upset by a revitalized Guomindang regime in Guangzhou, increasingly viewed with alarm by the foreign powers, which sought to change the rules of the game and restore China as a unified nation-state.

3

The Rise of the Guomindang and the Chinese Communist Party

The emergence of the Chinese Communist Party in 1921 and the reorganization of the Guomindang between 1923 and 1926 into a highly organized and disciplined political and military force introduced radical new elements into the Chinese scene. Both parties set themselves the task of overcoming the twin evils of warlordism and imperialism, and it was on this basis that a policy of joint collaboration was implemented. The Nationalist Revolution, symbolized by the military expedition (known as the Northern Expedition) launched by the Guomindang and its communist allies to reunify the country in 1926 from its base in Guangzhou, has usually been associated with growing anti-imperialism in the cities, the military defeat of the warlords, and the establishment of a new central government under Guomindang auspices in 1928. A recent study has also drawn attention to a wider process of 'national awakening' in material culture and intellectual thought during this period that intertwined with, and was ultimately absorbed into, the Guomindang's political agenda of forging a nation-state (Fitzgerald 1996). The Nationalist Revolution, furthermore, witnessed the first large-scale mobilization of women (Gilmartin 1995). During the course of the Northern Expedition the united front between the Guomindang and the CCP broke apart as irreconcilable differences over the issue of class revolution became more evident. While the CCP gradually retreated to the rural hinterlands, the Guomindang regime after 1928 set itself to achieve the tasks of a modernizing state. A combination of internal and external factors ultimately frustrated such ambitions, although the exact nature of the regime and its significance in China's twentieth-century history remain issues of debate amongst historians.

The First United Front

The first congress of the CCP in 1921, after much heated discussion, adopted an uncompromising stance towards other political organizations, including the Guomindang. In contrast to the loosely organized socialist and Marxist study groups formed in 1919 and 1920, the new party began the process of laying down strict organizational rules and membership requirements. Over the next few years, for example, anarchists either left, or were expelled from, the party (Dirlik 1989; 1991). Since the founding delegates in 1921 adopted both the orthodox Marxist view that the revolution would occur amongst the urban proletariat and the Leninist assumption that the party was the vanguard of the proletariat, priority was assigned to organizing urban labour with the aim of overthrowing 'the capitalist classes and all private ownership' (Harrison 1972: 34), although the question of whether to join the Moscow-based Communist International (Comintern) was not raised (Schwartz 1951: 34).

The reality of China's situation, however, belied the optimistic faith of early CCP leaders in promoting urban revolution. Although an urban proletariat had begun to emerge during the last years of the Qing dynasty (see chapter 1), China was still overwhelmingly rural in 1921. Despite the dramatic increase in the number of modern Chinese enterprises (e.g. in the textile industry) during and just after the First World War, as the attention of the powers elsewhere allowed more scope for native industry to develop (Feuerwerker 1968, 1983a; Bergère 1983, 1989), there were still only just under 1.5 million workers involved in large- and medium-scale production in 1919, less than 1 per cent of the total population (Chesneaux 1968: 41, 47). This proletariat was heavily concentrated in a few large cities, particularly Shanghai. To this figure should be added a further 12–14 million workers involved in mining, utilities, construction and handicrafts (Harrison 1972: 9; Wright: 1984), most of whom Chesneaux (1968), in his pioneering study of the

origins of the Chinese working class, excluded from his definition of a modern proletariat because they were still enmeshed
in pre-industrial labour organizations such as traditional guilds,
regional associations and labour contract gangs. Yet even
modern factory workers were often recruited by traditional-
style labour bosses or contractors, and since many of them were
rural migrants who would return to their home areas during
the busy harvest season, there was always a high turnover of
personnel.

In the 1920s only 6 per cent of China's population lived in
cities of more than 50,000 and another 6 per cent in towns of
between 10,000 and 50,000 (Harrison 1972: 9). As late as 1933,
out of a total working population of nearly 260 million, 250
million were engaged in agriculture. In 1933 agriculture contributed 65 per cent of the net domestic product, while the
output of factories, handicrafts, mining and utilities constituted
10.5 per cent of the net domestic product. Within this latter cat-
egory, however, modern factory production was overshadowed
by handicrafts; modern industry, in fact, accounted for only 2.2
per cent of the net domestic product in 1933 (Feuerwerker 1968:
6, 8, 10, 17). One economic historian (ibid.: 10) has argued that
the structure of China's mainland economy before 1949 was
typical of a 'pre-industrial society', although more recent work
on the Chinese economy before 1937 has underlined both the
(relatively) respectable rate of industrial growth during this
period despite recurrent political and economic crises and the
continued vitality of some traditional sectors of the economy
such as water junk transportation (Wright 1984; Rawski 1989).
Another recent analysis notes that although the modern sector
by the 1930s represented no more than one-tenth of GNP, it had
still grown on average at about 6 per cent over the preceding
three or four decades (Brandt 1997: 282 308).

The first congress of the CCP, nevertheless, established the
Chinese Labour Organization Secretariat (with branches in
other major cities) to promote the development of modern
labour unions. Between 1921 and 1923 communist activists were
involved in the launching of a number of strikes for improved
conditions, although they were only marginally involved in one
of the first strikes with national significance, that of the Chinese
Seamen's Union in Hong Kong (January to March 1922). Other
workers in Hong Kong and Guangzhou supported the strike,

which eventually involved about 100,000 men, brought Hong Kong to a virtual standstill and gained considerable wage increases (Kwan 1997). In 1922, also, Li Dazhao (co-founder of the CCP) in north China worked out an agreement with the warlord Wu Peifu to organize unions amongst railway workers along the Beijing–Hankou line. Communist activists also began organizing labour as far afield as Manchuria; by the end of 1923, for example, they had helped form unions among workers of the South Manchurian Railway. A case study of communist activities in Manchuria, however, has pointed out that such activists were handicapped by low levels of worker interest in communist appeals, their status as outsiders, lukewarm support from the CCP leadership (which tended to focus on central and south China) and the particularly hostile attitudes of both Zhang Zuolin's warlord regime and Japanese authorities of the South Manchurian Railway zone (Lee 1983: 41–5, 54–66).

One of the most prominent of these early communist labour organizers (all of whom were intellectuals rather than workers) was Deng Zhongxia (1894–1933). Born into a gentry family, Deng had attended Changsha Normal School in Hunan (where he met Mao Zedong) before enrolling at Beijing University in 1917. He became a student leader during the May Fourth demonstrations and participated in a workers' education movement organized by Beijing University students (Kwan 1997: 9–26). In 1921 Deng was elected general secretary of the Labour Secretariat, which convened the First National Labour Congress in May 1922 in Guangzhou. The congress was attended by 160 delegates claiming to represent 100 unions and up to 300,000 workers (Harrison 1972: 36). Mao Zedong's role in the labour movement during these years has also been highlighted by recent studies (e.g. Shaffer 1982), in contrast to earlier Mao biographies (Ch'en 1965; Schram 1966) which tend to gloss over this period in his revolutionary career. In 1921 he became head of the Hunan branch of the Labour Secretariat and during the next two years helped to organize successful strikes amongst miners, construction workers and printers, many of whom belonged to traditional guilds (Spence 1999b: 57–60). It might be noted here that recent research has highlighted the 'everyday forms of resistance' in urban factories and workshops, as opposed to focusing on specific and well-publicized strikes (Hershatter 1986), as well as exploring the ways in which native-place ties could facilitate, as much as hinder, mobilization in the factories (Perry 1993). These early CCP forays into the world of labour, however, were ultimately stymied by a number of factors. First, in cities such as Shanghai communist activists had to compete with underworld gangs and secret societies for influence over female textile workers, who constituted more than one-third of the proletariat there (Honig 1986: 4); in other urban centres such as Guangzhou they discovered that pioneering organizational activity (such as the establishment of workers' clubs and night schools) was already being carried out by anarchists – in Hunan, for example, Mao initially had to co-operate with prominent anarchist labour organizers (Shaffer 1982). Second, early CCP activity was often dangerously dependent on the support of local powerholders and the vagaries of warlord politics. In Hunan the loss of urban elite support and a change of military governor in 1923 led to the closure of many unions (McDonald 1978: 1–5, 143–4). The vulnerability of the early labour movement was dramatically illustrated in February 1923, when Wu Peifu, who had originally sanctioned CCP activity amongst railway workers in order to combat the influence of his major warlord rival, Zhang Zuolin, became alarmed at growing labour militance and brutally suppressed a strike (Wou 1978: 203–4, 223–4). Third, a recent study of Deng Zhongxia and the early CCP labour movement has argued that ideological and personal differences within the party itself, and the lack of faith Marxist intellectuals had in the potential political commitment of working-class labour activists, precluded the formulation (at least until early 1925) of a well-planned labour strategy (Kwan 1997: 47–9).

Meanwhile, the CCP came under increasing pressure from the Comintern to form an alliance with the Guomindang. In a 1920 speech to the Second Congress of the Comintern, later to be known as the Theses on the National and Colonial Questions, Lenin had argued that newly founded communist parties in the colonial world (in particular Asia) needed to co-operate initially with more powerful 'bourgeois nationalist' parties or groups since they shared common aims of national unification and freedom from foreign control and exploitation. In fact, initial Comintern assessment of Sun Yatsen and the Guomindang was not always positive, while the People's Commissariat for

Foreign Affairs (Narkomindel) at first looked to Wu Peifu as a potential ally (Whiting 1954: 90, 117–19), but it was finally decided that the CCP should co-operate with the Guomindang. Chen Duxiu, who had always mistrusted Sun Yatsen, was reluctant to go along with this policy, but the Comintern representative in China, Maring, was able to impose Moscow's authority on the fledgling CCP and by 1922, at the Second Party Congress, it was noted that the most urgent task of the proletariat was to unite with 'democratic groups' against feudal militarism and imperialism. The party made it clear, however, that within such a democratic alliance the workers had to continue fighting for their own interests (Schwartz 1951: 39–40; Feigon 1983: 168–70). The willingness of Chinese communist revolutionaries to submit themselves to Moscow's direction has always intrigued historians. One study argues that such willingness had its roots in the late Qing, when Chinese student revolutionaries perceived the Russian revolution as a universal struggle against oppression of which their own anti-Manchu movement was an integral part; the tendency to view Russia as a paradigm of universal moral progress thus foreshadowed acceptance of Russian leadership of the Chinese revolution in the 1920s and 1930s (Price 1974: 220).

Sun Yatsen at this time was seeking to expand his base in the south. Since 1917 he had been dependent on local warlords and had twice been ejected from Guangzhou by his main rival in Guangdong province, Chen Jiongming (in 1918 and 1922). Chen had been a member of Sun's *Tongmenghui* before 1911 and as governor of Guangdong in the early 1920s championed remarkably progressive policies. The relationship between Chen and Sun was always an uneasy one, since the latter's ambition to seek reconquest of the north and desire to appropriate sources for his 'national' government in Guangzhou clashed with the former's insistence that the needs of Guangdong province had to take priority. One historian notes that Guomindang denunciation of Chen Jiongming's 'rebellion' against Sun in 1922 as an act of moral betrayal and reactionary militaristic regionalism spelled the doom of federalism as a political ideal (i.e. that provincial autonomy should form the foundations for an eventual national unity) (Duara 1995: 194–200), an ideal that had its roots during the late Qing (see chapter 1) and to which even Mao Zedong briefly adhered in 1920 when he proposed the establishment of the Republic of Hunan (McDonald 1978: 42–3).

At the same time, Sun's quest since 1917 to gain western diplomatic recognition for his regime and subsequent financial assistance continued to prove fruitless (Wilbur 1976: 91–111), while his support for the 1922 Seamen's Union strike in Hong Kong marked him as a dangerous radical in the eyes of the western powers. Sun began to look to the Soviet Union as a possible source of aid. He had met Maring as early as 1921 and spoken highly of Lenin's New Economic Policy, which he compared to his own Principle of People's Livelihood. Sun was also attracted to Bolshevik Party organization, whose centralized discipline and *esprit de corps* he wanted the Guomindang to emulate.

In January 1923 Sun met with another Comintern representative, Adolph Joffe, in Shanghai and they issued a joint manifesto calling for co-operation between the Guomindang and the CCP. Sun agreed to allow the CCP to retain its separate existence but insisted that CCP members enter the Guomindang as individuals rather than as a party. One month later Sun returned triumphantly to Guangzhou, having used mercenaries from Yunnan province to oust Chen Jiongming. The first United Front was formalized later that year, despite opposition from the right wing of the Guomindang which viewed the CCP with suspicion. Leading communists such as Li Dazhao were enthusiastic about the new policy and Mao Zedong was to throw himself wholeheartedly into united front work, a fact that was later ignored by communist authorities after 1949. Yet it was natural that Li Dazhao and Mao Zedong, both ardent nationalists, should be attracted to the anti-imperialist programme of the United Front. For Mao, the desire to see a revived, strong and respected China was a crucial aspect of his early political thought (Schram 1989: 14–15).

With the establishment of the United Front, Sun Yatsen now had access to Soviet military and financial aid. He assumed, unlike his party's right wing, that the CCP would not present a threat and would ultimately be absorbed into the much larger Guomindang. The CCP, for its part, hoped to use the United Front to expand its membership and gain control of the mass organizations that began to be created under Guomindang auspices. For the Soviet Union, the United Front served its own national interests, since it could now hope to have an increasing influence over a potentially powerful force that would oppose the western powers in China; at the same time Moscow told CCP leaders that the party could eventually take over leadership of the revolution from within and hence fulfill long-term revolutionary aims.

The Soviet Union's tendency, however, to subordinate the interests of the Chinese revolution to its own national interests (illustrated by the fact that foreign policy was made by both the People's Commissariat for Foreign Affairs, whose priority was to enhance the interests of the Soviet state, and the Moscow-dominated Comintern, which promoted international revolution) was clearly seen in the attempt by Moscow to reach agreement with the Beijing-based warlord government at the same time as it was sponsoring the anti-warlord and anti-imperialist United Front in the south. This culminated in a 1924 treaty, which established diplomatic relations between Beijing and Moscow; the treaty also provided for joint-management of the Chinese Eastern Railway, a Russian concession that was originally to have been returned to China in accordance with the Karakhan Declaration of 1919 promising to return *all* concessions acquired by Russia in China during the nineteenth century (Whiting 1954: 208–35). A recent analysis of Soviet diplomacy in China during the 1920s emphasizes its self-serving and secret nature (e.g. two versions of the Karakhan Declaration were used, one of which omitted the reference to the return of the Chinese Eastern Railway without compensation and was used as the basis for the secret agreement with Beijing in 1924 giving the Soviet Union majority control over the railway) (Elleman 1994).

The Nationalist Revolution

With the help of Russian advisers, referred to in one account as 'missionaries of revolution' (Wilbur and How 1989: 12), and Soviet financial assistance, Sun proceeded to reorganize the Guomindang into a highly disciplined party (Wilbur 1983: 531–7; Wilbur and How 1989: 80–99). In particular he relied on Mikhail Borodin, the most important and energetic of the Soviet advisers, who was to remain in China until the break-up of the United Front in 1927 (Jacobs 1981). Borodin convinced

Sun that in order to defeat warlordism and imperialism the party would have to mobilize workers and peasants in a genuinely mass revolution. Party bureaux dealing with propaganda, organization, labour, peasants and women were soon created. At the same time a military academy was established at Whampoa (Huangpu), near Guangzhou, in May 1924 to train officers for a new and ideologically motivated army. Like the Russian Red Army, this new revolutionary army was to have political commissars attached to all units to ensure correct ideological training.

The commandant of the Whampoa Academy was Chiang Kai-shek (1887–1975), who had received military training in Japan before 1911 and had become closely associated with Sun. Chiang's association with Sun was also cemented by personal ties when he later (in 1927) married the sister of Sun Yatsen's wife, Song Qingling. The Songs were a wealthy family (the founder being a self-made man trained as a Christian missionary in the US who had become a wealthy entrepreneur in Shanghai) that was to exert considerable influence on Chinese politics during the following years; another sister was to marry H. H. Kong (K'ung), a future finance minister in the nationalist government after 1928, while a brother, Song Ziwen (T. V. Soong) was also to serve as finance minister and head numerous business and economic organizations after 1928 (Seagrave 1985). Chiang's connections to the Christian and western-educated Song family (all three Song sisters and their brother were educated in the US) brought him respectability and financial security, complementing his close links with the Shanghai underworld (not advertised at the time), which also paid dividends, especially after 1927 (see next section).

At the first National Congress of the Guomindang in January 1924 nationalism was redefined in terms of anti-imperialism and formal commitment was made to the mobilization of workers and peasants. For the first time Sun Yatsen was perceived as the spokesman for mass nationalism (Bergère 1998: 328–30, 341). The CCP also acquired influence and positions within the reorganized Guomindang. At the 1924 congress communists (including Li Dazhao and Mao Zedong) were elected to the Central Executive Committee. Others, such as Zhou Enlai (1898–1976), were political commissars at the Whampoa Academy. Communists also headed the Peasant and

Organization Bureaux, and held top positions in the Labour Bureau (Wilbur 1983: 538). In fact, it was through the United Front that the CCP began to pay more attention to the peasantry (Hofheinz 1977: 8). Although Peng Pai, the son of a landlord who had joined the CCP in 1921, had begun to organize tenant farmers near Guangzhou and helped to create a Peasants Union in 1922 (Marks 1984: 152–281; Galbiati 1985: 100–18), the CCP leadership was initially sceptical of the possibility of expanding into the rural areas. It was not until after 1923, for example, that the party created its own peasant committee. Peng Pai went on to become a leading member of the Peasant Bureau and was the first director of the Peasant Movement Training Institute set up by the Guomindang in 1924 to train rural cadrés. Peasant associations campaigning for rent reduction began to be formed throughout Guangdong province, and played a role in the Guomindang's struggle with local warlords. It was while serving as director of the Peasant Movement Training Institute in 1926 that Mao Zedong himself came to appreciate the enormous revolutionary potential of the peasantry (Womack 1982: 52–9; Schram 1989: 38–40).

Sun Yatsen's last political act was to leave for Beijing in November 1924 to negotiate peaceful reunification with the northern warlords (having abandoned earlier plans for a military expedition in alliance with southern militarists). Already seriously ill, nothing had been achieved by the time he died in Beijing in March 1925. Sun was soon canonized as the founder of the Chinese revolution and, especially after the establishment of the Nationalist government in 1928, his portrait appeared everywhere in schools and government offices (and was even printed on dollar bills and cigarette packets). The anniversaries of his birth and death became national holidays and by 1940 he was referred to as *Guofu* (the father of the nation) (Fitzgerald 1996: 27; Bergère 1998: 409–10). Although Sun ultimately failed in his quest for a united and democratic China, and his elaborate plans for national development – published in 1920 under the title *Jianguo Fanglue* (Plan for National Reconstruction) – have been described as the work of an impractical visionary (Wilbur 1976: 286–7), a recent assessment has highlighted the contemporary relevance of Sun's ideas (Bergère 1998: 284–5). Thus Sun's appeal for international economic co-operation, his focus on China's coastal zones and ports as the principal poles for future development, and his suggestions for a mixed economy are seen as anticipating the post-1976 reform programme of greater interaction with the West, use of foreign technology, emphasis on the special role of coastal development zones, and the introduction of a market economy to complement the existing state sector.

With the death of Sun Yatsen power within the Guomindang began to gravitate towards Chiang Kai-shek who, as commander of the National Revolutionary Army and chairman of the Military Council, exerted increasing influence over the civilian wing of the party, which was under the leadership of Wang Jingwei (1883–1941). Wang had been a close colleague of Sun's since their time spent together in the anti-dynastic cause before 1911 and was associated with the left wing of the party. Since both Wang and Chiang claimed the mantle of succession to Sun Yatsen, a conflict between them developed that was to result in a split within the party in 1926–7.

The Guomindang and the CCP, meanwhile, reaped the benefits of a growing anti-imperialist tide in China after 1923, and membership of both parties expanded rapidly. CCP membership, for example, grew from around 130 in 1922 to 60,000 in 1927 (Ch'en 1983: 526). Anti-imperialist feelings reached fever pitch with the May Thirtieth Incident in 1925. Ten days earlier Chinese workers protesting against the closure of a Japanese textile mill in Shanghai had been fired upon by Japanese guards and one worker had been killed. On 30 May students and workers held demonstrations to condemn the Japanese action in particular and to protest against foreign privilege in general. The British commander of the International Settlement police force in Shanghai ordered his men to fire on the crowd and twelve people were killed. The incident aroused a storm of protest not only in Shanghai but in all other major cities (Isaacs 1961: 70–3; Clifford 1979: 15–27). Strikes and boycotts in Shanghai and Guangzhou brought economic activity to a standstill, and British and Japanese consulates were attacked. Students were also able to elaborate on their 'protest scripts' first developed during the May Fourth Movement by re-enacting scenes of martyrdom on the streets to galvanize public opposition to foreign imperialism (Wasserstrom 1991: 109–10). Although the May Thirtieth Movement has usually been viewed as the turning point in the nationalist revolution and the subsequent defeat of the northern warlords in 1927–8, a recent study argues that it was two wars fought between two rival northern warlord cliques (associated with Wu Peifu and Zhang Zuolin) in 1924 that in fact marked the crucial turning point. The wars fatally weakened the Beijing regime, led to economic bankruptcy and instilled a pervasive loss of confidence in the status quo – all of which were the key determinants in the eventual success of the Guomindang's Northern Expedition in 1927–8 (Waldron 1995: 5–9).

During the course of the May Thirtieth Movement the Guangzhou regime declared itself the National government and plans were made for the military reunification of China. Chiang's National Revolutionary Army had already proved its worth in campaigns against the Guangdong governor, Chen Jiongming. Militarists from the neighbouring province of Guangxi decided to join forces with the Guomindang and their armies were renamed as units of the National Revolutionary Army. These militarists (Bai Chongxi and Li Zongren), known as the Guangxi clique, had been active in promoting reform in their own province and hoped to use their co-operation with the Guomindang as a springboard for national influence (Lary 1974; Levich 1993). A precedent had been set whereby former warlords and their armies were co-opted by the revolutionary forces.

Initially, both Chen Duxiu and Moscow were lukewarm towards the idea of a Northern Expedition. Chen, in particular, feared that such a campaign would merely enhance Chiang Kai-shek's military power. Chiang, meanwhile, demonstrated his growing influence within the Guomindang by carrying out what became known as the 'March Coup' of 1926. In that month he ordered that Russian advisers be placed under house arrest and declared that henceforth members of the CCP would not be permitted to head party bureaux. CCP membership on party committees was also reduced (Harrison 1972: 76–8). At the same time Wang Jingwei was forced into retirement.

Although Chiang now seemed to be publicly backing the Guomindang right wing, which had consistently demanded the expulsion of communists from the party, he adopted a more conciliatory tone after the 'coup' since he still needed the support of the CCP and Moscow in the coming campaign against the warlords. Stalin, for his part, was anxious that the United Front should continue. Within the Soviet Union Stalin's ideological and political differences with Trotsky (which were to lead to the latter's eventual expulsion from the Bolshevik Party and exile from the country) had repercussions on the perceptions he had of the situation in China. Thus while Trotsky opposed the CCP's co-operation with the bourgeoisie (i.e. the Guomindang) and called for the immediate establishment of soviets, Stalin insisted that the Guomindang represented a four-class bloc (large bourgeoisie, petty bourgeoisie, workers and peasants) and that therefore the CCP needed to remain in the United Front to guarantee its continuing influence over the masses. As will be noted later, Stalin's insistence that the CCP uphold the United Front policy – to have recommended withdrawal would have validated Trotsky's stance on China and hence would have weakened Stalin's attempt to assert his own ideological leadership – was very nearly to result in the CCP's total annihilation (Schwartz 1951; Brandt 1958; Isaacs 1961).

The United Front therefore held. Chiang released the Russian advisers and, with the support of the CCP and Moscow, the Northern Expedition got underway in the summer of 1926 (Spence 1999a: 323–30). Against the numerically superior but poorly co-ordinated warlord armies, the National Revolutionary Army was able to enlist considerable mass support (Wilbur 1968, 1983; Jordan 1976). Very often militant action by peasants and workers preceded the nationalist advance. There were widespread strikes in all major industrial centres, while in the central provinces of Hunan and Hubei there was an enormous increase in the number of peasant associations, with a reported membership of over two million by the beginning of 1927 (Isaacs 1961: 113). These associations went beyond the usual call for rent reductions and encouraged direct appropriation of the land, frequently attacking landlords in the process.

Mao Zedong visited Hunan in 1926, and witnessed at first hand the revolution that was occurring in the countryside. He wrote a report on his findings which has since become one of the classic texts of Chinese communism. In his 'Report of an Investigation into the Peasant Movement in Hunan', Mao drew the party's attention to the spontaneous struggle by peasants against 'corrupt officials, local bullies and evil gentry'. In contrast to the orthodox Marxist view, which portrayed peasants as essentially parochial and conservative and whose 'petty bourgeois' ambitions solely to secure title to their own plot of land meant that they would have to be led by a more revolutionary urban proletariat, Mao enthusiastically claimed that the real revolution was taking place in the countryside; he further implied that the party risked losing leadership of the revolution if it did not move quickly to involve itself in the peasants' struggle. By noting also that landlordism constituted the social foundation of imperialism and warlordism in China, Mao sought to shift attention from the cities and elevate rural class struggle as the principal determinant of the revolution:

> In a very short time, several hundred million peasants in China's central, southern and northern provinces will rise like a tornado or tempest – a force so extraordinarily swift and violent that no power, however great, will be able to suppress it. They will break through all the trammels that now bind them and push forward along the road to liberation. They will send all imperialists, warlords, corrupt officials, local bullies and evil gentry to their graves. All revolutionary parties and all revolutionary comrades will stand before them to be tested, to be accepted or rejected by them. To march at their head and lead them? To follow in the rear, gesticulating at them and criticizing them? To face them as opponents? Every Chinese is free to choose among the three, but circumstances demand that a quick decision be made. (Cited in Schram 1963: 179–80)

Although, as was noted earlier, Peng Pai had begun to organize peasant unions in the early 1920s (often overlooked in later CCP historiography because of the emphasis on Mao's pioneering role in mobilizing the peasantry), among the CCP leadership as a whole it was still assumed that the revolution would primarily be based in the cities. For the first time a prominent member of the CCP was claiming that the peasantry was the leading force of the revolution. Mao's report was also clear testimony to his populist faith, evident since May Fourth days, in the revolutionary potential of the masses. Furthermore, his implied criticism that the party had lost touch with real events going on in the countryside was a reflection of his disdain for 'bookish intellectuals' that was to remain with him throughout his life (although, ironically, Mao himself could be considered an intellectual, having attended both secondary school and teachers' training college).

Mao's confidence that a mobilized peasantry would sweep all before it (with no reference to the guidance and leadership to be provided by the party and urban proletariat) is an example of what has been called Mao's 'voluntaristic' belief in the ability of conscious human ability to overcome all objective factors. Such a belief implied that 'revolution in China was not dependent on any predetermined levels of social and economic development and that revolutionary action need not be restrained by inherited Marxist–Leninist orthodoxies' (Meisner 1999: 42). As such, Mao's report was the first significant step in the process whereby he would adapt Marxism–Leninism to Chinese conditions, a process that was later to be defined as the 'Sinification of Marxism' (see chapter 4). It might be noted that such a process involved detailed investigations by Mao of local conditions. Thus a report on the district of Xunwu (in southwest Jiangxi) that Mao compiled in May 1930 following the recent establishment of a local soviet, and recently translated into English (Thompson 1990), carried a wealth of detail on commerce, social customs, land tenure arrangements and education in the area.

By the end of 1926 the nationalist forces had taken control of the provinces of Hunan, Hubei, Jiangxi and Fujian. In addition to co-opting local warlords along the way, the nationalists also obtained the support of more important militarists like Yan Xishan and Feng Yuxiang who, like the Guangxi Clique, were to gain top positions in the Guomindang hierarchy while still retaining control of their own armies.

The increasingly militant mass movement, however, accentuated differences between the left and right wings of the Guomindang, with the former arguing that it was a positive development and the latter demanding that it be restrained. The foreign powers, too, viewed events with increasing alarm. As nationalist forces reached the Yangzi the British concession areas in Hankou and Jiujiang were overrun, while in early 1927 the British, American and Japanese consulates in Nanjing were attacked, which prompted quick reprisals in the form of joint British and American naval bombardment of the city.

As Wang Jingwei, Song Qingling and others associated with the Guomindang left wing began to set up a government in Wuhan, Chiang Kai-shek proceeded to Shanghai. A series of strikes during the previous nine months had paralysed the city and played an important part in preventing the local warlord, Sun Chuanfang, from mounting effective resistance against the advancing nationalist forces. In April 1927, less than one month after being welcomed by the workers, Chiang turned on his erstwhile leftist allies and brutally suppressed all trade unions in the city, arresting and executing all those accused of being in league with the communists. Chiang's actions were supported and abetted by both the Shanghai business and merchant classes, who feared the disruptive effects of militant labour activity, and the foreign powers, who favoured a quick return to normality. Chiang was also able to enlist the help of Shanghai's underworld, and in particular the Green Gang, a secret society involved in drug trafficking, labour racketeering, gambling and prostitution, in rounding up and shooting communists and their supporters (Marshall 1976; Martin 1996: 91–111). This 'White Terror' was extended to other cities under Chiang's control.

The Nationalist government at Wuhan condemned Chiang's action (prompting him to set up his own government in Nanjing), but its position became increasingly untenable. Although it had the support of a number of militarists jealous of Chiang's power, these generals were opposed to the continuing appropriation of land by peasant associations in the Hunan/Hubei countryside, since many of them owned land themselves or were related to landowners. Labour strikes in the city of Wuhan itself also placed the government in an awkward position as it attempted to steer a middle course between satisfying union demands and restraining the 'excesses' of the mass movement. It should be noted, however, that the Wuhan government did implement some progressive gender policies (such as extensive marriage, inheritance and legal rights for women) and a recent study has argued that this period witnessed the most enlightened attempt to tackle women's issues during the entire century (Gilmartin 1995: 181–94).

The CCP, meanwhile, was the victim of contradictory advice from Moscow. On the one hand Stalin instructed the CCP to co-operate with the Wuhan regime, on the basis that it represented the genuinely revolutionary wing of the Guomindang (now defined by Stalin as representing a 'three-class bloc', since Chiang Kai-shek, as the spokesman of the 'big bourgeoisie', had now revealed his true reactionary colours), and on the other, advised the party to arm the peasants, eliminate unreliable generals from the army, and strive to replace 'reactionary elements' within the Wuhan government itself.

Not surprisingly, Wuhan government leaders became increasingly suspicious of their CCP allies. Faced with sabotage from within and mutiny from its military supporters, who now began to take matters into their own hands by embarking on a ruthless campaign to suppress the peasant movement, the Wuhan regime dissolved itself, and the two wings of the Guomindang were formally united once more with Chiang's own power and prestige greatly enhanced. Chiang then continued with the Northern Expedition and in 1928, with the help of Yan Xishan and Feng Yuxiang, succeeded in taking Beijing and forcing Zhang Zuolin to flee northwards to his home base in Manchuria. A new national government was formally proclaimed, with its capital to be located in Nanjing. One immediate casualty of the end of the Wuhan regime was the women's movement. A conservative backlash against politically active women resulted in horrendous atrocities being perpetrated against women who by their dress, short-cropped hair and public visibility were condemned for upsetting the natural gender order and 'turning the world upside down' (Diamond 1975; Gilmartin 1995: 198–9).

The United Front had ended in total disaster for the CCP, with its membership decimated and urban base smashed. Chen Duxiu was made the scapegoat and accused of 'right-wing opportunism' (i.e. failure to encourage the mass movement). In August 1927 he was replaced as secretary-general of the party by Qu Qiubai. The party thereupon launched a series of insurrections, hoping to make use of mutinies within Guomindang army units and seize key towns and cities. One such insurrection, known as the Autumn Harvest Uprising and designed to capture Changsha (in Hunan province) in September 1927, was led by Mao. His insistence that a more organized military force be created under an independent CCP banner (rather than under the banner of the 'revolutionary left Guominding' as laid down by party leaders) and that a larger base area be formed instead of merely attacking a few cities, brought him a rebuke from the CCP Central Committee (now underground in Shanghai), which would come to view Mao as a reckless military adventurer (Harrison 1972: 129–34). The Autumn Harvest

Uprising failed and Mao took the remnants of his force, comprising landless peasants, vagrants and brigands, to Jingganshan, on the Hunan–Jiangxi border. There he was to meet up with Zhu De, one of the leaders of an earlier insurrection, and they began to build up a new military force which was to be the foundation of the Red Army. The CCP's woes were completed in December 1927, when its last attempt at urban insurrection in Guangzhou (where communists established a short-lived soviet, known as the Guangzhou Commune) was bloodily suppressed (ibid.: 137–9). Henceforth, the Chinese revolution would be based in the countryside.

The Nanjing Decade 1928–1937

When the Guomindang declared itself the national government in 1928 it was acting in accordance with Sun Yatsen's principle of political tutelage. By this Sun had meant that the party would have to guide the political destiny of the nation until such time as the people were prepared for democracy, after which a constitution would be promulgated. Yet although institutions of government were created in Nanjing (with the Guomindang retaining a separate identity), the nationalist regime was never able to exert total control of the country beyond the immediate surrounding provinces. Large areas of China, such as the province of Sichuan in the west, were still ruled by pre-1928 militarists, who recognized the Nanjing government but successfully blocked its attempts to reduce their power (Kapp 1973). Those militarists who had joined the Guomindang during the Northern Expedition, like Yan Xishan and Feng Yuxiang, were appointed members of the Guomindang Central Executive Committee but persistently refused to disband or reduce their armies. Furthermore, the government was beset throughout the 1930s with increasing Japanese encroachment in the north (see chapter 4), a growing communist threat in the south, and a series of revolts by disgruntled militarists (sometimes in alliance with Chiang Kai-shek's rivals within the Guomindang itself).

Chiang Kai-shek was to use his military campaigns against the communists to extend Nanjing's political control during the 1930s so that, according to one account, the Nationalist government ruled 25 per cent of the country (comprising 66 per cent of the population) by 1937 in contrast to the 8 per cent of the country (comprising 20 per cent of the population) it had controlled in 1929 (Eastman 1974: 281). However, a measure of the regime's weak hold over the country can be seen in the fact that Nanjing derived virtually all of its revenue from the modern sector concentrated in Shanghai. Furthermore, the government's expenditures in 1933 represented a mere 2.4 per cent of the country's total domestic product (Coble 1980: 9).

Although the Guomindang has been credited with laying the groundwork for the creation of a nation-state (Bedeski 1981), the regime itself was riddled with factionalism and corruption, and showed scant commitment to genuine social or economic reform (Eastman 1974). Such attempts as were made by state authorities after 1927 in provinces such as Zhejiang and Jiangsu to determine fair rents (a process that had begun in the early republican period) were largely abandoned by 1930 due to landlord opposition (Bernhardt 1992: 182–9). Other projects to which the regime was committed, such as the improvement of public health and hygiene, suffered from an urban bias and a lack of funds because of competing priorities (Yip 1996). Rural areas under Nanjing's control also suffered an increased tax burden as owner–cultivators were subjected to increased surcharges on the land tax imposed by local district governments. Since most of Nanjing's expenditures were used for military purposes little was done to promote economic development; the construction of roads and railways, for example, was carried out mainly for strategic purposes. Social reform consisted primarily of Chiang's New Life Movement, launched in 1934. An attempt to combine Prussian-style military values and Confucian ethics (both of which Chiang admired), and which has recently been described as a form of 'Confucian fascism' (Wakeman 1997), the New Life Movement sought to instil discipline, frugality, and the habit of hard work amongst the populace; it ultimately degenerated into meaningless exhortations for people to behave and dress 'properly' (such as not to spit in public, to be punctual at all times and to button up jackets and coats) (Dirlik 1975; Chu 1980; Kirby 1984: 176–85).

The Guomindang also took little heed of the interests of the urban business and merchant classes. Although earlier studies portrayed the Guomindang as either the hireling of the newly emerging urban bourgeoisie or as the representative of rural and urban elites (Isaacs 1961; Moore 1966), recent research has shown that it had no intention of allowing the urban capitalists to acquire political influence, while at the same time it resorted to extortion, increased taxes and forced purchase of government bonds in order to milk the modern sector of the economy (Coble 1980; Bergère 1983, 1989). Furthermore, a study of changing relations amongst the state, landlords and tenants in the Yangzi region from the mid-nineteenth century to the eve of the communist takeover in 1949 also demonstrates that the position of the landlord elite continued to decline during the period of Guomindang rule, as it was caught between rising state extractions on the one hand and tenant/state demands to maintain or lower rents on the other (Bernhardt 1992: 219).

Intimidation of the bourgeoisie (as well as of militant labour) was facilitated by the regime's symbiotic relationship with the Shanghai Green Gang, a 'working relationship' that also gave the Guomindang authorities a stake in the illegal opium trade (Martin 1996). By 1936 the government had taken control of the most important private banks, which were compelled to sub-scribe to government bonds; in this way, as one study notes (Coble 1980), the urban capitalists became dependent on the Nanjing regime. Speculation in government bonds was rife, particularly among government ministers themselves (some of whom also served as bank directors, such as H. Kong, a minis-ter of finance and Chiang's brother-in-law). Furthermore, Chiang's constant need for revenue to fuel his military cam-paigns against either the communists or recalcitrant militarists made him oblivious to the needs of native industry. Thus, even after tariff autonomy was achieved in 1929, rates on imports were not raised unduly (which might have enhanced the competitiveness of native industry) for fear that a resultant decline in imports would bring in less customs revenue for the government (Coble 1980: 83).

The Guomindang regime was therefore not the spokesman of urban capitalists. Yet neither did it plan to eliminate private enterprise altogether in favour of a planned economy, as the anti-capitalist bias of Guomindang propaganda might have sug-gested (capitalists were accused of being only concerned with their individual interests at the expense of those of the nation). As a recent study shows (Fewsmith 1985), despite the wishes of some Guomindang members to unite with the more radical and politically active elements of the merchant community – which tended to be representative of small-scale business and industry – against the merchant elite that had traditionally dominated the banking and industrial sectors, Chiang called a halt to further mass campaigns after 1928, arguing they would be detrimental to social unity. The merchant elite was not displaced, but rather co-opted by the regime.

The Guomindang itself was split into various cliques or factions, whose bitter rivalry Chiang was able skilfully to manipulate in order to ensure his own pre-eminence, a position that was given formal recognition in 1938 when he was awarded the title of 'leader' (*zongcai*). Yet it is a curious fact that although Chiang was able to impose strict press censorship and effectively hinder any attempt by liberal intellectuals to create new political organizations or pressure groups – for example, those demanding the promulgation of a permanent constitution which would establish full democracy – he was unable to eliminate corruption or inefficiency within the party or government itself. This was despite the fact that in 1932 Chiang sponsored the creation of an elite corps within the Guomindang to enhance his own personal leadership and stamp out corruption amongst party and government bureaucrats. Known as the Blue Shirts, the corps drew inspiration from European fascism (Eastman 1974), although one study has argued that the fascist elements of Chiang's regime have been much exaggerated, since its political and economic strategies have more in common with the 'national developmental state' of late nineteenth- and early twentieth-century Italy (Chang 1985). Nevertheless, even this organization made little impact and was disbanded in 1938, although Chiang's admiration for Nazi Germany resulted in the employment of high-ranking German officers during the 1930s to train selected regiments of his army and provide advice in his military campaigns against the communists (Kirby 1984: 55–9).

Although an earlier study of the Nationalist government in this period has concluded that it exhibited features of a military authoritarian regime whose corruption, factionalism and lack of commitment to reform 'aborted' any hopes for progressive and modernizing change (Eastman 1974), recent assessments have provided a more complex picture. In Shanghai, for example, the new municipal government (SMG) that was set up by the

Nationalist government after 1928 did make some attempt to expand Chinese control (*vis-à-vis* the Foreign Concessions) and instituted measures to improve the urban infrastructure; the experience of the SMG, in fact, demonstrated the multifaceted nature of Guomindang rule, with the SMG, the Shanghai branch of the Guomindang, and the Nationalist government in Nanjing all having different agendas at various times (Henriot 1993). More sinisterly, a recent study of policing in Shanghai has demonstrated the growing coercive power of the Guomindang state, whose control mechanisms anticipated those of the CCP after 1949 (Wakeman 1995). An additional legacy bequeathed by the Guomindang regime to the post-1949 communist state was the implementation of a rigorous film censorship, initially prompted by opposition to foreign films deemed offensive to China and its people (Xiao 1997: 36–8).

Another assessment argues that all republican governments from the 1910s to the Guomindang regime in the 1930s were characterized by a consistency in agenda and goals that focused on the achievement of centralized statism, underpinned by financial/administrative rationalization, state-controlled education and state-led industrial development; such aims were stymied by the limited extent of central government control, internal divisions and external military pressure-constraints that remained constant throughout the republican period (Strauss 1997: 333–4). In terms of foreign policy and diplomacy, the entire republican period (1912–49) has been described as 'one of stunning accomplishments from a position of unenviable weakness' (Kirby 1997: 436). The borders of the Qing multi-ethnic empire, for example, were inherited by the republic after 1912 (and redefined as a *Chinese* space) and then defended successfully to such an extent that they remain the borders of the People's Republic today – with the exception of Outer Mongolia, which declared itself a state under the aegis of the Soviet Union in 1924 and was recognized formally by China when Chiang Kai-shek signed a treaty with the Soviet Union in 1945. Although some border regions slipped from Chinese central government control after 1912 (e.g. Xinjiang in the west), all had been recovered by 1945 and the level of external influence in those regions was much less than it had been in 1911 (ibid.: 437–9). Furthermore, by the early 1930s Chinese control over maritime customs, tariffs, postal communications, salt monopoly revenues and many of the foreign concessions had been restored; although extra-territoriality was not formally ended until 1943, the nationalist regime had succeeded before then in regaining judiciary control over Chinese residents in the foreign concessions (ibid.: 441).

The Communist Revolution in the Countryside

By 1929 Mao Zedong, already relieved of his position on the party's central committee for the failure of the Autumn Harvest Uprising, had moved to southern Jiangxi, where he began to establish a base area (Spence 1999a: 385–96). During this time Mao virtually acted independently of the party leadership in Shanghai, which branded him a military adventurer for his strategy of guerrilla warfare and enlistment of the rural lumpenproletariat (agricultural labourers, landless peasants, bandits and secret society members) in his fledgling Red Army (Rue 1966; Schram 1966). Attention has been drawn, in fact, to the incorporation of bandit techniques by Mao and other local communists into their strategies, such as locating their base areas (and later, soviets) along remote provincial boundaries and using guerrilla methods (Billingsley 1988: 252–5).

Nevertheless, the CCP Central Committee, now under the leadership of Li Lisan, called on Mao's force to participate in a new campaign of co-ordinated rural and urban uprisings in accordance with Stalin's confident assertion that a new revolutionary 'high tide' existed throughout the world due to the great Depression (and also to take advantage of renewed fighting between Chiang and mutinous generals). In 1930 attempts to take and occupy the cities of Changsha, Nanchang and Wuhan failed, principally due to the lack of mass support, and Mao withdrew once more to his base area in Jiangxi convinced more than ever that the consolidation of a self-sufficient territorial base had to be given priority.

Li Lisan was recalled in disgrace to Moscow, where he was severely reprimanded for his 'adventurism' and 'petty bourgeois chauvinism'; this last charge was made because Li had proclaimed China as imperialism's weakest link and hence had attributed to the Chinese revolution worldwide significance, an assumption that was considered far too grandiose and ambitious by the Comintern (Thornton 1969: 123–9, 168–75). Party leadership now fell into the hands of a group known as the 'Twenty-Eight Bolsheviks', because they had all studied in Moscow between 1926 and 1930. Led by Wang Ming (Chen Shaoyu), Bo Gu (Qin Bangxian) and Luo Fu (Zhang Wentian), they were loyal supporters of the Comintern line and were even more critical of Mao than the previous leadership had been. In November 1931 Mao invited party leaders to attend the first All-China Congress of Soviets in Ruijin, which formally proclaimed the establishment of the Jiangxi Soviet Republic and elected Mao as chairman of the soviet government.

The Jiangxi Soviet was, in fact, one of a number of rural soviets created at this time in central China; these included four additional border soviets in Jiangxi province and two in Hubei province. The Central Soviet based at Ruijin, however, was the largest, comprising an estimated population of three million (Harrison 1972: 199). Studies of communist activists in these other soviets, such as the Min-Zhe-Gan Soviet (northeast Jiangxi) and the Oyuwan Soviet (northeast Hubei) are useful in demonstrating the flexible tactics used in communist mobiliza-tion of the peasantry, which included making use of kin and lineage ties, infiltrating modern schools and secret societies, and manipulating lineage or ethnic feuds (Polachek 1983; Sheel 1989; Wou 1994). The fact also that many communist activists came from traditional elite families helped them in Jiangxi, where they could challenge the old order due to the respect and status they commanded within it (Averill 1990). It might also be noted that the recent trend in shifting focus away from a Mao-centred analysis of the revolution (and even from a rural focus in general) has resulted in a study of the Shanghai Communist Party itself from 1927 to the onset of the Sino-Japanese War in 1937. Although forced to go underground after 1927 (and vir-tually ignored by later historiography of the revolution), the party in Shanghai continued to function and was able to con-struct a political role for itself in the city during the 1930s by joining with other disaffected groups, principally in protests against Chiang Kai-shek's appeasement policy *vis-à-vis* the Japanese (Stranahan 1998).

When members of the party leadership in Shanghai moved permanently to Ruijin in 1932–3, Mao's influence in the Jiangxi Central Soviet was gradually reduced. Although he retained his post as chairman of the soviet government it became largely an honorary one. Real power lay with the Politburo, the party's highest policy-making organ, which was dominated by the Twenty-Eight Bolsheviks. They were particularly critical of Mao's land distribution policy and his guerrilla tactics. In contrast to his more radical land policy while at Jingganshan in 1929, when land belonging to both landlords and rich peasants (i.e. landowning peasants who worked the land themselves as well as renting a part of it to others) was confiscated and redistributed to poor peasants, Mao's land reform law of 1931 allowed rich peasants to receive an allotment of land provided they tilled it themselves. This was considered by the party leadership as evidence of Mao's failure to adopt a strong class stand, and after 1933 a harsher attitude was taken towards rich peasants. Yet Mao's land distribution policy was in accord with his strategy of mobilizing as much rural support as possible, while at the same time his insistence that *poor peasant associations* participate actively in the confiscation and distribution of land reflected his belief that land reform was to have a political, as well as an economic, significance (Kim 1973: 118–43).

In a wider sense, the involvement of peasant associations in such a process was an important component of what Mao later would refer to as 'the mass line', a set of techniques and practices aimed at ensuring popular support and close identification of party policies with grassroots aspirations (Schram 1989: 45–6, 97–8). The concept also referred to a particular way in which party leadership was to be exercised. Thus a party resolution in 1943 elaborated on the concept in the following way:

In all practical work of the party, correct leadership can only be developed on the principle of 'from the masses to the masses'. This means summing up (i.e. co-ordinating and systematizing after careful study) the views of the masses (i.e. views scattered and unsystematic) then taking the resulting ideas back to the masses, explaining them and popularizing them until the masses embrace these ideas as their own, stand up for them, and translate them into action by way of testing their correctness. (Harrison 1972: 205)

After 1933 Mao's emphasis on flexible guerrilla warfare against invading nationalist forces was replaced by a stress on a more orthodox strategy of positional warfare. Between 1930 and 1934 Chiang Kai-shek launched five campaigns of 'encirclement and extermination' against the Jiangxi Soviet. The first four had failed but the fifth, begun in October 1933, was more success-ful. On the advice of General Hans von Seekt, head of the German military mission in Nanjing, Chiang adopted a policy of economic strangulation, blockading the soviet with an array of fortresses and pillboxes. The Red Army suffered a series of disastrous defeats and in October 1934 it was decided to evacu-ate the Jiangxi Soviet, a retreat that became known as the Long March. Leaving behind the elderly, children and most of the women, approximately 86,000 set off, initially heading west-wards but eventually deciding to establish a new base in the northwest. All the while pursued by nationalist troops and having to negotiate intimidating physical terrains, this commu-nist force (of which less than 4,000 survived) reached Shaanxi province one year later in 1935. One of the few women to embark on the Long March – about thirty in all (Lee and Wiles 1999) – was He Zizhen, Mao's second wife (his first wife, Yang Kaihui, had been executed by Guomindang authorities in Changsha in 1930 shortly after Mao's failed attack on the city). Badly wounded during the Long March, He Zizhen went to the Soviet Union in 1938 for medical treatment, by which time Mao had become involved with his future third wife, Jiang Qing, a minor movie actress who had travelled to the northwest from Shanghai in 1937 (Short 1999: 113–16, 225–6, 369–72; Terrill 1999: 107–61).

The Long March was accorded a near-mythical status in later communist historiography and helped to forge bonds amongst survivors, reinforced a collective *esprit de corps* and revitalized a sense of mission amidst what had, in effect, been a military defeat. It should be noted, however, that the traditional Mao-centred emphasis by western and Chinese historians of the Chinese revolution referred to earlier has meant that until recently the activities of those communist forces from other soviets in central China that remained behind enemy lines have been largely overlooked. A recent study (Benton 1992) has drawn attention to the almost forgotten guerrilla war carried out after 1934 by these communist forces, which were to re-emerge in 1938 with the formation of the Second United Front (see chapter 4) as an officially recognized unit (designated as the New Fourth Army) of the national resistance against Japan following its full-scale invasion of China in 1937.

During the course of the Long March Mao demanded the convening of an enlarged Politburo conference at Zunyi (Guizhou province) in January 1935, which criticized the errors of the party leadership during the last years of the Jiangxi Soviet. More importantly, the Zunyi conference marked the beginning of Mao's eventual leadership of the party. Mao was not only elected to the Politburo and appointed head of the General Secretariat but was also awarded the important post of director of the Military Affairs Committee (Harrison 1972: 246). By 1936 the CCP had established new headquarters at Yanan in north Shaanxi which, owing to its inhospitable terrain, was relatively safe from possible attack. It was here that Mao over the next few years was to consolidate his political and ideological leadership of the party. Meanwhile, there occurred a temporary respite in Chiang's campaign against the communists as both sides agreed to co-operate against a common enemy – Japan.

4

The War of Resistance Against Japan

The full-scale war that broke out between China and Japan in 1937 was the final act of a drama in which Japan had sought to preserve its economic and political rights in China in the face of both a reinvigorated Chinese nationalism and the increasing hostility of Britain and the US (Jansen 1975). At the same time Japan saw the war as the first step in the creation of a new order in East Asia, one in which China would finally realize that its true interests lay in partnership with Japan against the twin evils of Soviet communism and Anglo-Saxon liberal democracy (Storry 1979). Japan's actions in China, however, revealed the very fragile distinction between 'partnership' and domination, while at the same time Japanese government and military leaders failed to understand that the idea of a new order in East Asia never appealed to the Chinese because Chinese nationalism since the turn of the century had been directed just as much against Japan as it had against the West.

Contrary to initial assumptions on Japan's part that the 'China Incident' (as it was called) would be over in a few months, the war was to last eight years and represented an enormous drain of Japan's human and material resources. By 1941 Japan was also at war with the US and Britain and events were set in motion that would lead to the end of the European empires in Southeast Asia, Japan's eventual total military defeat, the emergence of two new superpowers in East Asia to fill the vacuum, and the creation of a communist state in China. Furthermore, a collection of essays has not only argued that the

Sino-Japanese War might well have been the key to the eventual outcome of the Second World War in the Pacific, but also emphasized its enormous political and economic impact within China itself (Hsiung and Levine 1992).

The Origins of Japanese Imperialism

Since the Meiji Restoration in 1868, when feudal rule had been replaced by a centralized government under the Meiji emperor, Japanese government policy had aimed to create a wealthy and militarily strong nation in order to meet the threat of an expanding West. Like China, Japan in the 1850s and 1860s had been compelled to sign 'unequal treaties' with the western powers that both opened a number of treaty ports in which foreign residents enjoyed extra-territoriality and impinged upon Japan's tariff autonomy. Also, until the 1880s Japan's external trade, modern banking and currency exchange operations were largely in foreign hands, leading one historian to refer to Japan at this time as a 'client' state of the West (Beasley 1989: 306). A quest for security was likewise an important motive in early Japanese expansionism, which sought to impose sovereignty over nearby islands (such as the Kuriles in the north and the Ryukyus in the south); a policy of expansionism was also supported by radical nationalists outside the government (who nevertheless had links with certain military and business circles) bent on extending Japanese influence in Asia, especially Korea and China. By the end of the nineteenth century it was assumed that Japan needed to become an imperialist power in order to both emulate and compete with the West (Jansen 1984). Such an assumption, in addition to increasing Japanese contempt for China as a 'backward' nation that was unwilling to modernize, dispelled earlier hopes (especially in the 1870s) among some Japanese that Japan could repay its cultural debt to China (dating from the eighth century, when Japan assimilated the Chinese writing system and Confucian philosophy) by joining with China in a common cause against western encroachment.

In 1895 Japan formally entered the ranks of the imperialist powers in Asia after defeating China in a war fought over dominant influence in Korea. By the Treaty of Shimonoseki, not only was Japan's predominance in Korea recognized but it also gained all the rights and privileges enjoyed by the western powers in China and acquired the island of Taiwan (only just integrated by the Qing into the province of Fujian). Although security reasons may have been a factor in the acquisition – the Japanese navy, for example, saw the possession of Taiwan as crucial in its long-term project to make Japan a viable naval power in East Asian waters and the Pacific – economic motives also played a part; Taiwan was to be developed as a 'model' colony serving the economic interests of the metropole, while also serving as a convenient staging post for Japanese penetration of the China market. In 1900, for the first time, Japan joined the western powers in military action in China when it participated in the allied expedition to relieve the foreign legations besieged by the Boxers (see chapter 1). Japan's status was further enhanced in 1902 when Tokyo signed an alliance with Britain, the principal aim of which was to check Russian influence in Asia.

Russia's growing presence in Manchuria (especially in the wake of the Boxer uprising) and attempts to extend its economic influence in north Korea were regarded by Tokyo as a threat to Japan's security. Conflict between the two countries broke out in 1904, and by 1905 Russia sued for peace. For the first time in modern history an Asian country had defeated a western power, a fact not overlooked by reformers and revolutionaries throughout Asia struggling against their European colonial masters. More importantly, as far as Japan was concerned, the Treaty of Portsmouth (brought about by the mediation of the US) which ended the war awarded the former Russian leased territory of the Liaodong (in Japanese, Kwantung) peninsula and the South Manchuria Railway to Japan. Over the next thirty years the Japanese presence in Manchuria was to expand considerably and its rights and privileges there came to be regarded as sacred, bought with Japanese blood. A Japanese military force, known as the Kwantung Army, was stationed in the Liaodong peninsula, while the Japanese-controlled South Manchuria Railway Company gradually acquired mining concessions and the right to station railway guards along the line.

As an imperialist power in China on a par with the western powers, it seemed that Japan had now attained equality with the West (in 1899 extra-territoriality in Japan was formally ended, while in 1911 Japan's tariff autonomy was restored). Yet the relationship between the two remained uneasy. The US, in particular, began to voice increasing concern after 1905 over the potential threat Japan posed to its security interests in the Pacific, while the blatantly racist nature of anti-Japanese immigration policy in Hawaii (annexed by the US in 1898) and California soured relations between the two countries. Furthermore, the US espousal of the Open Door doctrine (first enunciated in 1899), which called for equality of commercial opportunity among the powers in China irrespective of spheres of influence, clashed with Japan's determination to preserve its economic dominance in Manchuria.

Japan's relationship with China was also ambiguous. On the one hand, there were private Japanese individuals (inspired by pan-Asian ideals) who sincerely desired to work and co-operate with Chinese revolutionaries such as Sun Yatsen in the creation of a modern and democratic China (Jansen 1954); on the other, Japanese governments, despite frequent pious statements that Japan desired to repay its cultural debt to China by helping it to modernize, treated China with the same arrogance and contempt shown by the other powers and continually sought to expand Japan's privileges there, particularly in Manchuria. Ironically, it was the thousands of admiring Chinese students who flocked to Japan in the early years of the twentieth century who were the first to become painfully aware of the inferior status assigned to the Chinese by many Japanese. Ominously for the future, there were also elements within the Japanese military, especially the Kwantung Army, who began to argue that Japan should go its own way in China and disregard potential criticism or opposition from the western powers.

American and British suspicion of Japan intensified both in the wake of the 1911 revolution, when the Kwantung Army attempted to foster an autonomy movement in Manchuria, and during the First World War, when Japan seized the opportunity to take over the German leased territory of Qingdao in Shandong and impose the Twenty-One Demands on Yuan Shikai's government (see chapter 2).

The Washington System and its Breakdown

In 1921–2 the US organized the Washington Conference, which affirmed the powers' respect for the sovereignty and territorial integrity of China. The principle of equal economic opportunity was also upheld and the notion of 'spheres of influence' condemned. Much to the satisfaction of the US, the Anglo-Japanese Alliance was allowed to lapse, to be replaced by a four-power treaty (US, Britain, Japan and France) which provided for mutual consultation if any threats arose with regard to their interests in China. As further indication of potential harmony and co-operation among the powers, a naval treaty limited construction of capital ships (with Japan accepting a lower ratio *vis-à-vis* Britain and the US) and halted any further build-up of fortifications in the western Pacific. Finally, Japan agreed at the Washington Conference to return the Qingdao leasehold and the Jinan–Qingdao railway to China (Thorne 1972: 27–8).

A detailed study of the Washington Conference and its consequences (Iriye 1965) has argued that the period from 1922 to 1925 represented a lost opportunity for the powers to implement the ideals animating the conference by creating a new framework of international relations in East Asia. Chronic instability in China and the bewildering succession of warlord regimes, the emergence of a new factor in Chinese politics in the shape of the CCP–Guomindang United Front backed by a power (the Soviet Union) not party to the conference, and continuing suspicion among the powers themselves, are all cited as reasons for a scenario in which each power ultimately decided to act unilaterally in China to safeguard its interests. Nevertheless, it should not be forgotten that despite the Washington Conference's rhetorical support for China's independence and territorial integrity, the powers did not at this time envisage an end to the unequal treaty system (China had not even been invited to the conference). The one concession that *was* made involved a proposal to convene a tariff conference in 1925–6 to negotiate the gradual return of tariff autonomy to China. Disagreements arose at the conference, however, and each power decided to make its own arrangements with the Chinese government. Although tariff autonomy for China was formally recognized in 1929, it was not to be until 1943 that Britain and the US, as a sop to Chiang Kai-shek whose role in the war against Japan was considered vital, would agree to end their privilege of extra-territoriality in China (a privilege that had become largely irrelevant anyway because of the Japanese occupation).

What none of the powers had anticipated, however, was the rapid growth of anti-imperialism during the 1920s and the increasing importance of the United Front. While Britain and the US wavered between armed intervention to 'punish' the excesses of the Northern Expedition and an attitude of 'wait and see', Japan, perceiving the growing split between the left and right wings of the Guomindang, sought to negotiate with Chiang Kai-shek. At the same time Tokyo was determined, as it had always been, that the country's economic interests in China would not be threatened by continuing war and instability. Thus twice, in 1927 and 1928, Japanese prime minister Tanaka Giichi despatched troops to Shandong to protect Japanese lives and property there, which resulted in armed clashes with Chiang's advancing nationalist forces. A new wave of anti-Japanese sentiment led to boycotts of Japanese goods, ironically at the very time Britain and the US were adopting a more conciliatory attitude towards Chiang Kai-shek, whose promise to put an end to all anti-foreign excesses and crack down on labour unions and communists gave him credibility as an upholder of 'law and order'. Britain's coming to terms with Chinese nationalism (and recognition of its diminishing political and military capacity as an imperialist power in China), in particular, was demonstrated by the formal retrocession of its concession areas in Jiujiang and Hankou in 1927 (Louis 1971), and the return of its Weihaiwei leasehold in 1930 after several years of stalling (strictly speaking, the leasehold had expired in 1923) (Atwell 1985: 131, 157–62).

Japan's economic stake in China, particularly in Manchuria, was far greater than that of either Britain and the US. Whereas by 1931, for example, China represented 81.9 per cent of Japan's total foreign investment (two-thirds of which was in Manchuria), it represented only 6 per cent of Britain's total overseas investments and less than 1.5 per cent for the US (Thorne 1972: 32–3). Japan also supplied one-quarter (in value) of China's imports and took a similar proportion of its exports, again the largest share coming from Manchuria. Manchuria, in fact, had become a vital source of minerals essential for Japan's programme of industrial and military development. It was also increasingly perceived as a suitable region of migration for Japan's own hard-pressed rural population. By 1930 military planners in the Kwantung Army, such as Ishiwara Kanji, were predicting that Manchuria would be crucial for any future war effort against either the Soviet Union or the US (Peattie 1975). It was precisely because of this greater economic stake that Japan stood to lose the most in the wake of a resurgent Chinese nationalism (Duus 1989: xviii–xix). Thus, just at the time when Japan was surpassing Britain as the dominant foreign economic presence in China within the framework of the unequal treaty system – referred to as 'collective informal empire' (ibid.: xxiv) – it decided to break with this arrangement by resorting to direct military occupation of Manchuria.

Already, in 1928, the Kwantung Army had engineered the assassination of Zhang Zuolin as he returned to his Manchurian base in Mukden after fleeing Beijing, shortly to be occupied by nationalist forces. The Kwantung Army had feared that Zhang's continuing national ambitions would suck Manchuria into conflict with the new nationalist regime and hence exacerbate instability in the region. In 1931 another crisis 'incident' was fabricated by lower-ranking officers of the Kwantung Army (a section of the South Manchuria Railway was blown up), and used as a pretext to launch a full-scale military offensive in Manchuria (Ogata 1964). Despite calls from Tokyo for restraint, the Kwantung Army extended its sphere of operations and Manchuria was overrun within five months. In 1932 hostilities between Chinese and Japanese troops also broke out in Shanghai. Chiang Kai-shek, preoccupied with his campaign against the communists, appealed to the League of Nations. Despite a report issued by a League of Nations investigative mission (the Lytton Commission), which pointed to Japan as the aggressor, and the announcement by US Secretary of State Henry Stimson that Washington would not recognize any settlement brought about by force (known as the non-recognition doctrine), little was done. In 1932 the Kwantung Army created the puppet state of Manchukuo and installed Puyi, the last Qing emperor, as a figurehead ruler. The government in Tokyo was presented with a *fait accompli* and henceforth was to be subject to increasing pressure from the Kwantung Army, which had supporters within the Army General Staff, to adopt a stronger line with regard to its China policy.

Mutual mistrust between Britain and the US, in addition to their reluctance to antagonize Japan, overtly prevented an effective common stance to deal with Japanese aggression in

Manchuria (Thorne 1972). The League of Nations resorted to a moral condemnation, but the idea of imposing sanctions on Japan was shelved. This was enough, however, to alienate Tokyo, and Japan withdrew its membership of the League in 1933. Japan's political isolation from the world community was worsened by the effects of the great Depression. With the erection of tariff barriers throughout the world in the 1930s, which threatened Japan's foreign trade, a 'siege mentality' increasingly took hold of Japanese leaders. It was in this context that the East Asian mainland assumed an even more vital importance for Japan.

Meanwhile, from 1933 onwards, the Japanese army in Manchuria attempted to expand its influence in north China. Guomindang political authority in the region was gradually whittled away and in 1935 the Japanese sponsored the creation of an East Hebei Autonomous Council under their influence. With Japanese connivance large-scale silver and narcotics smuggling also became prevalent in north China (Boyle 1972). In 1936 the Japanese foreign minister, Hirota Koki, announced a number of conditions that he insisted had to form the basis of any *modus vivendi* with Chiang Kai-shek's regime – recognition of Japan's special position in north China, an end to all anti-Japanese demonstrations in the region, Sino-Japanese collaboration against communism, and the employment of Japanese advisers by the Chinese government. Japan's increasingly aggressive stance was further illustrated when Tokyo signed the anti-Comintern pact with Nazi Germany the same year.

The Second United Front

Throughout the early 1930s Chiang Kai-shek argued that defeat of the CCP had to take precedence over everything else, but increasing numbers of people began to criticize what they saw as Chiang's appeasement of Japan. Interestingly, during the Manchurian crisis of 1931–2 elements within the Guomindang had favoured support for anti-Japanese boycotts in what has been termed 'revolutionary diplomacy' (Jordan 1991), but Chiang's fear of mass movements that might escape the regime's control always inhibited him from taking a strong anti-Japanese stance (Coble 1991). In 1933 a division of Chiang's own army, the Nineteenth Route Army, which was stationed in Fujian to fight the communists and had previously fought the Japanese at Shanghai in 1932, rose up in revolt and proclaimed the creation of a new government. The rebels called for an end to internal strife and united resistance against Japan (Eastman 1974: 86–127). Although Chiang succeeded in suppressing the insurrection in 1934, criticism of his policy continued. The CCP itself in Jiangxi began calling for a united front of all democratic forces in the country to resist Japan, and during the course of the Long March in 1935 the Comintern issued instructions to communist parties to form alliances with anti-fascist groups. Finally, in December 1935 there were huge student demonstrations in Beijing protesting against the government's lack of resolve in dealing with Japanese aggression in north China (Israel and Klein 1976).

When Chiang flew to Xian in 1936 to reproach his troops for their lacklustre performance against the communists in Shaanxi, he was promptly placed under house arrest by the commander, Zhang Xueliang. Zhang, the son of the Manchurian warlord, Zhang Zuolin, had suffered the ignominy of seeing his native Manchuria overrun by the Japanese in 1931–2 and demanded that the military campaign against the communists cease and that all Chinese unite to confront the Japanese threat. He even intimated that he might have Chiang executed as a traitor. Ironically, it was through CCP intercession that Zhang was persuaded to release Chiang, on condition that he promise to halt his anti-communist campaign and form a united front. It was felt that Chiang's symbolic importance as the head of the central government in Nanjing could contribute to a more effective national unity, a feeling that was shared by the US and Britain, as well as by the Soviet Union (Wu 1976).

With Chiang's release in December 1936, the second United Front was established. Unlike in 1923, however, the second United Front that was gradually formalized during 1937 was an alliance between two separate groups; the CCP was now in a much stronger position, possessing its own military units (with the principal unit based in Yanan now redesignated as the Eighth Route Army) and controlling specific territory. Nevertheless, the CCP accepted Chiang's overall command and promised to modify its radical policy of land confiscation in the interests of national unity. When, in July 1937, Japanese and Chinese troops clashed near Beijing both sides refused to compromise. Chiang sent reinforcements and proclaimed all-out resistance to Japan.

The Sino-Japanese War 1937–1945

Tokyo was confident that the war would not last long. By 1938 Japanese forces had taken Beijing, Shanghai, Nanjing (where atrocities against the civilian population were committed), Guangzhou and Wuhan. The Nationalist government retreated west to Chongqing, in Sichuan province, which was to remain Chiang's headquarters throughout the rest of the war. Since Chiang's regime had relied heavily on the lower Yangzi region for its revenues, its retreat westwards weakened it economically and politically, especially as the Nationalist government was now located in an area where local warlords still held sway. Although Japanese forces occupied the coastal regions and key urban centres in the north and along the lower Yangzi, they found it impossible to conquer the vast rural hinterlands. After 1939 a virtual stalemate ensued punctuated by occasional clashes and skirmishes. Yet the China war represented a considerable drain on Japanese manpower. Between 1937 and 1941 up to 750,000 troops were engaged in China, approximately one half of the total strength of the army. By 1945 there were to be 1.2 million Japanese troops (out of a total overseas force of 2.3 million) stationed in China (Hsu 2000: 611).

In the northwest the communist Eighth Route Army conducted a guerrilla campaign against the Japanese, often behind Japanese lines. The CCP also created border governments in the region, the most important one being the Shaanxi–Gansu–Ningxia Border Region with Yanan as its capital. During the course of the war the communists were able gradually to enlarge the territory under their control throughout north China. It is important to note, however, that this was not the only region in which communist military action took place. For a long time the Shaan–Gan–Ning Border Region and the Eighth Route Army dominated narratives of the communist revolution during the anti-Japanese war because of their association with the central leadership under Mao. A recent study (Benton 1999) has charted the activities of another communist military force, the New Fourth Army in central and eastern China (Jiangsu and Anhui provinces), which represented the reconstituted guerrilla units that had fought the nationalists between 1934 and 1937.

The second United Front was tenuous from the beginning. Although there were CCP representatives (including Wang Ming and Zhou Enlai) in Chongqing, Chiang's mistrust of the communists persisted, while Mao and other CCP leaders made no secret of the fact that they intended to expand communist influence during the war of resistance. Chiang virtually imposed an economic blockade on Yanan, while mutual antagonism often resulted in armed skirmishes between communist and nationalist forces, the most serious one being the New Fourth Army Incident in 1941 when the New Fourth Army was attacked by nationalist troops as it deployed north of the Yangzi. During the course of the war, however, Yanan, rather than Chongqing, became for many Chinese the symbol of national resistance to the Japanese; thousands of students and intellectuals from cities such as Beijing made their way to the northwest to join the struggle. Such a large influx of outsiders into the region, many of whom became CCP members, was to cause Mao concern about the ideological 'soundness' of the party.

For the first years of the war China virtually stood alone against Japan. The Soviet Union initially extended credit to the Nationalist government for military supplies and sent volunteer pilots to take part in the defence of Chongqing and other cities such as Xian and Hankou. In 1938 and 1939 large-scale fighting broke out between Russian and Japanese troops along the border between the Soviet Union and Manchuria, in which the Japanese suffered heavy losses. Yet after 1939 Soviet aid to China diminished as Stalin's attention became increasingly focused on meeting a possible threat from Nazi Germany. In 1941 Stalin signed a non-aggression treaty with Japan, which signalled the end of Soviet involvement in the China war. Chiang received little or no aid either from Britain and the US. Although a small group of American volunteer pilots (the 'Flying Tigers') operated from southwest China, it was not until early 1941 that the US provided significant credit to Chongqing for the purchase of miltary goods in accordance with the Lend Lease Act (Schaller 1979; Mancall 1984: 303–5).

By 1938 Tokyo had decided it could no longer deal with Chiang Kai-shek and in November of that year Prime Minister

Konoe Fumimaro announced the creation of a New Order in East Asia. Since China and Japan were racially and culturally akin, Konoe argued, it was natural that the two should co-operate – politically and economically – in defeating communism and western imperialism. The New Order entailed the promotion of an alternative Chinese regime with whom Tokyo could deal, although such an attempt was always obstructed by the manoeuvres of various Japanese army commands in China, which had already begun to sponsor various client regimes in Beijing, Nanjing and Shanghai (Boyle 1972).

Nevertheless, Wang Jingwei responded to Tokyo's overtures and left Chongqing at the end of 1938, initially in the hope of mediating between Chiang and the Japanese but ultimately with the aim of establishing a new Guomindang regime in Nanjing. A study of this 'peace movement', as it was called, maintains that Wang was motivated partly by his keen personal rivalry with Chiang Kai-shek that dated from the mid-1920s after Sun Yatsen's death, and partly by a sincere desire to bring an end to the war (Bunker 1971). Although Wang inaugurated a new government in 1940, his hopes of bringing about peace and genuine Sino-Japanese co-operation never materialized. Tokyo was unwilling to grant Wang real influence or power, and the regime lacked credibility from the start (it was recognized only by Japan and the European fascist powers). Denounced by both the CCP and Chiang Kai-shek as a traitor and having to suffer repeated humiliation at the hands of the Japanese (a fate shared by the hapless Puyi in Manchukuo), Wang died in 1944 a bitterly disillusioned man, his only achievement being that Tokyo in 1943 had allowed his regime to take over the foreign concessions in Shanghai.

Japan's ever-increasing need for mineral resources (especially oil), which ironically could not be entirely met by the self-sufficient bloc (of Japan, China and Manchukuo) supposedly inaugurated by the New Order, prompted more ambitious plans for a southward expansion in Asia to embrace the rich oil-fields of the Dutch East Indies (Indonesia). By 1940 Japanese troops were in Indochina. Relations with the US deteriorated and Washington placed an embargo on the export of petroleum to Japan. Tokyo's decision to launch a pre-emptive strike on the American naval base at Pearl Harbor in December 1941, which was quickly followed by the occupation of Hong Kong, Malaya,

Singapore, the Dutch East Indies and the Philippines, dramatically changed the nature of the Sino-Japanese War. With the US and Britain now directly at war with Japan as well as with Germany (which had declared war on the US shortly after the Japanese attack on Pearl Harbor), China's resistance to the Japanese was seen as a heroic contribution to the worldwide struggle against fascism (Schaller 1979). US aid to China henceforth increased and during the years 1942–5 would amount to over US$1 billion (Mancall 1984: 306).

For Japan the defeat of western imperialism in Southeast Asia heralded the birth of what Tokyo called the Greater East Asia Co-Prosperity Sphere, but as in China the realities of the Japanese occupation often belied the grandiose rhetoric of partnership. Nevertheless, the ease with which Japanese forces had overrun the former western colonies had an enormous impact on the development of Asian nationalism. The myth of the white man's invincibility had been irretrievably shattered, and the former colonial masters would have to confront vigorous liberation movements when they returned in 1945 to reclaim their 'possessions'. Interestingly, it is precisely *this* consequence of the Japanese occupation (which in the end proved disastrous for the peoples of Southeast Asia) to which some right-wing circles in present-day Japan refer when emphasizing the more positive aspects of Japan's role in Asia during the Second World War.

Although Chiang was made supreme commander of the China Theatre of War (within the larger Burma–China–India Theatre) and was now assured substantial US aid, he remained unwilling to use his troops in large-scale offensives against the Japanese, preferring to keep his forces intact for the future showdown with the CCP he knew must come. The American General Joseph Stilwell, who was attached to Chiang's command after 1942, was continually frustrated in his efforts to persuade Chiang to show greater urgency and constantly complained to Washington of the inefficiency and corruption he saw prevailing in Chongqing (Tuchman 1971; Schaller 1979). Stilwell's complaints were reinforced by the negative reports on the Chongqing government by American foreign service officers in China such as John Service and John Paton Davies. President Roosevelt, however, continued to place his faith in Chiang; his continued leadership was seen as a crucial element in

Roosevelt's plans for the postwar world in which a united and democratic China would become one of the Big Four (along with the US, Britain and the Soviet Union) guaranteeing stability in the international arena. Although observers on the spot often commented on the corruption of Chiang's regime, studies have also underlined the limitations on Chiang's power (Ch'i 1982; Eastman 1984). The Guomindang's political control had diminished after 1937 when the government had been compelled to abandon its political and economic stronghold in the east, particularly the provinces of Jiangsu and Zhejiang. Furthermore, Chiang's central government troops constituted only approximately one-fifth of all the nationalist forces. The loyalty and commitment of many army commanders to Chiang Kai-shek were never absolute. In provinces such as Sichuan, Shanxi and Yunnan military governors frequently obstructed central government control. Mutual rivalries and suspicions prompted everyone to play a waiting game, with no one commander (including Chiang) willing to risk losing troops in any large-scale action. Throughout the war, in fact, there continued to be illicit trade between unoccupied and occupied China, a trade tolerated by the local commanders of both sides (Eastman 1980). The activities and outlook of writers and businessmen in Japanese-occupied Shanghai also demonstrated a considerable 'grey' area between active resistance and open collaboration (Fu 1993). Very often it seemed that more hostility was directed against the communists than against the Japanese. One historian, citing Hubei provincial reports of 1942–3, notes that nationalist operations against the Japanese tended to be defensive and reactive in nature, while those against the communists were more offensive in nature and involved larger numbers of troops (Eastman 1984: 138). This is not the whole picture, however. Recent research has drawn attention to the anti-Japanese activities of nationalist guerrilla forces in the northern province of Shandong (Paulson 1989), and to the murky world of political terrorism in occupied Shanghai, where nationalist secret services and assassination squads targeted collaborators and traitors (*hanjian*) (Wakeman 1996, 2000; Yeh 1998).

The overall ineffectiveness of the nationalist forces was highlighted in stark clarity in 1944 when the Japanese launched their one and only major offensive after 1938 (the Ichigo offensive), which led to advances in the south and southwest. Nationalist resistance was swept aside with brutal ease, prompting Stilwell to insist afterwards that he be given overall command of Chinese troops. Understandably, this was unacceptable to Chiang and he was able to have Stilwell recalled, an interesting example of the leverage Chiang was able to exert on Washington.

It was a measure of the increasing alienation of the peasantry in the areas under nationalist control that the retreating Chinese troops in the wake of the Ichigo offensive were actually attacked by peasants. Increased taxes and 'contributions', such as the military grain levy, had already worsened the economic plight of the peasantry, and this was aggravated by the arbitrary use of military and labour conscription. In Henan a famine in 1942–3 as a result of poor harvests and the military grain levy led to the death of several million people (Eastman 1984: 67–8). By 1945 famine was widespread.

Although the Ichigo offensive enabled Japanese troops to advance to Yunnan and Guizhou in the southwest, the China war by 1944 had, in a sense, assumed a secondary importance in the overall American strategy against Japan. Originally, it had been assumed that the US air force would be able to carry out bombing raids on Japan from bases in China, but the focus shifted when the US decided to concentrate its efforts on taking the Japanese-held islands in the Pacific. The dropping of atomic bombs on Hiroshima (6 August 1945) and Nagasaki (9 August 1945) brought the war to an abrupt end, with Japan announcing its surrender on 15 August 1945.

Barely twenty-four hours before the dropping of the second atomic bomb, the Soviet Union declared war on Japan and Russian troops poured into Manchuria. Stalin, in response to the urging of his western allies, had promised at Yalta in February 1945 that he would enter the war against Japan once Germany was defeated. The unexpected end to the war in Asia obviated the need for Soviet intervention, but Stalin went ahead anyway, especially as he had gained allied approval for the Soviet Union's 'pre-eminent interests' in Manchuria (Mancall 1984: 297). On the day Japan surrendered, Stalin signed a thirty-year treaty of friendship with Chiang Kai-shek, which promised future Soviet withdrawal from Manchuria while also granting the Soviet Union the use of Port Arthur (present-day Lushun) and continued involvement in the management of the Chinese

Eastern Railway. As in the early 1920s the Soviet Union was playing a skilful 'double game'.

The end of the China war thus bequeathed a tense and complicated situation in which Russian troops occupied key cities in Manchuria and a race developed between the CCP and the nationalists (aided by the US) to accept the surrender of Japanese forces in China, most of which remained intact. Before discussing the civil war that resulted and the subsequent victory of the CCP, it is first necessary to describe communist policy in Yanan and the emergence of Mao Zedong as undisputed leader of the CCP.

The Yanan Period 1937–1945

After 1945 Mao was often wistfully to refer to the Yanan period as a time when close links were forged between the party and the people, and when a spirit of self-sacrifice and egalitarianism prevailed in the struggle to overcome both the Japanese menace and the economic blockade imposed on Yanan by the Guomindang (Meisner 1999: 47–51). The Yanan period also witnessed Mao's final victory over the 'Internationalist' faction (those with close links to the Comintern, such as Wang Ming and Bo Gu) in the rivalry for leadership of the CCP. In the process Mao affirmed his *ideological* pre-eminence within the party, which was to mark the beginnings of a personal cult (Wylie 1980).

In accord with the United Front, the CCP after 1937 stressed national unity and halted its radical programme of land confiscation, although land belonging to those who had collaborated with the Japanese continued to be appropriated. In 1940 Mao wrote an important article entitled 'On New Democracy' which presented the CCP as a genuine *national* movement leading an alliance of 'revolutionary classes' (the proletariat, peasantry, petty bourgeoisie, and national bourgeoisie). For Mao the 'new democratic' period began in the wake of the May Fourth Movement and the formation of the CCP – thus making the former entirely synonymous with the latter, an assumption of orthodox CCP historiography that has persisted to the present; furthermore, according to Mao, 'new democracy' under the leadership of the proletariat (i.e. CCP) would complete the tasks unfulfilled by the 'old' bourgeois–democratic revolution of 1911 before proceeding to the socialist stage (Wylie 1980: 119–21). Mao thus

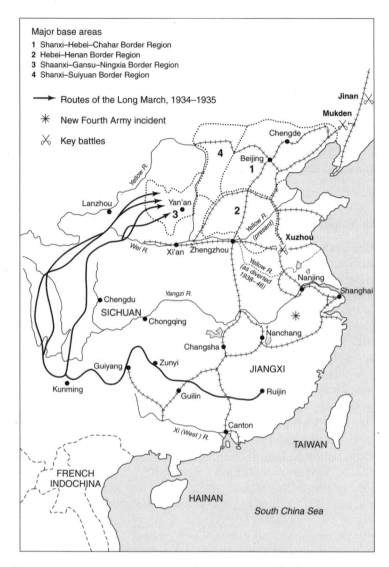

Map 3 Chinese communist activity, 1930s and 1940s. From R. Keith Schoppa, *The Columbia Guide to Modern Chinese History*, Columbia University Press: New York, 2000.

not only asserted the CCP's national role, but also advanced its claim to be the legitimate heir of Sun Yatsen's revolutionary legacy (Shum 1988: 165–9). At the same time Mao remained committed to the strategy of rural revolution and the consolidation of CCP-controlled base areas, in contrast to Wang Ming who wanted to use the United Front to expand and legalize the CCP's role in the cities and who believed that without a firm urban stronghold the CCP would lose its Marxist–Leninist character and become mired in 'petty bourgeois' peasant concerns (Van Slyke 1986: 617–18).

Official CCP policy during the Yanan period therefore sought to protect private enterprise and encourage non-CCP participation in administration, especially at grassroots level (without, however, compromising the CCP's leadership role). Land policy aimed at improving the economic situation of the poor peasants through a campaign of rent and interest reduction (while also guaranteeing the payment of rents). In areas where tenants were compelled to hand over as much as 50 per cent of their crop in rent and where tenants and landowning peasants alike were victims of unscrupulous moneylenders and landlords who charged exorbitant rates of interest on any loan extended, this campaign had a significant impact in galvanizing peasant support (Gillin 1964; Selden 1971).

By 1940–1, however, Mao began to feel that a number of problems needed to be urgently dealt with. The Shaan–Gan–Ning border region had by now expanded to cover an area of 23 counties with a population of 1.5 million. At the same time membership of the CCP increased from 40,000 in 1937 to 800,000 in 1940 (Wylie 1980: 164), due to the influx of large numbers of intellectuals and students from the cities. An overstaffed bureaucracy, particularly at higher levels, had developed. For Mao this led to the evil of 'bureaucratism', which threatened to divorce officials from the needs and concerns of the people. Mao also expressed concern that the party itself lacked internal cohesion, with higher-level cadres possessing a mainly urban and intellectual background and lower-level cadres coming mostly from local rural areas. He was also keen to eliminate all vestiges of what he called 'dogmatism' or 'formalism' within the party, by which he meant an inflexible and rigid approach to Marxist doctrine without taking into account the concrete Chinese situation. Mao's target was clearly the 'Internationalist'

faction led by Wang Ming, although his criticisms were also levelled at the growing number of 'bookish' intellectuals in Yanan.
These political and ideological problems were compounded by
the worsening economic situation as a result of the Guomindang
blockade.

In 1942–3 Mao launched a 'rectification' campaign designed
to 're-educate' cadres and combat the 'evils' of bureaucratism
and formalism. Since Mao's own writings formed an important
component of the study materials used (Compton 1966), this
campaign confirmed Mao's ideological leadership of the party.
In particular, Mao stressed the importance of the 'Sinification'
of Marxism (the creative adaptation of Marxism to Chinese conditions), a concept to which he had first referred in 1938 and
which owed much to the writings of Chen Boda (Wylie 1980).
Chen, who was to become Mao's political secretary and director of the China Problems Research Section of the CCP's
Central Party School in Yanan, had insisted since the 1930s that
Marxism had roots in the Chinese past – for example, he noted
that the fifth-century BCE thinker Mo Zi had shown an awareness of the class struggle – and condemned wholesale imitation
from abroad. In promoting the Sinification of Marxism Mao was
not only attacking those in the party closely associated with the
Comintern but also, ultimately, asserting his ideological independence from Moscow.

Mao's leadership of the party was formally recognized in
1943 when he was elected chairman of the Politburo and the
Central Committee. Furthermore, although the day to day work
of the party was delegated to a three-man secretariat (Mao, Liu
Shaoqi and Ren Bishi), Mao as chairman was to have the final
say (Schram 1987: 210). The increasing prominence given to
Mao's writings was also accompanied by the emergence of a
Maoist cult. As early as 1937 Mao's portrait, with a personal
quotation, appeared in a party journal, while the first published
collection of his writings appeared at the end of that year (Wylie
1980: 41). In 1943–4 messages from 'labour heroes' and other
activists published in the CCP official newspaper *Jiefang ribao*
(Liberation Daily) hailed Mao as the 'star of salvation' (*jiuxing*)
of the Chinese people. At the beginning of 1944, as part of the
Chinese New Year festivities, Mao was even invited to plant
grain in person near Yanan – a bizarre resemblance to the planting rituals that had traditionally been performed by Chinese

emperors at the start of the agricultural season (Schram 1987: 213). Finally, in 1944 the first edition of Mao's *Selected Works* was published, and the new party constitution drawn up by the Seventh Party Congress (April–June 1945) noted that 'Mao's Thought' (*Mao Zedong sixiang*) constituted the 'single ideological guide' for the CCP (Wylie 1980: 217, 273). The most fulsome praise at the party congress was delivered by Liu Shaoqi (1898–1969), a prominent labour organizer in the 1920s who was now ranked directly after Mao, when he declared: 'Our Comrade Mao Zedong is not only the greatest revolutionary and statesman in all of Chinese history; he is also the greatest theoretician and scientist in all of Chinese history' (Schram 1987: 213). Ironically (and tragically), Liu was to fall victim two decades later to the very personality cult that he had helped to foster (Dittmer 1998).

In the wake of the rectification campaign attempts were made to reduce the numbers of bureaucratic personnel; higher-level party cadres, administrators and intellectuals were encouraged to participate in manual labour at the local level, in what was termed 'going down to the countryside' (*xiafang*). Army units, also, were expected to take part in agricultural production, especially during the planting and harvesting seasons. Rural part-time schools were set up to spread both literacy and practical skills. To counter the effects of the economic blockade local, small-scale industry (such as iron-smelting) was promoted and the party mobilized rural women in a production campaign to increase cloth supplies (Davin 1976: 35–42; Stranahan 1983: 58–60). For the first time, in a region where women were generally confined to the home, large numbers of peasant women enjoyed access to a 'public sphere' and were able to mix together socially; the income they earned during the campaign brought them enhanced status and a certain amount of economic independence.

It might be noted here that official CCP policy towards women was always conditioned by the perceived need to balance emancipation with family stability. Thus during the Jiangxi Soviet period the CCP's commitment to improving the lives of women was manifested in a 1931 Marriage Law that proscribed concubinage and child betrothals, provided for free choice in marriage, and granted women divorce and property rights (Meijer 1983). The establishment of women's associations was also encouraged to provide a platform for women's voices and represent women's interests. The gender concerns of women's associations, however, sometimes clashed with the class focus of CCP-sponsored peasant associations; in such cases the class interests of the peasantry generally had priority. Also, since in most cases it was women who were more likely to utilize the law and petition for divorce and the CCP was anxious to preserve the morale of male peasants in the Red Army, the unconditional right of soldiers' wives to seek divorce was later restricted – both in Jiangxi and later during the Yanan period (Johnson 1983: 60, 66). Interestingly, the CCP's aim of encouraging stable and harmonious families – in the words of one study, to 'reknit' families at a time when decades of war, economic insecurity and worsening living conditions had broken up stable communities, increased social instability and led to a permanent floating population of rural migrants (Stacey 1983) – meant that after 1944 party leaders often stressed the important role hard-working and loyal housewives could play in ensuring family well-being and advancing the cause of the liberation struggle (Stranahan 1983: 79–80).

A classic study of the Yanan period (Selden 1971) described the policies and leadership style of the CCP – with its emphasis on the 'mass line', local economic initiative, grassroots participation in elections and administration, and close links between the army and people – as a pioneering contribution to the theory and practice of revolutionary change and social transformation (the 'Yanan Way') within the context of an anti-colonial liberation movement. In a recently revised edition (Selden 1995a), however, the author – while affirming the basic validity of his earlier thesis – notes that the 'dark side' of mobilization politics during the Yanan period that would later (after 1949) manifest itself in party despotism, ideological fundamentalism and a personality cult had been underestimated. Thus one little-studied aspect of the rectification campaign in 1942 was the 'investigation' of cadres in order to root out 'erroneous' thinking and practice; a key figure in this process was Kang Sheng (d. 1975), who had returned from Moscow in 1937 after studying Soviet secret police techniques (Schram 1987: 213). Kang Sheng was to play an important, if shadowy, role after 1949 in the party's security operations.

The rectification campaign was also used to clamp-down on intellectual freedom. In May 1942, in his 'Talks at the Yanan Forum on Art and Literature', Mao criticized the elitism of certain writers and intellectuals, urging them to cultivate a deeper understanding of the 'masses' so as to create a more genuine 'revolutionary literature' that would represent the 'proletarian standpoint'. Mao also insisted that literature's task was to reflect the glories of revolutionary society rather than to critique its less exalted aspects. In a sense, Mao's prescriptions signalled the beginnings of greater party control over intellectuals, especially those who had first come to prominence in the wake of the May Fourth Movement. A recent study, however, has also noted that the war period in general witnessed a more widespread 'popularization' of culture as urban intellectuals (now ensconced in the rural hinterlands) adapted and remoulded new cultural forms that had flourished in the cities since the early years of the twentieth century (such as newspapers, drama and cartoons) in order to expound on patriotic and anti-Japanese themes accessible to rural folk (Hung 1994). Mao's criticism in 1942 notwithstanding, communist intellectuals during the Yanan period also skilfully exploited traditional popular culture by infusing new political content into songs, dances and folk plays traditionally performed in north China (Holm 1991).

The principal victim of the clamp-down on intellectuals in the wake of Mao's 'Talks' was Wang Shiwei (1907–47). A student at Beijing University in the 1920s, Wang had come to Yanan in 1937 as a translator and writer of fiction. He aroused the wrath of the party leadership when he wrote a series of articles in early 1942 (ironically responding to Mao's criticism of 'bureaucratism') that denounced an emerging privileged hierarchy in Yanan as well as the party's resort to authoritarian methods (Spence 1982: 292–4; Benton and Hunter 1995: 7–13, 69–75). Wang refused to recant and was dismissed from his translating job and sent to work in a factory (he was later executed on party orders). The party's increasing intolerance of outspoken intellectuals was also demonstrated in the fierce criticism levelled at Ding Ling (1904–86), a noted female writer who had been active in the revolution since the mid-1920s and had been imprisoned by the Guomindang for several years. In March 1942 (on International Women's Day) Ding Ling published an article in the party's official newspaper that bewailed the lack of sexual equality in Yanan and satirized male double standards in their judgement of women (Spence 1982: 288–91; Stranahan 1983: 55; Benton and Hunter 1995: 78–82). Ding Ling was denounced as a bourgeois feminist and for the next few years desisted from writing. Recent research has also uncovered another 'dark side' to the Yanan 'myth' that was assiduously cultivated during this period and subsequently after 1949 (Apter 1995). The Shaan–Gan–Ning Border Region, hard-pressed by the Guomindang-imposed economic blockade, surreptitiously relied on opium revenues (Chen 1995).

Foreign visitors to Yanan throughout this period, however, consistently remarked upon the high morale and dedication shown by the communists. The American journalist, Edgar Snow, had first brought Mao and his colleagues to the world's attention when he visited Yanan in 1936 and then wrote his classic account of the CCP, *Red Star Over China* (1938), which depicted the communists as sincere revolutionaries dedicated to socio-economic reform. By 1944 American official interest in the CCP was sufficient to prompt the sending to Yanan of an army observer group, known as the Dixie Mission, under Colonel Barrett. Mao was keen to obtain American aid for the struggle against Japan, and in an interview in August 1944 with John Service, a foreign affairs officer attached to the Dixie Mission, Mao expressed his hope that Washington might mediate between Yanan and Chongqing. Later in the same year President Roosevelt sent his personal emissary, Patrick Hurley, to Yanan and a five-point draft programme was agreed as a basis for CCP–Guomindang reconciliation, including the formation of a coalition government and legal status for the CCP (Reardon-Anderson 1980: 51–7). Chiang Kai-shek's unwillingness to accept the draft programme effectively put an end to any hopes of a *modus vivendi*.

Although Hurley's mission to Yanan was not a success (Hurley's own lukewarm and condescending attitude towards the communists did not help much), Mao continued at certain times to believe that the US might play a constructive role in postwar China (Hunt 1996: 153–7). This has led to an assumption that CCP foreign policy in the 1940s was driven as much by pragmatic aims (underpinned by nationalism) as ideological imperatives (e.g. Reardon-Anderson 1980). Such a view has recently been critiqued in a study of CCP relations with the Soviet Union and the US from 1935 to 1949 (Sheng 1997). The study argues that since the CCP and Mao consistently adhered to a 'class-struggle ideology' and that their sense of identity was bound up with a commitment to a higher 'moral value than that of nationalism' (i.e. 'proletarian internationalism', which meant following Moscow's instructions in most cases) (ibid.: 6–10), Mao's 'flirtations' with the US in 1944–6 were purely tactical in nature. In effect, Mao, in dealing with the US, was simply applying domestic united-front tactics to the realm of diplomacy (ibid.: 74–85) and there was never any intention of forging a long-term relationship with the US at Moscow's expense.

Although Mao never did receive the American aid he had hoped for in 1944–5, by the time the war ended Yanan had considerably expanded its influence, controlling eighteen base areas (with a population of 100 million), mainly throughout north China.

5

The New Communist Government

The war against Japan took an enormous toll on the Chinese people. Large areas of the country were devastated and communications destroyed. Eight years of war had resulted in 1.5 million Chinese killed and almost 2 million wounded, while the country's war debt had escalated to 1,464 billion Chinese dollars (Hsu 2000: 611). Over a longer period, from 1931 to 1945, official Chinese reports claim that Japan was responsible for the death of 3.8 million soldiers, the killing or wounding of 18 million civilians, and the destruction of US$120 billion worth of property (Feuerwerker 1989: 431–2). All hopes, however, that peace and stability might prevail were cruelly dashed as increasing hostility between Chiang Kai-shek and the CCP, whose forces now totalled 1 million regular troops and 2 million militia, erupted into a bloody civil war – the first conflict of the Cold War era because of the involvement of the US and the Soviet Union (Westad 1993).

The eventual victory of Mao Zedong's CCP in October 1949 and the establishment of the People's Republic of China (PRC) has long been regarded as a major watershed in modern Chinese history. Mao himself described the CCP victory as the culmination of a 100-year struggle against imperialism (dating from the Opium War) and the quest for an independent and respected nation-state that would assume its rightful place in the world. On the eve of the CCP victory Mao's second-in-command, Liu Shaoqi, also declared that the rural-based Chinese revolution based on self-reliance and the Sinification (i.e. indigenization) of Marxism would serve as a model and an inspiration for other oppressed countries in the colonial world, especially in Asia and Africa. Not quite representing the first accession to power by a national communist party without outside assistance since the Bolshevik Revolution of 1917 – in September 1945 Ho Chi Minh's communist-led Vietminh declared Vietnamese independence and inaugurated the Democratic Republic of Vietnam, although it subsequently had to engage in a thirty-year military struggle, first against the returning French determined to restore their colonial rule in Indochina and then against the US and its South Vietnamese proxies – the CCP victory of 1949 also remained a focal point of attention amongst western scholars. Although there was much disagreement about the causes and nature of that event (Hartford and Goldstein 1989), until recently it occupied the dominant position in accounts of modern Chinese history (Hershatter, Honig and Stross 1996: 7). From the 1950s to the 1970s, also, the assumption that 1949 marked a crucial dividing line in modern Chinese history explains why studies of post-1949 China (especially in the US) were more likely to be the domain of political scientists or sociologists than historians *per se* (Stross 1996: 261).

However, just as within the last couple of decades studies have sought to unravel the Mao-centred approach to the Chinese revolution by focusing on the rural revolution from the 1920s to the 1940s in other regions ignored by Maoist historiography, such as eastern and central China (Chen 1986; Wou 1994), examining the local contexts in which communist activists operated and how such activists responded and adapted to grassroots concerns (Sheel 1989; Thaxton 1983, 1997), and explored the CCP's use of united-front tactics and its involvement in student movements in cities such as Beijing and Tianjin during the civil war (Yick 1995), so scholars have transgressed the 'border' of 1949 in order to illuminate historical perspectives that embrace all of the twentieth century. Thus, for example, recent studies have analysed student 'repertoires' of protest during the twentieth century (Wasserstrom 1991), suggested the relevance of changing attitudes towards popular education at the turn of the century to Maoist educational thought after 1949 (Bailey 1990), underlined the significance of the military during the late Qing, republican and post-1949 periods (Van de Ven

1997), and explored the contemporary relevance of ethnic identities that were 'constructed' in the late nineteenth and early twentieth centuries (Honig 1992).

Furthermore, the continuities that are now seen as transcending the 1949 dividing line have led some historians to argue that Guomindang rule was as much a precursor to the communist revolution as its enemy. Thus a study shows that Chiang Kai-shek's use of German advisers and assistance during the Nanjing decade to implement Sun Yatsen's vision of a state-run industrial sector led to plans being formulated in 1932–5 designed to create a fully 'planned economy' (Kirby 1984: 81, 95–6). Also, the Guomindang's reorganization as a Leninist-style party and the creation of a party army in the early 1920s, as well as its campaigns against 'superstitious' beliefs and customs, all echo aspects of communist rule and practice (Esherick 1995: 47–8).

Nevertheless, the creation of the PRC in 1949, as far as Mao and his colleagues were concerned, marked the beginning of a project to create a new society and lay the foundations for an economically prosperous state. The gradual divergence of views between Mao and his closest associates within the party over how such ambitions might be realized were to have momentous, and ultimately disastrous, consequences for the Chinese people.

The Civil War

With the formal ending of the Second World War in Asia in August 1945 there was an immediate rush to accept the Japanese surrender in China and hence acquire their weapons. Chiang Kai-shek issued orders that Japanese troops were to surrender only to nationalist forces, and even commanded that until then they be responsible (along with former collaborators) for maintaining law and order in the cities. Inevitably, this caused much resentment amongst the urban population (Pepper 1978: 9; 1986: 738–9). At the same time Chiang relied on American assistance to airlift his troops to Beijing, Tianjin, Nanjing and Shanghai. American marines also landed in north China to await the arrival of nationalist troops (Schaller 1979). Chiang's attempt to take over the cities in Manchuria, however, was hindered by the continued presence of Soviet troops in the region, despite Stalin's promise that they would be withdrawn after the

Japanese surrender. By the time they did leave, in May 1946, taking with them much of Manchuria's heavy industrial plant worth an estimated $858 million (Mancall 1984: 319), the CCP had succeeded in extending its control throughout most of the Manchurian countryside.

By this time large-scale fighting had already broken out between communist and nationalist forces. Although Mao had flown to Chongqing in August 1945 to negotiate with Chiang, talks soon broke down as Chiang insisted that communist troops be placed under nationalist control before he would consider Mao's demand for a coalition government. Chiang's intransigence was bolstered by his confidence in US support, although, ironically, the new American president, Harry Truman, who had succeeded Franklin Roosevelt on his death in April 1945, was far more circumspect in his support for Chiang than his predecessor had been. In December 1945 Truman sent his special ambassador, General George Marshall, to China in order to act as a mediator. A temporary ceasefire was arranged and a Political Consultative Conference convened, but co-operation proved impossible. With the renewal of fighting in April 1946 Chiang convened a Guomindang-dominated national assembly without CCP participation. Marshall returned to the US in January 1947, his mediation attempt having totally failed. As secretary of state after 1947, Marshall was to adopt a cautious policy with regard to China and even reduced financial aid to Chiang. This has led one historian to argue that the unwillingness and inability of the US to attempt a sustained armed intervention on behalf of the Guomindang regime 'created a favourable international environment for the Chinese Communist revolution' (Levine 1987: 8).

Chiang, however, was confident of success. His troops outnumbered those of the CCP and were also better equipped. In March 1947 the communists were even forced to evacuate Yanan. Yet the fatal flaws which had characterized the nationalist armies during the war against Japan continued to exist. They were poorly led and badly co-ordinated. Enforced recruitment of civilians and the undisciplined behaviour of the troops alienated growing numbers of the population. Conditions within the armies themselves were so brutal that desertion from the ranks was common. At the same time areas under nationalist control experienced an accelerated rate of inflation and the currency virtually collapsed. Efforts to implement economic reform were consistently undermined by corruption within Guomindang ranks. Chiang himself remarked in January 1948 that 'never, in China or abroad, has there been a revolutionary party as decrepit and degenerate as we are today; nor has there been one as lacking in spirit, in discipline, and even more in standards of right and wrong as we are today' (Eastman 1984: 203).

Manchuria, where Chiang had committed some of his best troops, was the first region to fall to the communists, when a decisive CCP campaign under the military command of Lin Biao (1907–71) between September and November 1948 put over 400,000 nationalist soldiers out of action (Levine 1987: 134–6). By early 1949 the nationalist garrisons at Beijing and Tianjin had surrendered wholesale. The US became increasingly reluctant to bale Chiang out, although growing criticism from the administration's Republican opponents, some of whom formed an effective pressure group known as the China Lobby, compelled President Truman in February 1948 to recommend a grant-in-aid of US$570 million (less than Chiang had asked for). US government policy in the end satisfied no one. Chiang Kai-shek complained bitterly about the inadequate amount of American financial aid, while the CCP accused the US of actively interfering in China's internal affairs. Furthermore, the administration's domestic critics were to accuse the government (and, in particular, the State Department) of having 'betrayed' Chiang Kai-shek and hence of having 'lost' China to the communists (Tucker 1983).

With CCP military forces (now called the People's Liberation Army) poised to take south China in early 1949, Stalin in January of that year advised caution, and even suggested that negotiations with the Guomindang might be a serious option. In line with current Soviet thinking, which divided the world into two hostile camps – the socialist and the imperialist – Stalin argued that nothing should be done which might provoke US military intervention in China and hence involve the Soviet Union, as the leader of the socialist camp, in a world war. No doubt Stalin's advice also reflected his mixed feelings concerning the prospect of having a potential rival communist power as a near neighbour. Mao, however, had argued in 1946 that an 'intermediate zone' (of colonial and semi-colonial countries) existed between the two camps in which active resistance against the US could roll back the tide of imperialist aggression and hence *avoid* world war (Gittings 1974: 142–8; Yahuda 1978: 32–3). Mao also at this time dismissed the potential threat of American military and nuclear power as a 'paper tiger' that could be overcome by a 'people's war' drawing on the unstinting commitment of the whole population. Although Mao by 1947–8 had come round to the Soviet 'two camp' thesis, the possibility of opening talks with the Guomindang was rejected and CCP forces crossed the Yangzi in April 1949 to embark on the conquest of south China. Mao's ignoring of Stalin's advice showed that just as the Yanan period had witnessed an emphasis on 'self-reliance' (*zili gengsheng*) in the economic sphere, so too would Mao adhere to a certain 'self-reliance' in foreign policy, an important contributory factor to the future Sino-Soviet dispute.

In October 1949, from the Gate of Heavenly Peace (Tian'anmen) – the entrance to the former imperial Forbidden City in Beijing – Mao proclaimed the establishment of the People's Republic of China (PRC). By the end of the year the Guomindang government had retreated to the island of Taiwan, from where it was to continue to insist that it represented the true 'Republic of China'. Although the US government did not consider military protection of Taiwan at this time, its relations with the new communist government had deteriorated sufficiently for Washington to impose a trade embargo on the PRC. Over the next few years, moreover, the US was to associate itself more closely with the Guomindang regime in Taiwan, constituting for the CCP direct interference in China's internal affairs (by preventing Taiwan's reunification with the mainland) and virtually ruling out meaningful relations between the two countries until the 1970s. On the mainland, however, the last act of national reunification was carried out in October 1950 when PLA troops occupied Tibet and compelled its spiritual leader, the Dalai Lama, to accept full Chinese sovereignty (in March 1959 a rebellion was brutally suppressed and the Dalai Lama fled to India to set up a government in exile) (Spence 1999a: 500, 556).

There has been much debate amongst historians over the reasons for the communist victory in 1949. Interestingly, writings about the CCP in the pre-1949 period (mainly by journalists and freelance writers, many of whom had intimate knowledge of Guomindang China) focused on issues that were to re-emerge in writings of the 1960s and 1970s (Hartford and Goldstein 1989: 4–11; Selden 1995b: 11–12). In seeking to explain CCP success such writings drew attention to popular support for the party's socio-economic reforms as well as to its ability to mobilize national resistance against the Japanese. With the Cold War in the 1950s, the study of the CCP revolution became virtually synonymous with the study of Soviet foreign policy and Comintern machinations in China (accompanied by a stress on the CCP's instrumental use of organization and Manchiavellian manipulation in its quest for power), although one pioneering study in this period (Schwartz 1951) was the first to highlight Mao's independence from Moscow and an indigenous Chinese development of the 'Leninist' model that was applied to a rural-based revolution. In the 1960s and 1970s attention was once again focused on the reasons why the CCP gained popular support. One study (Johnson 1962) argued that it was essentially the war against Japan that brought the CCP to national power because of its appeal to 'peasant nationalism' and the public legitimacy it gained (in contrast to the Guomindang) by engaging in committed resistance against the Japanese invaders. A later study of Manchuria (Lee 1983: 238–50, 263–4, 314) supported this hypothesis by demonstrating that it was not until the local CCP branch in the region was able to pursue an active anti-Japanese policy after 1933 (and especially after 1935 with the Comintern's formal sanction of a united-front policy against Japan because it was now in the Soviet Union's interest) that it gained widespread popular support; although the Manchurian branch of the CCP had been decimated by Japanese forces by 1937, the grassroots support it had cultivated after 1933 stood the party in good stead during the civil-war period.

In response to the 'peasant nationalism' thesis, other scholars in the 1960s and 1970s emphasized the ability of the party to gain popular support through its social and economic policies (e.g. Gillin 1964). One, in particular, focused for the first time on the Shaan–Gan–Ning Border Region (Selden 1971), and stressed the revolutionary quality of the party's policies in meeting the basic economic needs of the peasantry through reduction of land rent and interest rates – although more importance is now attributed to equitable tax policies (Selden 1995b:

22–3) – and creating political structures allowing for genuine popular participation. Significantly, a classic study of the communist revolution in the countryside, based on first-hand observations of land reform in a Shanxi village (northwest China) during the spring and summer of 1948, was also published at this time (Hinton 1966). The expropriation of land belonging to rural elites and its redistribution among poor peasants was compared to Lincoln's Emancipation Proclamation, destroying the power and privilege of landlords and local 'bosses' and allowing for a radical change in status and self-perception for poor peasants, a process referred to as *fanshen* (lit. 'to turn the body over', used in the sense of freeing oneself and standing up on one's own two feet) (ibid.: x, 8).

Another study at this time (Kataoka 1974) drew attention to the anti-Japanese war as a crucial factor in CCP success, although not in accordance with the 'peasant nationalism' thesis. In the view of this study, the United Front and the war immobilized the urban-based power of the Guomindang and hence provided a respite for the CCP-led rural revolution, allowing the party to extend and consolidate its organizational and military control over a parochial and tradition-bound peasantry. The importance of the United Front during the war has also been recently highlighted, but more in terms of the party's ability to appeal to (and gain the support of) rural elites – referred to as 'intermediate elements' (*zhongjian fenzi*), that included petty bourgeoisie, rich peasants and small landlords – as well as of poor peasants through its moderate and pragmatic policies (Shum 1985; 1988: 5, 14, 189–90, 231–5).

Studies since the early 1980s have delved more into local revolutionary milieux (in areas other than the Shaan–Gan–Ning Border Region) to describe how CCP activists successfully forged coalitions of interest, established structures of power in the countryside, or adapted to local contexts and concerns. A study of four base areas in eastern Henan (central China) from the 1920s to the end of the war sees the CCP revolution as a dual and 'incremental' process of power politics and social revolution (Wou 1994). In the period after 1937, especially, the CCP resorted to 'coalition politics', which involved tactical compromises with local commanders and authorities, incorporation of bandit and sectarian groups, and infiltration of village and community defence networks. In particular, the CCP in eastern Henan was able to exploit skilfully divisions amongst local elite groups and adapt its mobilization tactics according to local conditions, in general restricting the targets of class attack and emphasizing security and collective interests (ibid.: 210–11, 373–9, 382–3). A study of eastern and central China (Jiangsu, Anhui and Hubei provinces), by way of contrast, underlines the party's deliberate resort to class struggle against rural elites (under the facade of trans-class unity) as a means of engineering some redistribution of wealth and co-opting poor peasant support (Chen 1986: 501–2). The recruitment of peasant activists into CCP-organized peasant associations, militia and rural administration also enabled the CCP to establish structures of power at all levels in the countryside, a factor that became crucial in the CCP–Guomindang conflict in central China in 1948, when the party was able to rely on a dependable supply of manpower and provisions (ibid.: 504–5, 509).

A third approach has been to analyse long-term grassroots concerns of particular areas and to see how CCP activists gained support by involving themselves with such concerns (Thaxton 1983, 1997). Thus a study of the north China plain (where Hebei, Shandong and Henan provinces converge) has revealed that for peasants of this region the Japanese invasion and war of resistance were not necessarily perceived (as it was by CCP leaders) as a defining historical moment (Thaxton 1997). What concerned them was an ongoing struggle (that both preceded and persisted beyond the war of resistance) against an intrusive Guomindang state bent on monopolizing the salt trade and eliminating the informal free-market trade in locally manufactured salt so crucial to peasant income. CCP activists in this region thus gained popular support by joining with local elites and peasant producers in this 'struggle for the market' (ibid.: xv, 2, 12–13, 22–9). This CCP tactical political alliance with 'market-bound country people' against Guomindang state repression gave the party legitimacy and convinced people that a CCP-led revolution was the surest way of escaping the economic consequences of centralized state power and its 'extractive revenue machinery' (ibid.: 280–1, 319–20). The study concludes that the CCP gained power by supporting peasant expectations of unrestricted participation in market activities, although after 1949 the CCP in effect carried on where the Guomindang left off with a more effective 'centralized political assault on the private sector' (ibid.: 332). As has been pointed out, there was nothing in the revolutionary process before 1949 to suggest that popular rural support for the CCP's economic programme envisaged anything other than the preservation of small peasant farming, the establishment of private and voluntary co-operatives, and the guarantee of free-market activity (Esherick 1995: 69). Since large-scale structural change only occurred *after* 1949, in the form of collectivization in the mid-1950s (see later), any assessment of the '1949 revolution', it is suggested, must take into account developments in the subsequent decade (Huang 1995: 105).

A recent general overview of peasant responses to CCP mobilization policies during the anti-Japanese war has argued that at the outset peasants were unresponsive to national defence appeals (hence compelling the party to rely more on elites and the floating population) and that peasants were more motivated by guarantees of security and the prospect of economic redistributive policies (without necessarily calling into question the legitimacy of the landlord system itself). In the final analysis, however, the peasants' willingness to co-operate with the CCP had more to do with their keen awareness of the party's intimidating power and its capacity for repression (Bianco 1995).

Most studies of the CCP revolution have tended to dwell on the war period. One of the few to focus on the civil-war period, which takes Manchuria as its subject, argues that far from being an inevitable outcome of socio-economic forces, the CCP triumph in Manchuria was a contingent victory dependent on political, military and international factors (Levine 1987: 7), a point also made by a recent article in relation to the CCP victory as a whole (Esherick 1995: 53–6). In this view, a favourable environment for CCP success was initially created by the unwillingness and inability of the US to intervene in a substantial way, an informal 'understanding' between the US and the Soviet Union not to make China another area for competition between the two powers, and a certain amount of Soviet technical and medical assistance to the CCP (Levine 1987: 238–9) – although the Soviet presence in Manchuria until March 1946, which allowed for CCP penetration of the region, was a double-edged sword as far as the CCP was concerned since the behaviour of Soviet troops did not always endear them to the local population (Westad 1993: 90–1). In the final analysis, however, it was the CCP's ability to create its own political structures from village to provincial levels (in August 1946 the CCP established a regional government for all of Manchuria), which allowed it to displace traditional elites isolated and fragmented by the Japanese occupation and to monopolize coercive power. In order to consolidate further its power in the countryside, the CCP then took the strategic political decision to implement land reform in 1946–8. The popular and logistical support the party gained (through redistribution of land, equitable tax and corvee policies, and the promise held out to poor peasants for advancement and upper mobility in party organizations) enabled the CCP successfully to fight a *large-sale conventional war* against the nationalists in Manchuria (ibid.: 9–13, 228–35, 245–6). Whereas earlier studies (e.g. Selden 1971) underlined the party's commitment to social and economic justice as a motivation behind its reforms in the countryside, land reform in Manchuria is viewed more in instrumentalist terms. Although dramatic – for example, at the end of 1946 a party newspaper reported that 4.2 million peasants in northern Manchuria had acquired 5.5 million acres of land (Levine 1987: 228) – land reform did not represent a peasant revolution *per se* (in the sense of a radical transformation led by peasant leaders committed to reordering relations in the countryside), but rather a specific instrument of political warfare in which the CCP sought to mobilize both rural and urban populations in its war against the nationalists (ibid.: 243).

In seeking to explain the CCP victory of 1949, it is also necessary to see how the Guomindang *lost* the war. Thus after 1945 the Guomindang government progressively alienated students, intellectuals and the urban bourgeoisie through its determination to prosecute an unpopular civil war and its failure to stem economic collapse in the cities and stamp out corruption amongst officialdom (Pepper 1978, 1986). In many nationalist-controlled areas peasants simply withdrew their support from the regime as result of forced labour and military conscription (Eastman 1984). An intriguing anthology of personal essays and letters written on a particular day (21 May 1936) and published in September the same year by a group of celebrated Chinese writers – now partially translated into English (Cochran and Hsieh 1983) – already revealed a growing disillusionment with the nationalist government (ibid.: 71–137); this became much more evident after 1945. For example, one of the most loyal higher education institutions during the war was the National Southwest Associated University (Lianda). An amalgam of Beijing, Qinghua and Nankai universities which had moved from their campuses in Beijing and Tianjin after the Japanese invasion in 1937 to Kunming (Yunnan provine) in the south-west, Lianda after the war gradually emerged as a centre of criticism of the Nationalist government and its uncompromising policy *vis-à-vis* the communists. Anti-war rallies and student strikes at the end of 1945 resulted in a military assault on the campus and the deaths of four intellectuals. The following year (in July 1946), one of Lianda's most noted professors and an outspoken critic of the Guomindang, Wen Yiduo, was assassinated. By 1949, as a recent study has noted, most of Lianda's faculty and student body were prepared to accept communist rule (Israel 1998).

A study of postwar cinema in Shanghai also demonstrates a widespread feeling of malaise and disillusionment (Pickowicz 2000). Many of the negative characters in these films, most of which were made by those who had worked for nationalist cultural organizations during the war, were wartime profiteers and opportunists in the nationalist wartime capital of Chongqing passing themselves off as 'patriots'. Although the main theme of such films (which proved to be enormously popular) was the erosion of traditional family values brought about by the war (for which the Guomindang was not specifically blamed), the portrayal of corrupt wartime officials (and contrasting them with the long-suffering Shanghai populace under Japanese occupation) 'eroded public confidence in the post-war state' (ibid.: 392–4). In many ways, then, authority and legitimacy simply ebbed away from the Guomindang regime.

The People's Democratic Dictatorship

With the establishment of the PRC in October 1949, the CCP, after more than twenty years of revolutionary struggle, now faced the daunting task of administering the entire country. On the eve of the communist vitory, Mao wrote an important article entitled 'On the People's Democratic Dictatorship', in which he set forth the aims of the future communist government. In line with his concept of 'New Democracy', Mao claimed that the CCP was leading an alliance of four classes (the proletariat, peasantry, petty bourgeoisie and national bourgeoisie), all of which were to enjoy democratic rights and freedoms. This CCP-led alliance would exercise 'dictatorship' over what Mao assumed to be a minority of counter-revolutionaries, former Guomindang members, comprador bourgeoisie (i.e. those who had worked for, or were linked with, foreign economic interests) and landlords (Brugger 1981: 51–2; Meisner 1999: 56–61).

Shortly after Mao wrote this article, in September 1949, he convened the Chinese People's Political Consultative Conference (CPPCC) in Beijing to which a large number of non-CCP personalities were invited. A Common Programme was drawn up which announced the elimination of all foreign privileges and property, and the confiscation of Guomindang capital. At the same time, the Common Programme called for the implementation of land and marriage reform, and envisaged a transitional period to socialism during which the private urban economy would continue to exist. Non-CCP members also participated in the new government, with several being appointed to the Government Administrative Council (under Zhou Enlai); furthermore, three of the six vice-chairpersons of the People's Republic (purely honorary positions) were non-communists, one of whom was Song Qingling, the widow of Sun Yatsen.

Nevertheless, it was made clear that leadership was to be in the hands of the CCP. Until 1954, in fact, China was divided into six military – administrative regions (under the control of the various communist front armies), and it was a measure of the speed with which the party imposed centralized authority that it was able to dismantle these regional administrations and replace them with district and provincial governments under the direct control of the centre. A State Constitution was also promulgated in 1954, which allowed for the creation of People's Congresses at the local, provincial and central levels, the last one to be called the National People's Congress. Only the 'basic level' congresses were to be directly elected (under close CCP supervision), the membership of the higher congresses being nominated by the congress immediately below. Although in theory the People's Congresses were to oversee the administration at the equivalent level, they were primarily used to provide a platform for official party policy. The CCP ensured overall control by establishing party committees to supervise each level of administration (very often there was an overlap of personnel), while at the centre the CCP's Politburo (and, in particular, its five-member standing committee) wielded decisive influence over the formal government structure, which now comprised a State Council and a host of ministries and commissions (Lieberthal 1995: 77–9). Here, too, an overlap of personnel was evident, the most obvious examples being that of Mao, who was concurrently president of the PRC and chairman of the CCP, and Zhou Enlai, who was both state premier and a member of the Politburo Standing Committee (Meisner 1999: 61–4).

High on the agenda of the new communist government was the completion of land reform, a process already begun after 1945 in those areas under communist control and one which involved appropriation of land belonging to landlords and its redistribution to poor peasants. In some areas, particularly in 1947–8, the process had quickly got out of hand, leading to what was called 'leftist deviations', with rich peasants (and even middle peasants) as well as landlords being attacked (Hinton 1966: xi, 125–6). The Agrarian Reform Law of June 1950 aimed to extend land reform to the whole country and to set limits on its targets. Only the land and property owned by landlords (comprising 4 per cent of the rural population and owning 30 per cent of the land) were to be confiscated and redistributed – although land owned for industrial and commercial enterprises was left intact, in line with the official policy of protecting the private industrial sector. Middle and rich peasants were specifically protected, and rich peasants could even rent out land provided it did not exceed the amount they tilled themselves (Lieberthal 1995: 90–1; Meisner 1999: 91–102).

The impact of land reform, however, was dramatic enough (Shue 1980: 41–91). Not only did it result in a large increase in the number of peasant smallholders, but it also ensured the elimination of the social and political influence of the rural elite. Peasant associations were encouraged by the party to stage mass rallies during which individual peasants were invited to confront landlords and publicly denounce them. These 'speak bitterness' meetings, as they were called, led not only to the public humiliation of landlords but, in many cases, their execution as well. The CCP insisted on whipping up 'class struggle' (*jieji douzheng*) during these rallies as part of a stage-managed moral drama that legitimized the party's view of the revolution (Anagnost 1997: 28–35). Ominously for the future, however, class labels of 'landlord' and 'class enemy' (*jieji diren*) were often arbitrarily imposed; thus in north China wealthy 'managerial farmers' (employing wage labour) tended to be lumped together with landlords, while in the Yangzi region, where many of the landlords were absentee and rent and wage labour relations often occurred between middle and poor peasants, the former were often 'struggled' against (Huang 1995: 115–19). In this way class labels became more symbolic and moral in nature rather than reflecting material reality. Such a disjuncture between what has been described as 'representational and objective reality' was to become especially acute during the Cultural Revolution (ibid.: 111). Land reform took longer to complete in south China because many local cadres responsible for implementation were also members of lineages (traditionally more pervasive in the south) and hence were caught between loyalty to the state and kinship solidarity with the targets of the reform. It was not until 1952 that the whole process had been completed.

Another early priority of the new government was the implementation of marriage reform, which the CCP had pioneered during the Jiangxi Soviet period. A Marriage Reform Law was promulgated in 1950 designed to end the traditional practices of arranged marriages and concubinage, set minimum ages for marriage, allow for free choice of marriage partner, and grant freedom of divorce. By insisting also that all marriages henceforth had to be registered with the communist authorities (traditionally marriages took place as a result of negotiations and bargaining between the elders of two families or lineages), the government hoped to shift the focus of loyalty from the family to the state. Thousands of rural women (many of whom were in arranged marriages) sought to use the law to petition for divorce or marry someone of their choice. Many faced obstruction from local (male) cadres or suffered mistreatment from unwilling husbands and in-laws (in some cases even leading to death). By the end of 1953, some studies have argued, the party began to wind down its active implementation of the law and to stress instead the importance of harmonious families as the foundation of the socialist order – women seeking divorce, for example, were now criticized for exhibiting the 'bourgeois' trait of selfish individualism (Johnson 1983). In any event, one study has noted, the party's aim in 1950 was to establish stable and monogamous household units rather than to bring about absolute equality between the sexes; in effect a 'new democratic patriarchy' was created (Stacey 1983) in which women now had certain rights but authority still rested with the male head of the household – it might be noted in this respect that although women were allocated land under the land reform law it was still registered in the name of the male head of the household, whether a father or husband.

A recent study (Diamant 2000), based on previously inaccessible party archives, has questioned this view that the Marriage Reform Law was undermined by patriarchal authority at the top and traditionalist rural officials from below, arguing that rural women *were* able to use the law to their advantage (even beyond 1953) by appealing directly to district and county courts that tended to be more sympathetic than lower-level and uneducated village officials. Higher-ranking officials in the cities (many of whom were themselves former peasants in arranged marriages) were also enthusiastic about the law, especially as it allowed them to divorce their peasant wives and marry, in their eyes, more 'alluring' urban women. Furthermore, many local cadres and village officials interpreted the Marriage Reform Law as a political movement similar to land reform, targeting the older generation (rather than landlords) as the oppressors. The older generation (and especially older women) were thus as much victims of the law as its diehard opponents. Women continued to use the law's language of freedom to gain leverage over husbands and families after 1953, while those married to PLA soldiers were often able to obtain divorce without prior approval of their husbands (a condition laid down in the law) because of the connivance of village cadres – some of whom, it would seem, were carrying on adulterous affairs with soldiers' wives.

Mass campaigns were also organized in the cities, where the government was determined to stamp out all vestiges of corruption within the bureaucracy (many administrators from the previous regime remained in place, simply because the party lacked the personnel to take over from them) and in economic enterprises (Meisner 1999: 75–87). Other aspects of urban life such as gambling, drug-trafficking and prostitution (which Mao referred to as 'sugar-coated bullets' that might tempt unsuspecting party cadres as they entered the cities) were also strictly proscribed. Studies of individual cities such as Guangzhou, Tianjin and Shanghai have shown how successful the CCP was in imposing discipline and moral order on the urban landscape (Vogel 1969; Lieberthal 1980; Gaulton 1981; Hershatter 1997: 304–20).

While private enterprise in the cities was initially protected, a gradual process of nationalization began in 1953 and was completed in 1956. At the same time the new government launched its first Five-Year Plan, which emphasized the promotion of heavy industry. In this China relied heavily on the support of the Soviet Union. Although Mao had stated in his article on the People's Democratic Dictatorship that the new government would be prepared to deal with any country on the basis of equality and mutual respect, he also admitted that China would need to 'lean to one side' (i.e. towards the socialist camp headed by the Soviet Union). In any event, increasing American hostility, illustrated by Washington's imposition of a trade embargo on the PRC in November 1949, inevitably forced Mao to look to the Soviet Union for economic assistance. A recent study, however, has argued that Mao's decision to 'lean to one side' in 1949 was the logical end-product of CCP–Moscow relations since 1935 (Sheng 1997: 162).

Mao therefore went to Moscow between December 1949 and February 1950 (his first trip abroad) and concluded a thirty-year alliance with the Soviet Union. Moscow promised to come to China's aid in the event of an attack by 'Japan or any other state which should unite in any form with Japan in acts of aggression' (a clear reference to the US). Moscow also agreed to extend a fixed credit worth US$300 million (repayable at 1 per cent interest per annum) with which to purchase Soviet machinery and equipment. Further credits were to be extended in 1954. At the same time Stalin secured a number of concessions from Mao that included recognition of the Soviet Union's rights in southern Manchuria originally granted by Chiang Kai-shek in his 1945 treaty with Stalin (i.e. continued Soviet naval use of Lushun, formerly Port Arthur, and Dairen), continued joint Sino-Soviet administration of the Chinese Eastern Railway, and Beijing's recognition of the independence of Outer Mongolia (now within the Soviet Union's sphere of influence). Later agreements also provided for the creation of Sino-Soviet joint-stock companies to exploit mineral resources in Xinjiang as well as to run a number of civil airline routes. Although by 1954 Moscow had returned Lushun, Dairen and the Chinese Eastern Railway to sole Chinese control and had sold its shares in the joint-stock companies, the very fact that Mao had been obliged to grant these concessions in the first place had been a great shock, and he was later to refer bitterly to the arduous negotiations of 1950.

The tough bargain Stalin drove in 1950 has prompted a description of the Sino-Soviet alliance as an 'unequal relationship' (Mancall 1984: 368), but it is important to note the benefits that the PRC gained from it. First, the alliance provided a nuclear umbrella for China at a time when relations with the US were extremely tense. In 1950 the invasion of South Korea by communist North Korea (Korea had been partitioned in 1945) led to the intervention of United Nations forces, mainly comprising American troops, under General MacArthur. When UN forces in turn went on the offensive and advanced deep into North Korean territory, almost as far as the Sino-Korean border, Beijing sent 'volunteers' in October 1950 to participate in the fighting on the North Korean side (Whiting 1960). A war of attrition followed, ended by an armistice in 1953 that settled virtually on the original line of demarcation – the 38th parallel. The Sino-Soviet alliance may very well have been a factor in deterring a direct American attack on China, although, it should be noted, Soviet material assistance to China during the war was minimal and arrived late on in the proceedings.

Second, the Sino-Soviet alliance paved the way for Soviet assistance in China's first Five-Year Plan. Moscow contributed to the construction of over a hundred industrial plants (machine-building, metallurgy, coal, iron and steel), and sent thousands of experts to offer advice and help with training. At the same time Chinese students were sent to the Soviet Union. Overall, the 1950s witnessed considerable Soviet influence in China; Soviet textbooks and technical manuals, for example, were translated wholesale into Chinese and used extensively in education. Furthermore, the first Five-Year Plan was itself based very much on the Soviet development model, with an emphasis on both heavy industry and centralized planning. It has recently been pointed out that the adoption of the Soviet model in the 1950s was a logical consequence of close Sino-Soviet relations and Soviet influence on CCP policy *before* 1949 that has hitherto been overlooked – for example, two figures who returned to Yanan in the late 1930s after training in Moscow (Chen Yun and Kang Sheng) were to play important roles in applying Soviet models to economic planning and party rectification (Esherick 1995: 50–3).

The Sino-Soviet relationship, however, was fraught with potential tension, especially after Stalin's death in 1953. During the course of the 1950s Mao became increasingly dissatisfied, not only with the Soviet model of economic development, but also with Moscow's attempt to exert control over China's defence and foreign policies, in particular its reluctance to share nuclear technology with Beijing and its lukewarm support for Beijing's campaign to retrieve Taiwan – now linked to the US by a 1954 defence treaty. It was significant that the first crisis within the CCP leadership after 1949 involved the condemnation and purge of Gao Gang, head of the party apparatus in Manchuria and of the newly created State Planning Commission, in 1953. Gao was known to have had close ties with Moscow and was accused of attempting to set up an 'independent kingdom' in the northeast (Brugger 1981: 101–3; Meisner 1999: 120–2).

Collectivization and the Hundred Flowers Campaign

Since the principal domestic source of finance for industrialization was to be the agricultural sector, it was hoped that land reform would lead to increased production in the countryside. At the same time a gradual process of collectivization was envisaged, beginning with the formation of mutual and teams and ultimately ending with the creation of 'higher agricultural producers' co-operatives' (APCs), when private ownership of land would be eliminated. The first Five-Year Plan, for example, originally set a target suggesting that by 1957 one-third of all peasant households would join lower APCs, in which land, although still privately owned, would be pooled and farmed collectively.

Burdened by heavy state taxes and its efficiency hampered by the fragmentation of landholdings, the agricultural sector did

not achieve the hoped-for increase in production. Poorer peasants, always at a disadvantage because of the lack of appropriate credit facilities and their inability to purchase modern
equipment, quickly became indebted to their richer neighbours,
often losing their land in the process. Mao began to fear the
restoration of exploitative class relations in the countryside and
referred to the emergence of a new 'rich peasant class' (Meisner
1999: 132–3). Although the Central Committee of the party
called for a speeding up of collectivization in mid-1955, Mao was
still not satisfied and in July 1955, in a speech addressed to a
meeting of provincial and regional party secretaries, he criticized the party's caution in the wake of what Mao perceived as
'spontaneous' enthusiasm for collectivization amongst the peasants themselves. On this basis he called for the schedule to be
brought forward, declaring that one-half of all peasant households should join lower APCs by early 1958. This was the first,
and by no means the last, occasion when Mao went over the
heads of his colleagues in the Politburo to appeal to a wider
audience. He implicitly rejected the view held by many 'planners' in the party leadership, including the vice-chairman of
the party, Liu Shaoqi, that the socialization of agriculture was
dependent on the prior development of industry and extensive
mechanization in the countryside. For Mao the very process of
collectivization itself would stimulate mass enthusiasm and
hence lead to increased production.

Ironically, even Mao's target was quickly overtaken during
the winter of 1955–6 as the movement took on a momentum of
its own. By mid-1956 virtually all peasant households had joined
lower APCs, and the final stage of collectivization was then
completed soon afterwards when most lower APCs were transformed into higher APCs in the spring of 1957. Although higher
APCs, initially comprising 250 households but later reduced to
150, ended the individual ownership of land, private plots were
permitted, principally for domestic use (ibid.: 134–43).

Mao also moved decisively in launching a campaign to
combat bureaucratism within the party. Mao's concern about
this dated from the Yanan period, but he saw the problem as
being especially serious during the first years of the new government, with the proliferation of central government ministries and commissions and the growth of a party bureaucracy
increasingly differentiated by elaborate grade and salary scales

(Harding 1981: 67–86). It is significant that the lesson Mao drew
from Khrushchev's secret speech of February 1956 denouncing Stalin's crimes (apart from the irritation felt that the CCP
leadership had not been informed beforehand about such a
momentous step) was that communist parties had to be aware
of alienating the people. Proclaiming the slogan 'Let a hundred
flowers blossom and a hundred schools of thought contend',
Mao called on the non-party intelligentsia to offer criticisms of
the party's work-style; in the process, Mao believed, greater
unity would be achieved and the party would be revitalized. This
'open-door rectification', as Mao called it, did not meet with
the unequivocal approval of some of Mao's colleagues, who,
although quite willing to agree to criticisms made of party
bureaucrats 'behind closed doors', were not happy to see such
a process extended beyond the inner confines of the party.
Intellectuals themselves were initially cautious, but criticisms
began to appear in the press during the summer of 1956
(Meisner 1999: 162–9).

The party's lukewarm reaction to Mao's initiative was clearly
shown at the Eighth Party Congress in September 1956, when
mere formal approval was given. The implicit condemnation of
'personality cults' contained in the new Soviet leader's secret
speech of February 1956 also made Mao's position vulnerable.
The reference to 'Mao Zedong Thought' was deleted from the
new party constitution, while the post of party secretary-general
was revived and awarded to Deng Xiaoping, who, like Liu
Shaoqi, was unenthusiastic about 'open-door rectification'.
Riots in Poland and the anti-Soviet uprising in Hungary during
the latter half of 1956 only confirmed fears of what might
happen if the party lowered its guard.

Mao revived the debate in February 1957 in a speech entitled 'On the Correct Handling of Contradictions Among the
People', which he addressed to a Supreme State Conference
(therefore once again bypassing the party leadership). Mao
argued that unless the party was willing to listen to criticisms
from outside, a 'non-antagonistic' contradiction between the
party and the people could be transformed into an 'antagonis-
tic' one, a bold statement to make for someone who was a
communist party chairman (MacFarquhar 1974: 184–6; Meisner
1999: 170–4). Again, after initial timidity, intellectuals and
students began to express their criticisms in the summer of 1957.

On university campuses students, for example, displayed 'big character posters' (*dazibao*) accusing party cadres of becoming a new elite of arrogant and insensitive bureaucrats. Some intellectuals even went so far as to criticize one-party rule and to question the validity of socialism itself (MacFarquhar 1960).

The ferocity of the criticisms took Mao by surprise, as he had assumed that the intelligentsia was united in its general sympathy for socialism. He now backtracked from his original position (no doubt encouraged by his colleagues) and in June 1957 a revised version of his February speech was published, which defined 'correct criticism' as that which strengthened party leadership and upheld the socialist system. Intellectuals were condemned as 'poisonous weeds' and subjected to public denunciation in an anti-rightist campaign that resulted in many of them having to undergo 'labour reform'. Although the Hundred Flowers Campaign had failed as far as Mao was concerned, the growing dissatisfaction he felt with the way the party was developing (which had led him to launch the campaign in the first place), as well as with the Soviet model of economic development that the first Five-Year Plan had adopted, prompted Mao to change direction in 1958 and look to the countryside rather than intellectuals for inspiration.

6

Mao's Road to Socialism

As early as 1956 Mao had questioned the validity of the Soviet model as a guide to Chinese development. In a speech entitled 'On the Ten Great Relationships' (details of which were only known a decade later) Mao emphasized the importance of light industry and agriculture, the industrialization of the country-side, the decentralization of planning, labour-intensive projects (as opposed to capital-intensive ones), the development of inland areas, and the use of moral incentives rather than material ones in stimulating revolutionary commitment (Schram 1974: 61–83; 1989: 114). This collection of strategies, in Mao's view, would lead to rapid economic development and allow China to overtake the capitalist West. The Great Leap Forward campaign that was launched in 1958 to realize this aim also represented Mao's utopian vision of creating a specifically Chinese form of socialism, which entailed a renewed emphasis on the key role of the peasantry and the ultimate achievement of a 'collectivist cornucopia' (MacFarquhar 1997: 467).

The campaign ended in disaster and recent studies have highlighted its enormous cost in lives lost to famine and the drastic decline of agricultural production (Yang 1996: 33–9; MacFarquhar 1997: 1–6). The subsequent retreat from Great Leap policies and Mao's increasing perception that both he and 'his' revolution were being sidelined engendered an obsession in his mind by the mid-1960s that nothing short of a 'spiritual metamorphosis' (MacFarquhar 1997: 6) was required to revive a flagging revolutionary *élan* and commitment. The Cultural

Revolution was to be Mao's last major initiative of his political career – an audacious and orchestrated attempt to dismantle current party authority in order to rebuild the foundations of a new revolutionary society and polity. As with the case of the Great Leap Forward, however, the Cultural Revolution led to unintended consequences that ruined countless numbers of lives.

The Great Leap Forward

The slogan 'Great Leap Forward' (*dayue jin*) was first used at the end of 1957 in connection with a water conservancy campaign that had required a greater mobilization of manpower than that provided by the higher APCs. The slogan soon began to take on a much wider meaning, reflecting Mao's boundless confidence that radical social, economic and ideological transformation would lead not only to a communist society but also to a rapid increase in industrial production (Meisner 1999: 191–213). As in 1955, Mao would insist that social and ideological change was the prerequisite, rather than the result, of economic development. In Politburo meetings during the first months of 1958 Mao outlined his plans with the call to 'go all out, aim high, and achieve greater, faster, better and more economical results' (MacFarquhar 1983: 42).

In this Mao was supported by the 'planners' in the party hierarchy such as vice-chairman Liu Shaoqi, who had confidently predicted at the end of 1957 that China would surpass Britain in the production of iron, steel and other industrial products (Schram 1973; MacFarquhar 1983: 17). There was, however, a difference in approach, with Liu stressing the need for the masses' enthusiasm to be harnessed and guided by the party leadership, whereas Mao, as we shall see, saw the Great Leap as a means to 'unleash' the masses (ibid.: 54). A recent study, rather than simply describing the launch of the Great Leap as Mao's personal initiative, has argued for an *institutional* approach that attributes the origins of the economic policies associated with the Great Leap to the complex interplay of competing bureaucratic coalitions (Bachman 1991). Far from exercising autonomy, Mao was constrained to choose amongst different policy options advanced by those connected with planning and heavy industry on the one hand, and those connected with finance, agriculture and light industry (championing market-reform measures) on the other. What Mao did was to add his own calls for mass mobilization and an accelerated growth rate to the programme advocated by the planners and heavy-industry coalition. Significantly, the second Five-Year Plan (due to start in 1958) was virtually scrapped, as provincial cadres, taking their cue from the ambitious statements publicized by the central leadership, substantially revised output figures upwards. In Guangdong province, for example, the planned increase in industrial production for 1958 had been set at 5.8 per cent in October 1957. By early February 1958 the planned increase was revised upwards to 33.2 per cent (Brugger 1981: 182).

A pioneering study of the origins of the Great Leap, focusing on Henan province, has also highlighted the profound sense of social crisis that pervaded the country in 1956–7, and which formed the background against which the decision to launch the campaign was taken (Domenach 1995: 17–18, 29, 42–3, 54–5). Dissatisfaction amongst the peasantry (due to more rigid state control of the grain trade, decline of 'secondary activities' vital to peasant income, and reductions in distribution of cash and grain because of greater APC investment in machinery) led to peasant withdrawal from the APCs, attacks on cadres and 'economic disobedience' (ibid.: 58–61). Rural discontent was accompanied by considerable worker unrest in the cities at this time as a result of falling living standards. Between October 1956 and March 1957, for example, there were 10,000 labour disputes, most of which were instigated by 'marginal' workers – temporary or contract workers, and those involved in the service sector or small-scale enterprises – as opposed to those in the privileged state sector that guaranteed its workers job security, higher wages and welfare benefits. Resentment against this system on the part of those excluded was, in fact, an important factor in bouts of labour unrest that broke out after 1949 (Perry 1995: 306–8; Sheehan 1998). The Great Leap has been described as a rational response to this economic and social crisis that ultimately engendered a 'frenzy' (Domenach 1995: 166).

Economically, Mao hoped that the Great Leap would reduce the gap between town and countryside by promoting the development of small-scale industry such as crop processing and tool manufacture in the rural areas. Labour-intensive projects, in particular, would utilize China's one advantage – a surplus of manpower – and thereby eliminate both underemployment in the countryside and unemployment in the cities (caused by migrations from the rural areas). Mao's voluntaristic faith in the potential of mass mobilization was well illustrated in his description of China as 'poor and blank', which he saw as positive attributes because there would be more scope for development. It should be noted, however, that the Great Leap in effect brought a temporary halt to a nascent debate over the need to control China's birthrate (an idea that was to be taken up again in the early 1960s) (White 1994), and also brought in its wake tighter state controls on population movement from the rural areas to the cities; this involved the creation of a household registration system (*hukou*) that clearly differentiated the agricultural and urban populations (Davin 1999: 4–9).

Mao further argued that in the process of industrializing the countryside the masses themselves would master technology and thereby reduce their dependence on a technocratic elite, the emergence of which Mao saw as an inevitable consequence of the first Five-Year Plan. In a wider sense, the Great Leap would promote self-reliance (*zili gengsheng*) and hence assert China's independence *vis-à-vis* the Soviet Union. The following two complaints raised by Mao at a party conference in Chengdu, in March 1958, provide revealing testimony to his dissatisfaction with the Sino-Soviet relationship.

First, having noted that China in recent years had been compelled to import foreign (i.e. Soviet) methods, even in the realm of education, Mao continued:

> The same applied to our public health work with the result that I could not have eggs or chicken soup for three years because an article appeared in the Soviet Union which said one should not eat them. . . . We lacked understanding of the whole economic situation and understood still less the differences between the Soviet Union and China. So all we could do was follow blindly. (Meisner 1999: 210)

Second, Mao referred to the unequal nature of the Sino-Soviet relationship by noting that

Chinese people used to be slaves and it appeared that they would continue that way. Whenever a Chinese artist painted a picture of me with Stalin, I was always shown shorter than Stalin. (MacFarquhar 1983: 38)

In order to modify the structure of centralized planning that had emerged in the early 1950s, the Great Leap also involved decentralization. By June 1959 80 per cent of centrally controlled state enterprises were under provincial jurisdiction while, at the same time, the number of central government ministries was reduced from 41 in 1957 to 30 in 1959 (ibid.: 59–60). In particular, adopting a distinction that has been made between decentralization which transfers decision-making power to the production units themselves ('decentralization I') and that which transfers decision-making power only to some lower level of regional administration ('decentralization II'), the Great Leap implemented the latter (Schurmann 1968: 175–6). More importantly, however, such a decentralization gave the party more control over the economy, since it was *provincial party committees* that supervised economic enterprises and performed a co-ordinating role, thereby further reducing the influence of the central planning ministries. Greater party control was needed, Mao argued, because ideological soundness was just as, if not more, important than technical expertise. Hence cadres were expected to be both 'red' and 'expert', encapsulated by the slogan current at the time, 'politics are in command'.

The symbol of the Great Leap was the commune (Meisner 1999: 217–28). In December 1957 Mao had called for an amalgamation of collectives to facilitate the mobilization of larger groups of people for water conservancy work. By April 1958 an experimental commune was formed in Henan, followed by others in Hebei and the northeast. Mao encouraged this development, although it was not until July 1958 that the term 'people's commune' (*renmin gongshe*) appeared in a party publication and not until August 1958 that the party formally ratified the creation of communes at the Beidaihe conference, noting that they marked the transition stage to full-blown communism. The emergence of the communes is an intriguing example of how policy formation sometimes involved a dialectical process, whereby Mao publicly endorsed a local or provincial initiative (often in response to suggestions raised in Mao's reported speeches) which then subsequently became formal party policy. By November 1958, 99.1 per cent of rural households had been enrolled in 26,500 communes, each one averaging 4,756 households (Yang 1996: 36).

The communes, which combined political, social and economic roles, were not only to promote the 'industrialization' of the countryside, but also to help lessen the gap between urban and rural areas by encouraging the expansion of rural part-time schools and clinics. Since modern hospitals and western-trained doctors were generally concentrated in the towns and cities, increased use was also made of 'barefoot doctors' – paramedic personnel with a training in Chinese traditional medicine – to ensure that health care was enjoyed by the more remote rural areas. The very distinction between mental and manual labour was also to be eliminated (an ideal that had motivated work-study promoters in the 1910s) with the creation of commune-funded half-work/half-study schools. Thousands of students and intellectuals were 'sent down' to the countryside to live among the peasants and participate in production work, although a study of the phenomenon has shown that peasants did not always view these 'outsiders' positively, while many students themselves were resentful at having to forego a comfortable urban education (Bernstein 1977). Lest anyone be unclear about official policy, however, the official media made sure to publicize orchestrated tours of the countryside by party leaders such as Mao and Zhou Enlai; newspaper photographs and news-reels showed them engaging in friendly banter with local peasants and demonstrating enthusiasm for manual work.

Another function assigned to the commune was the formation of a people's militia; the slogan 'everyone a soldier' was publicized with particular fervour in July–August 1958, since this was a period of increasing tension with the US over the Taiwan issue (Yahuda 1978: 106–7). Much of the terminology of the period, moreover, had a distinctly militarist flavour (Van de Ven 1997). In a wider sense, Mao's enthusiasm for a people's militia revealed a difference in emphasis from that of the defence minister, Peng Dehuai, a military hero of both the Sino-Japanese and Korean wars and a marshal of the PLA. While Mao was keen to develop nuclear weapons so that China could play an independent world role and reduce its dependence on a professionalized army (relying more on a people's militia and using surplus funds for industrialization), Peng Dehuai preferred to rely on the Soviet nuclear shield so that China could build up a modernized and highly professional army (MacFarquhar 1983: 14). Peng may not have been over-enthusiastic, for example, about Mao's insistence that officers of the PLA spend time in the ranks as ordinary soldiers, or that the role of political commissars within the army be enhanced.

Meanwhile, by the end of 1958, it became apparent that the Great Leap had generated serious problems. Despite the relative moderation of the party's Beidaihe resolution in August 1958 ratifying the creation of communes (for example, the size of the commune was not to exceed 2,000 households; the arrival of communism was still described as a long-term eventuality; and cadres were to exercise restraint in their dealings with peasants), there was a frenzied rush by commune administrators to usher in the communist utopia, which only succeeded in arousing popular antagonism. Peasants were compelled to eat in communal mess halls as part of an effort to reduce the importance of the family unit and mobilize larger numbers of women in production (Andors 1983: 47–53). Household goods and property (including the private plots individual households had been allowed to keep) were confiscated; in connection with the 'backyard steel production' campaign, for example, even cooking utensils were appropriated by the commune (much of this 'home-made steel' proved to be useless). Large-scale construction projects took peasants away from crucial agricultural work. The transportation system was inadequate to meet the demands made of it, and it was not uncommon for food supplies destined for other areas to be left to rot as priority was given to the transportation of steel and other products.

Furthermore, organizational chaos abounded as local cadres competed with each other in the frequent raising of unrealistic output quotas. In this they took their cue from the centre. In August 1958, for example, the steel target was set at 10.7 million tons (double the 1957 output); the previous February it had been raised to 6.2 million tons and in May to 8.5 million tons (MacFarquhar 1983: 85, 89). Mao himself had confidently predicted that by 1960 China would be the world's third largest steel producer. More ominously, the unrealistic raising of grain quotas by local cadres led to increasing hardship as the state's compulsory grain taxes (the amount of which was based on these inflated quota figures) left diminishing supplies for the peasants' own consumption (Yang 1996: 37).

Amidst growing food shortages, party leaders met at Wuhan in December 1958 and called for moderation. They stressed once again the long-term achievement of communism and criticized 'commandism' (i.e. imposition of measures without duly taking into account the desires of the masses). Individual ownership of personal goods was restored and households were once again to enjoy the use of private plots. The principle of distribution according to work was reaffirmed in criticism of those communes that had attempted to implement a 'free supply system'. It was at the Wuhan plenum that Mao confirmed an earlier decision he had made to step down as president of the People's Republic – Liu Shaoqi was formally to replace him in April 1959. Although Mao retained the chairmanship of the party he was later to complain that he was increasingly ignored when important decisions were made, accusing his colleagues (in particular Liu Shaoqi and Deng Xiaoping) of treating him 'like a dead ancestor'.

The food shortages were exacerbated by natural disasters in 1959 and 1960, with drought affecting large areas of north China and floods devastating southern China. The resulting famine of 1959–61 (affecting mainly rural areas), which some have described as the worst in human history (Yang 1996: vii), led to an estimated 30 million deaths (MacFarquhar 1983: 330; Yang 1996: 38–9). Figures for individual provinces are equally dramatic. In the province of Anhui (central China), in 1960, 2.2 million people died – nearly ten times the death rate of a normal year – and the population dropped by 11.2 per cent. Grain production in the province fell from 10 million tons in 1957 to just over 6 million tons in 1961. In Sichuan, China's most populous province, the population dropped from nearly 71 million in 1957 to 64.5 million in 1961, while grain output in the province fell from a 1958 peak of nearly 22.5 million tons to just under 13.4 million tons in 1960 (MacFarquhar 1997: 2). In the wake of this famine and drastic reductions in grain output, the government was compelled to import large amounts of grain from Canada and Australia after 1961. In 1961 alone nearly six million tons were imported, *six times* the total that had been imported during the previous eleven years since the establishment of the People's Republic (ibid.: 27). A recent study has argued that the traumas of the Great Leap famine experienced by ordinary peasants provided the impetus for widespread popular acceptance of the post-1978 rural reforms (and subsequent 'delegitimization' of the communes), and that such reforms were as much due to grassroots initiative as they were to policy dictated from above (Yang 1996: 240–2).

At the Lushan (Jiangxi province) plenum during July and August 1959 Peng Dehuai sternly criticized the follies of the Great Leap. Mao, viewing Peng's criticism as a questioning of the entire Great Leap strategy, denounced Peng for breaking party ranks and accused him of leading an 'anti-party clique'. Other party leaders, however, supported Mao; after all, Liu Shaoqi himself had initially been an enthusiastic supporter of the Great Leap. An ominous portent of the future was Mao's extraordinary threat during the confrontation with Peng that he would retreat to the countryside and lead another guerrilla war against the government if the party leadership did not fully back him (Breslin 1998: 98). By insisting on Peng's dismissal, also, Mao had broken with accepted norms of inner-party behaviour, whereby leaders could feel free to express differing opinions at party gatherings provided they accepted any final decision reached (Lieberthal 1993: 108).

Peng Dehuai's case was not helped by the fact that his criticisms coincided with increasing condemnation of the Great Leap by Soviet Union leaders. Already before 1958 serious ideological differences had arisen with the Soviet Union over Khrushchev's espousal of 'peaceful coexistence' with the capitalist world and what Mao regarded as Moscow's lukewarm support for national wars of liberation in the 'Third World'. Another source of disagreement concerned Beijing's insistence that communist parties work together on an equal basis rather than automatically accept Moscow's leadership in doctrinal and strategic matters. In July 1958 Khrushchev had visited Beijing and further antagonized Mao with his suggestion that the two countries enter into joint military arrangements, which would have restricted Beijing's freedom of manoeuvre. Khrushchev was also reluctant fully to support Beijing in its dispute with the US over Taiwan, viewing Beijing's threat in 1958 to bombard the offshore island of Quemoy (under nationalist control) as dangerous 'brinkmanship'.

By 1959 Khrushchev was openly criticizing the communes and belittled Beijing's claim that China had entered the transitional stage to communism. In the same year he scrapped a 1957 nuclear agreement, which had promised Soviet assistance for China's nuclear weapons programme, and in 1960 withdrew all Soviet advisers and experts from China. Over 200 co-operative projects had to be abandoned. From 1960 both sides publicly attacked each other, with Khrushchev very publicly refusing to support Beijing in the Sino-Indian border conflict of October–November 1962, and Beijing accusing Khrushchev of capitulating to the US in the Cuban missile crisis during the autumn of 1962. With the signing of the Test Ban Treaty by the Soviet Union, US and Britain in 1963, Beijing formally announced its intention to 'go its own way' in international affairs and the Sino-Soviet partnership was effectively ended (Gittings 1968; Yahuda 1978; MacFarquhar 1997: 351–8).

Although the party leadership had closed ranks behind Mao in his clash with Peng Dehuai, the Great Leap was formally brought to an end in 1960, and in the ensuing years Mao was compelled to witness a retreat from Great Leap policies as Liu Shaoqi and Deng Xiaoping sought to reassert centralized control and implement more pragmatic economic measures.

The Great Proletarian Cultural Revolution

After 1960 Liu Shaoqi and Deng Xiaoping proceeded to reverse many Great Leap policies, in what has been described as a 'Thermidorean Reaction' (Meisner 1999). Bureaucratic control from the centre was restored. The socio-economic functions of the communes were reduced and the production team (coinciding with the natural village) was made the basic production and accounting unit. Private plots and free rural markets were tolerated. Many rural part-time schools and clinics were closed down as resources were once again shifted in favour of urban areas. There was a general tendency to play down the importance of ideological campaigns as emphasis was now placed on expertise (as opposed to 'redness') and economic recovery. The pragmatic atmosphere of the time was well illustrated in 1962 by Deng Xiaoping's endorsement of a peasant saying in his justification of more flexible rural policies: 'It doesn't matter if a cat is black or white, so long as it catches the mouse it's a good cat' (MacFarquhar 1997: 233).

In 1962 Mao first began to voice his fears of a 'restoration' of reactionary classes, arguing that even in a socialist society 'bourgeois elements' might emerge. More importantly, by September 1962 Mao was calling for class struggle against 'revisionism' – the appearance of bourgeois elements *within* the party itself. He particularly expressed concern that China should not go down the same path as the Soviet Union, whose abandonment of Marxism–Leninism and capitulationist foreign policy (Mao insisted) proved the 'revisionist' nature of its leadership.

Mao hoped to restore his own influence and combat 'revisionist tendencies' through two campaigns that were promoted in the early 1960s. In 1964 Lin Biao, who had succeeded Peng Dehuai as defence minister in 1958 and was a Mao supporter, launched the 'Learn from the PLA' campaign (Gittings 1967: 254–8). The army was portrayed as the model of socialist virtues, whose example the people were to emulate. Regular political study sessions became a feature of the soldiers' routines, and it was during this campaign that the 'little red book' was compiled and published – an anthology of pithy sayings taken from Mao's speeches and articles. Individual PLA soldiers such as Lei Feng were held up as models and praised for their conscientious study of Mao's thought and tireless devotion to the people and to socialism. Extracts from Lei Feng's diary were published in the media to encourage total loyalty and devotion to Mao and the party; one such extract noted:

> I felt particularly happy this morning when I got up, because last night I had dreamt of our great leader Chairman Mao. And it so happens that today is the Party's fortieth anniversary. Today I have so much to tell the Party, so much gratitude to the Party, so much determination to fight for the Party. (MacFarquhar 1997: 338)

Mao also hoped to revive ideological fervour with the Socialist Education Movement (1962–5), which aimed to correct 'unhealthy tendencies' in the countryside amongst both cadres and masses as a result of the retreat from Great Leap policies (ibid.: 334–48). These included too much attention being paid to private plots at the expense of the collective, and corruption amongst village officials and cadres (such as the acceptance of bribes and embezzling of accounts). Mao wanted to revive poor and lower-middle peasant associations so that they could play an important role in the supervision of cadres' work (and, in the process, to mobilize peasants behind socialist goals), but as a study of the movement shows (Baum 1975), Liu Shaoqi and Deng Xiaoping preferred to send party-controlled 'work teams' from outside the locality to criticize and supervise local cadres. Mao's colleagues in effect blunted the impact of the movement and transformed it into a mere party-imposed and controlled rectification of errant cadres. Mao's frustration over the way in which the movement had been restricted was clearly shown in 1965 when he ominously referred to 'those people in positions of authority within the party who take the capitalist road' (Meisner 1999: 277).

Mao's fear of 'revisionism' was compounded by two other factors. First, there was his concern, first voiced in 1964, over 'revolutionary successors'. Since even the Soviet leadership was plainly revisionist, Mao wondered, was it not possible that China's younger generation, born after 1949 and thus having no experience of the arduous struggle to achieve liberation, would lose sight of the socialist ideals for which the party had fought? It is no coincidence that it was precisely at this time that Mao launched a scathing attack on the education system, condemning its emphasis on academic achievement (thereby neglecting ideological commitment as a criterion of advancement) and book-learning divorced from productive labour (Chen 1981: 63–80).

Second, Mao became dissatisfied with developments in the cultural sphere. Not only had satirical articles appeared in 1961–2 criticizing the Great Leap – some of which, notably by the former editor-in-chief of the party newspaper *Renmin Ribao* (People's Daily) and Beijing Party Committee member Deng Tuo, were thinly veiled attacks on Mao himself – but various views put forward by party intellectuals and writers seemed to question Maoist belief in the necessity for continued class struggle and radical ideological transformation. Historians and philosophers, for example, played down the importance of class struggle in Chinese history and affirmed the universal and timeless value of certain Confucian beliefs; they equated the Confucian concept of *jen* (compassionate benevolence) with humanism and asserted that it had no class nature. In the literary field, writers stressed the utility of depicting 'middle characters' instead of simply portraying characters who were all good or all bad (Goldman 1973). To Mao such views were a dangerous manifestation of ideological neutrality.

In 1964 Mao called for a 'rectification' in the cultural domain, but once again found himself thwarted by his party colleagues. A five-person party group was set up under Peng Zhen (head of the Beijing Party Committee and close associate of Liu Shaoqi) to investigate 'erroneous' views, but its activities were limited and the rectification Mao had called for petered out at the end of 1965. This was not surprising, since many of the party intellectuals who had aired their views in the early 1960s had close links with, or worked for, the Beijing Party Committee, and hence must have had at least the unofficial support of both Peng Zhen and Liu Shaoqi. One result of this brief 'rectification' was the public emergence of Mao's wife, Jiang Qing, who had kept a low profile throughout the 1950s but now became involved in a campaign both to reform traditional Beijing opera and to produce 'revolutionary opera' that would accurately portray the heroic struggles of the party and its individual members to achieve liberation in 1949 (Terrill 1999: 216–27).

It was evidently at this point that Mao decided to launch a frontal assault on the party itself, which was to become known as the Great Proletarian Cultural Revolution (*wuchan jieji wenhua da geming*). It began innocuously enough, with an article written in November 1965 by Yao Wenyuan, editor of the Shanghai *Wenhui bao* (Cultural Review), which criticized a play written five years earlier (and staged in February 1961) by Wu Han, a historian and vice-mayor of Beijing who was a close associate of Peng Zhen. Entitled 'Hai Rui Dismissed From Office', the play concerned the efforts of a local official during the Ming dynasty to protect the peasants from rapacious gentry and landlords and how vested interests at court ensured his dismissal by the emperor. Yao claimed that the play was a thinly veiled attack on Mao, interpreting the emperor's dismissal of Hai Rui as an allegory for Mao's arbitrary dismissal of Peng Dehuai in 1959 for having opposed the communes. Yao declared that such a play was typical of the current revisionist line in the cultural domain and urged a more widespread rectification campaign.

Yao's reference to a seemingly innocuous historical play is an interesting example of how political debate in both pre- and post-1949 China has often been carried out in the form of historical allegories and allusions to the past, which serve to reflect views on current issues or problems. An intriguing study of post-1949 intellectuals demonstrates that between 1960 and 1976 the Maoists and their opponents recruited writers to their cause and that a vigorous philosophical and ideological debate occurred (at a time when free intellectual activity was being suppressed), often in the form of obscure and apparently harmless articles devoted to historical topics (Goldman 1981). The study also distinguishes between two groups of intellectuals. Writers such as Wu Han, who had the backing of the Beijing party hierarchy, tended to be of an older generation and more cosmopolitan – the heirs of the May Fourth generation who believed in both change and flexibility. The writers associated with Maoist policies, by way of contrast, were of a younger generation and less cosmopolitan – akin to a group of late nineteenth-century officials and scholars known as the *qingyi* (pure speech) faction, who had argued for a revival and strengthening of fundamental Confucian principles in the wake of the western military threat. In the same way, Maoist writers were urging a return to fundamental socialist principles (ibid.: 6–8).

There were two other interesting aspects to Yao's article. First, the fact that it was published in a Shanghai newspaper rather than in the party's principal media organ, the *Renmin Ribao* (People's Daily), may have indicated reluctance amongst some of Mao's party colleagues to encourage further debate on the issue of 'revisionism'. Second, the utility of Yao's critique as a means to embarrass the Beijing party hierarchy may have been uppermost in Mao's mind when he endorsed Yao's position, since six years before, when Wu Han had first begun writing a series of articles on Hai Rui, Mao had actually called on party members to emulate the courageous and outspoken Ming official (MacFarquhar 1997: 252–3).

Following the publication of Yao's article attacks on Wu Han and other party intellectuals considered to be critics of the Maoist line became more common. Although Mao was away from Beijing during the first half of 1966 he secured the dissolution of Peng Zhen's five-person group in May (in the name of the Central Committee) and replaced it with his own Cultural

Revolution group under the direction of Chen Boda and Jiang Qing. The Beijing Party Committee was also purged and Peng Zhen, Wu Han's patron, was dismissed. Peng's dismissal was the culmination of a series of individual purges following the publication of Yao Wenyuan's article clearly designed to secure Maoist control of the capital, party propaganda and the army – these included Yang Shangkun (later to become state president in 1988), head of the Central Committee's General Office and hence in charge of the flow of party documents, Luo Ruiqing, who had been in daily control of the PLA, and Lu Dingyi, head of the party's propaganda department. Liu Shaoqi's position was becoming increasingly vulnerable.

Mao now encouraged spontaneous struggle against all forms of bureaucratic authority. The first of such 'struggles' occurred at Beijing University, where students wrote big-character posters (*dazibao*) denouncing university administrators in May–June 1966 for having attempted to dampen the students' political enthusiasm and deflect criticism of Wu Han (Nee 1969). In June it was announced that university entrance examinations would be postponed for six months while the education system was being reconstructed. With such slogans as 'to rebel is justified' (*zaofan you daoli*) students increasingly took to the streets criticizing teachers, intellectuals, and government and party cadres. From out of these demonstrations (and struggles amongst the student themselves) emerged the Red Guards (*hong weibing*), high school and university students who saw themselves as the genuine upholders of Mao's thought. Mao welcomed these developments. In his view youth would gain a unique opportunity to experience revolution by participating in 'struggles' against those in authority and hence earn the right to acquire the title of 'revolutionary successors'. Mao's appeal to youth was also a conscious attempt to revive the rhetoric of the May Fourth period, when the dynamic, progressive and iconoclastic role of the young had been especially emphasized (Lupher 1995: 326).

In July Mao returned to Beijing after a very public swim in the Yangzi River (near Wuhan) clearly aimed to show his colleagues that he remained vigorously in charge of affairs. Openly criticizing Liu Shaoqi and Deng Xiaoping for dampening down the student movement on Beijing University campuses by sending in party-controlled 'work-teams' to supervise debate,

Mao convened an enlarged Central Committe plenum in August at which a sixteen-point programme was drafted to define the aims of the Cultural Revolution. Not only was it to overthrow 'those within the party who are in authority and taking the capitalist road', but it was also to destroy the 'four olds': old ideas, old culture, old customs and old habits. Mao was aiming at nothing less than a total transformation of people's thought and behaviour. At the August plenum Liu Shaoqi and Deng Xiaoping were demoted in the party hierarchy, and after November 1966 disappeared from public view. Liu himself was formally expelled from the party in 1968 and increasingly demonized as 'China's Khrushchev' (Dittmer 1998). Lin Biao emerged as Mao's 'closest comrade-in-arms' and was elevated to second position in the party leadership. In the words of a recent study the August plenum finally shattered the 'Yanan Round Table' – the tightly knit party group that had been together since the days of the anti-Japanese war (MacFarquhar 1997: 462–3).

Shortly after the August plenum Mao greeted thousands of Red Guards in Tian'anmen Square at a 'Nuremberg-style' rally (ibid.: 464). Mao's public endorsement of the Red Guards in Beijing (wearing a Red Guard armband) ensured the formation of Red Guard units nationwide. There were to be seven more such rallies in the next three months and the frenzied adulation of Mao and his thought was to attain fanatical proportions. With schools and universities closed until further notice, Red Guards were encouraged to travel around the country (often being given free rail passes) exchanging revolutionary experiences and to 'bombard the headquarters' of local and regional party organizations.

Despite the premise laid down by the Sixteen Points that 'contradictions' among the people were to be resolved by reason and not coercion, and that even 'anti-socialist rightists' should be allowed to repent, anarchy and violence became the order of the day. Party officials were publicly humiliated and paraded through the streets in 'dunces' caps; teachers, intellectuals and writers were verbally and physically assaulted (many of them were killed or committed suicide) and their personal libraries and residences vandalized. Not only symbols of the past, such as temples, were the target of attack; anyone professing an interest in western culture (for example in western

classical music) was also criticized and humiliated, notwithstanding the grotesque irony that 'revolutionary opera', virtually the only form of artistic performance allowed at this
time, made use of western musical instruments. The Cultural
Revolution, in effect, witnessed an unprecedented interference
in people's daily lives; even hobbies such as fishing, stamp-
collecting, growing flowers and keeping pet birds were
condemned as 'petty bourgeois amusements' (Wang 1995: 155).

Mao's thought, Red Guards claimed, would be used to 'turn
the old world upside down, smash it to pieces, pulverize it, create
chaos and make a tremendous mess, the bigger the better'
(Gittings 1989: 63). Red Guards also often resorted to bitter
fighting amongst themselves, each faction claiming to be the
true upholders of Mao's thought (Hinton 1972). Memoirs published in the 1980s by former Red Guards have attested to the
increasingly violent nature of such clashes (Liang and Shapiro
1983; Gao 1987). For many youth who became Red Guards the
experience initially was an exhilarating liberation from parental
control; this was especially so for young women, as a recent
memoir has noted (Yang 1997). Yet while female participation
in the Red Guard movement was empowering to a certain
extent, the Cultural Revolution had decidedly ambivalent consequences as far as women were concerned. Since the primary
focus of debate and 'struggle' was to assert the supremacy of
the 'proletarian' class viewpoint, specific gender issues were
marginalized. Although women were encouraged to engage
actively in the political movement, they had to undergo a
certain 'androgynization' (i.e. they were expected to act and
look like men); all forms of femininity (including hairstyle), for
example, were condemned as 'bourgeois'. It was not unknown,
either, for female Red Guards to be the target of sexual harass-
ment or assault, especially after being sent to the countryside
after 1968. Ultimately, the Red Guard experience (for both men
and women) was to be a profoundly disillusioning one (see
chapter 7).

In cities such as Shanghai there were also clashes between
rival workers' organizations that reflected divisions between
those workers in the state sector who enjoyed permanent
employment and welfare facilities and temporary or contract
workers who enjoyed no such privileges. Thus the more conservative Scarlet Guards comprised older state-sector workers,

while the more radical Revolutionary Rebels represented a younger generation, many of whom were unskilled temporary workers (Perry 1995: 311–12). It was the Revolutionary Rebels who attacked officials from the party-controlled Shanghai Federation of Trade Unions (many of whom were former skilled craftsmen), using 'protest repertoires' that had been used in the 1920s. Thus in 1967 the director of the SFTU was forced to kneel in front of a hostile crowd with a 'dunce' cap and a placard across his chest accusing him of being a 'revisionist', just as hated foremen (capitalist 'running dogs') had been so humiliated by Shanghai textile workers in the 1920s (ibid.: 313–14). In February 1967 all party organization in Shanghai was virtually dismantled and replaced by workers' organizations that called themselves the Shanghai Commune (Meisner 1999: 324–33). At this point Mao feared things had gone too far. Criticizing the establishment of the Shanghai Commune as sheer anarchy, Mao insisted on the need to create revolutionary committees that would not only comprise representatives from mass organizations but also members of the PLA and 'unpurged' pro-Maoist party cadres. Chaos and violence continued throughout 1967, however. The PLA itself came under attack by radical Red Guard factions, and in August 1967 the British chancery in Beijing was burnt down.

The first years of the Cultural Revolution (1966–9), in fact, witnessed China's near-total isolation in the international arena. Diplomatic relations with most countries were broken off in 1967 as Maoists declared that the Cultural Revolution served as an inspirational model for socialist revolutionaries throughout the world (in 1965 Lin Biao had authored a treatise entitled 'Long Live the Victory of the People's War', which predicted that China's revolutionary experience would soon be replicated worldwide in the sense that the 'revolutionary countryside' of Asia, Africa and Latin America was on the verge of surrounding the advanced 'cities' of Europe and North America). Condemnation of *both* Soviet 'revisionism' and US imperialism also reached its highest pitch at this time. Significantly, although American military involvement in Vietnam had steadily increased since 1964, which included bombing raids on North Vietnam by 1967, Mao rejected any possibility that China and the Soviet Union might co-operate in assisting North Vietnam. This is even more remarkable given the fact that the Cultural

Revolution coincided with implementation of a policy known as the Third Front (*sanxian*), details of which were shrouded in secrecy until recently (Naughton 1991: 157–8). Against the background of increasing US aggression in North Vietnam, it was decided after 1965 to allocate more resources for the development of a state-controlled heavy industrial base in remote inland provinces (factories were also transferred to these areas from the coastal regions) in order both to provide a strategic line of defence and to bring modern industry to a third major region (the other two being the coastal and central-south provinces). Although this 'Third Front' region received over 50 per cent of national investment from 1965 to 1971, however, there was no considerable increase in industrial output (ibid.: 160–2).

In September 1967 Mao called on the PLA to restore order and there followed a brutal suppression of the Red Guard movement in which thousands were killed. One historian has argued that PLA atrocities against radical Maoists in 1967–8 made the latter as much victims of the Cultural Revolution as party functionaries and intellectuals (Meisner 1999: 344–5, 354–5). Many Red Guards were sent off to the countryside to 'learn from the peasants' and take part in manual labour. At the party's Ninth Congress in April 1969 priority was given to the task of party rebuilding. Ironically, a movement that had begun with an attack on all forms of authority ended with the military firmly in control. PLA-directed Mao Zedong Thought Propaganda Teams entered factories, work units and villages to maintain order and supervise study sessions devoted to Mao's writings, and the PLA was also involved in the Campaign to Purify Class Ranks in 1967–9 that 'investigated' suspect party cadres; many cadres and intellectuals were sent to the countryside, where they studied Mao's thought and performed manual labour for periods up to two years in May 7 Cadres Schools (first set up in 1968). PLA officers constituted a majority of revolutionary committee chairmen, while half of the Central Committee elected at the Ninth Congress comprised PLA representatives. Lin Biao himself had reached the apogee of his career, being officially proclaimed at the congress as Mao's successor.

At a time, also, when the mass movement had virtually ended after 1968, the glorification of Mao's thought and persona attained its most extreme manifestations. When once wedding couples might pay reverence to ancestral tablets, they now swore undying loyalty before Mao's portrait. Villages erected communal 'rooms of loyalty' dedicated to Mao, while individual household shrines were set up before which families paid homage to Mao (Meisner 1999: 346–7). A study of a Guangdong village notes that meetings at this time always began with the 'loyalty dance' accompanied by the song 'Sailing the Seas Depends on the Helmsman, Making Revolution Depends on Mao Zedong's Thought'. Most families in the village displayed the four volumes of Mao's *Selected Works* in their homes, and every family meal began with bows before Mao's portrait (Chan, Madsen and Unger 1992: 169–70). In contrast to the spontaneous fervour for Mao and his thought at the beginning of the Cultural Revolution (when the 'little red book' was attributed almost magical qualities), deference to Mao now took on a more ritualized form.

Interpretations of the Cultural Revolution

Early western interpretations of the Cultural Revolution focused on Mao himself and the possible 'psychological' reasons for his actions. Thus for one observer the Cultural Revolution was the vehicle for the promotion of a fanatical personality cult, and Mao's sanction for this was the desperate attempt of an ageing revolutionary to achieve 'immortality' (Lifton 1968). Mao's encouragement of mass defiance against authority was also portrayed as a natural outcome of his own personality, which had been marked by youthful rebellion against his own father and a proclivity for *luan* (disorder, chaos) in reaction against the strictures of traditional authority (Solomon 1971). Later studies in the 1970s focused on the political background to the Cultural Revolution, describing it as the culmination of a struggle between two visions, or 'lines', of socialist development represented by Mao and Liu Shaoqi (Rice 1972; Chang 1975; Ahn 1976). A recent study argues that Mao's principal concern in the 1960s was how China could avoid the fate of the Soviet Union (embarked on a 'capitalist restoration') and reinvigorate its revolution. By the mid-1960s he was running out of options; for Mao, if the party was incapable of changing society then society had to be 'unleashed' through the Cultural Revolution to change the party (MacFarquhar 1997: 468–70).

Yet it is also necessary to place the Cultural Revolution in the larger context of China's twentieth century revolution(s) (Schram 1973). From the end of the nineteenth century, when officials and scholars began to come to terms with China's weakness *vis-à-vis* the West, political and intellectual debate had revolved around the central issue of *how* to make the country wealthy, strong and united. In such a quest it was increasingly argued that political, economic and military reforms had to be accompanied by a transformation of cultural and social norms. In fact, the idea of cultural revolution has been uppermost in the minds of the Chinese intelligentsia since the beginning of the twentieth century. Thus Liang Qichao during his years of exile in Japan during the early years of the century urged the training of a 'new people' (*xinmin*) who would be self-reliant, disciplined and public-spirited. May Fourth intellectuals during the 1910s condemned traditional attitudes and social customs, and advocated the inculcation of a democratic and scientific spirit amongst the people as a prerequisite for political change; like Mao, they thus emphasized the primary importance of 'correct consciousness' and cultural–intellectual change in the making of history (Meisner 1999: 295). For Mao, therefore, the Cultural Revolution was not just a ploy to remove his opponents in the party hierarchy or an attempt to galvanize mass activism (especially that of youth) in order to root out revisionism within the party, but also the means by which people's consciousness would be 'proletarianized' – the prerequisite for the destruction of both feudal and modern bourgeois culture and the achievement of a socialist society. In this sense Mao's concept of cultural revolution differed from that of Lenin after the Bolshevik Revolution of 1917, which referred to a gradual process led by intellectuals and the advanced urban working class (and dependent on the prior consolidation of a modern industrial economy) to make pre-1917 bourgeois culture more accessible to the 'backward' masses (ibid.: 296–8). One historian has pointed out, however, that Mao was reluctant to identify revisionist party and government bureaucrats as a new ruling class since this would have implied the need for a *political* and not just a cultural revolution. In this view, the Cultural Revolution was ultimately 'reformist' rather than revolutionary since Mao assumed that most of his opponents in the party could be ideologically remoulded (ibid.: 307).

The fact remains, nonetheless, that the Cultural Revolution ushered in a wave of disorder and often gratuitous violence, and other recent studies have shifted attention away from the policy debates of the late 1950s and early 1960s among party leaders such as Mao and Liu Shaoqi in order to focus on the impact of long-term party policies on social groups, as well as on the actions and agendas of grassroots actors themselves, to explain the chaos of the Cultural Revolution.

Thus a study of the Cultural Revolution in Shanghai attributes the causes of the mass violence of 1966–8 to three sets of administrative policies of the 1950s designed to manipulate people for short-term ends but which over time caused alienation and frustration (White 1989). First, the party labelled people according to their class background, thus creating status groups in society; those with 'good class' labels were advantaged over those with 'bad class' labels in terms of job allocation, housing, education and health care. Second, everyone was assigned a work-unit (*danwei*) under local party bosses (or official monitors). Since the work-unit governed all aspects of an individual's life (job prospects, housing, health care), a system of 'clientelism' emerged in which compliance and deference were essential. Third, the party legitimized violence (as well as instilling fear amongst the population) through its use of threats and intimidation during mass campaigns that were targeted at specific groups and aimed to root out certain 'evils' or 'vices' in society; such campaigns included the 1951 campaign against 'counter-revolutionaries' (mainly those who had been members of the Guomindang or who had served in Guomindang armies), the 1951 'Three Antis' campaign (*sanfan*) aimed at denouncing corruption and waste among party members, bureaucrats and factory managers, and the 1952 'Five Antis' campaign (*wufan*), which specifically targeted industrialists and businessmen who had stayed on after 1949 and were accused of bribery, tax evasion and theft of state property (Spence 1999a: 509–13). Mao's legitimation of rebellion and protest in 1966 therefore gave the green light for the unleashing of accumulated grievances and resentments, and served to aggravate deep cleavages within society (White 1991; Harding 1991).

As one scholar has pointed out, the Cultural Revolution began on school campuses and the reform of the education system had been one of Mao's aims in launching the movement (Pepper 1991; 1996: 352–64); it was in the domain of education that another source of alienation and resentment existed. Studies of communist education after 1949 have noted that right from the start, despite the official rhetoric concerning the need to encourage co-operation in the classroom, an acrimonious and potentially damaging climate of competition emerged within urban high schools because a student's moral worth was a major criterion of advancement, a phenomenon referred to as 'virtuocracy' (Shirk 1982: 4). The use of such 'virtuocratic' criteria was not only subjective and often arbitrary, but also generated hidden resentments as students competed to demonstrate their activism and moral credentials through mutual surveillance and public criticism of one's peers (ibid.: 13–15, 57; Unger 1982: 95). Such competition was exacerbated by decreasing opportunities to advance beyond high-school level after the late 1950s and limited urban job prospects (college and job assignments were controlled by the party).

Furthermore, the situation was complicated by the fact that alongside the criteria of an individual's beliefs and actions, schools also highlighted an individual's 'redness' or family class background as a criterion for advancement. Use of class labels was resurrected after 1962 (based on the economic status of a person's father or grandfather three years before Liberation), and further encouraged competition since one way to gain acceptance as an activist (and hence to become eligible for membership of the Communist Youth League, an essential requirement for superior college or job allocations) for those with 'bad class' backgrounds was to criticize one's classmates in public; such a situation bred opportunism and cynicism in equal measure (Shirk 1982: 91, 183). Not surprisingly, those with 'good class' backgrounds, especially the children of revolutionary and party cadres, sought to defend their privileged position by emphasizing the absolute importance of class background as a determinant of political behaviour (a concept referred to during the Cultural Revolution as the 'bloodline theory'). Mao himself wavered between these two sets of criteria, but by 1965 attention was focused once again on individual political performance. This meant that during the Cultural Revolution the use of 'proletarian' and 'bourgeois' became increasingly arbitrary and personalized.

A study of education in Guangzhou has further illustrated the fierce competition to gain entrance to the better-quality secondary schools – known as 'keypoint' (*zhongdian*) schools – and universities in the early 1960s (Unger 1982). While working-class youths tended to be concentrated in the poorer junior high schools, the children of 'middle-class' (e.g. intellectuals) and 'bad-class' (e.g. former capitalists and landlords) backgrounds competed with the children of revolutionary and party cadres in the keypoint schools to gain access to university (ibid.: 23–38). At the start of the Cultural Revolution students of good class background (many of whom had not done so well academically) drew on Mao's criticism of the 'revisionist' education system because of its elitism and undue emphasis on 'bourgeois' academic criteria to criticize openly teachers and administrators for showing preference to students from middle- and bad-class backgrounds and attributing too much importance to academic examination results (the keypoint schools were also condemned as 'little treasure pagodas'). Students of middle-class background, however, also joined in the criticism of school authorities to demonstrate their activism and by early 1967 had formed their own Red Guard units (known as the Rebel Red Guards) in contradistinction to the Loyalist Red Guards, comprised of students from good-class backgrounds. Ironically, it was the Rebel Red Guards that tended to be more radical in their denunciation of party authority (and who insisted on their greater loyalty to Mao) than the Loyalist Red Guards, with whom they often came into conflict. The Rebel Red Guards were also joined by the students of working-class background, who likewise felt disadvantaged by the system (ibid.: 102–26).

Recent studies of worker activism during the Cultural Revolution – especially in Shanghai, the one urban centre in which the leaders of workers' mass organizations actually took power albeit for only a short time – have also underlined the spontaneous emergence of grassroots workers' organizations that sought to act autonomously and collectively in their own interests (Perry and Li 1997; Sheehan 1998: 103–38). While some of these organizations were linked with party authorities, others were not beholden to party leaders and challenged party authority or made specific socio-economic demands (such as ending the division between permanent and contract workers).

Such activism drew on a subculture of dissent and opposition that dated from the 1920s and persisted beyond 1949.

Yet another aspect to the Cultural Revolution violence has been suggested by a new study of marriage and divorce in the PRC (Diamant 2000), arguing that differing conceptions of 'proper' marital and sexual behaviour shaped criticism and forms of collective action. The 'sexualization of political critique' (whereby party propaganda related sexual behaviour to class status) meant that an attack on capitalist or bourgeois culture could mutate into condemnation of the sexual behaviour of other classes. The puritanical urban youth who comprised the Red Guards often carried out vicious assaults on those (e.g. teachers, prominent party officials) accused of contravening sexual codes (ibid.: 282–92).

Finally, the rationale of the Cultural Revolution has been described in terms of a Stalinist-style quest to unmask and purge 'capitalist roaders' and 'hidden enemies' (Walder 1991: 42–6). The ensuing persecution and violence were thus not aberrations or departures from original ideals, but rather the natural outcome of a Maoist political mentality (more influenced by the Stalinist political culture of the 1930s than has hitherto been recognized) and the movement's intrinsic aim of saving socialism from the domestic and international forces of subversion. Furthermore, such 'hidden conspiracy' fears were taken seriously by Cultural Revolution radicals of all stripes and were not simply the pretext to vanquish opponents or promote particular group interests. Inevitably, however, confusion arose as to the exact identity of 'class enemies' – they might be members of the former 'exploiting' classes, corrupt party or government officials, previous critics of party policy, or even those who enjoyed a privileged life-style. While some radical groups (usually linked to party organizations and drawing on people from 'good-class' backgrounds) saw the danger coming from outside the revolutionary ranks, which were being infiltrated by the former exploiting classes or by those with links to foreign countries, others (mostly from middle- or working-class backgrounds) emphasized the deterioration of revolutionary ideals within the party; a smaller group within this constituency, and known as the Provincial Proletarian Alliance (*shengwulian*), condemned the entire system of power and privilege, and referred to a 'red bourgeoisie' running the country (ibid.: 57–9).

The End of the Maoist Era

The gradual process of rebuilding the party began in April 1969 at its Ninth Congress, at which the principal theme was that of reconstruction. Schools and colleges were also reopened, although university entrance examinations (abolished at the start of the Cultural Revolution) were not restored; potential students were now to be recommended by their work-units on the basis of political criteria and were expected to spend time performing manual labour before entering college (Meisner 1999: 362–3). In 1970 Mao, clearly uneasy with the pervasive influence of the PLA, sanctioned the subordination of PLA-dominated revolutionary committees to newly (re)formed party committees (which were set up in all the provinces between December 1970 and August 1971) and called for the rehabilitation of pre-Cultural Revolution cadres purged in 1966–8. Lin Biao may have seen such moves as an attempt to reduce the influence of the PLA and hence threaten his power base. Mao's criticism of the 'arrogant' and 'careless' work-style of the PLA (especially with regard to its involvement in the Campaign to Purify Class Ranks) and the dropping of some of Lin's associates from the party's Military Affairs Commission in 1971 certainly added to tensions between the two (ibid.: 376–84).

There were two other sources of disagreement. In March 1970 Mao had made it known that the post of state chairman (vacant since the demise of Liu Shaoqi) should be removed from the constitution, but at the Lushan plenum of August 1970 Lin unsuccessfully attempted to have the post restored – a move, some historians have argued, that illustrated Lin's ambition to become head of state (MacFarquhar 1991). In any event, Mao's suspicions of Lin seem to have increased after the Lushan plenum. There was also disagreement over the shift in foreign policy after 1970. Mao increasingly regarded Soviet 'hegemonism' as the greatest threat to world peace, especially after the Soviet invasion of Czechoslovakia in 1968 and border clashes in 1969 between Chinese and Soviet troops on China's northeastern frontiers that had nearly escalated into all-out war (Robinson 1991). At the same time Mao made it known that a tactical accommodation with the US, whose intention to withdraw from Vietnam seemed to make it less of a threat, might be desirable. Mao's changing views were reflected in premier

Zhou Enlai's call for peaceful coexistence and friendly relations between states with different social systems. Lin opposed such developments, arguing that opposition to US imperialism should be the cornerstone of China's foreign policy (Yahuda 1978: 221).

Lin's misgivings notwithstanding, US Secretary of State Henry Kissinger was received unofficially in April 1971 to prepare the way for an official visit to China by US President Richard Nixon the following year. In October 1971 China's diplomatic isolation during the Cultural Revolution was dramatically ended when the United Nations General Assembly voted to admit the People's Republic as a member (hitherto, China's seat at the UN had been occupied by Taiwan, which had claimed, with the support of the US, to represent the legitimate government of China). By the time Nixon became the first US president to visit the People's Republic, in February 1972, Lin Biao had disappeared from public view. Nixon's visit began the gradual process of normalizing Sino-American relations after decades of mutual hostility; Nixon formally recognized Taiwan as part of China (affirming US interest in 'a peaceful settlement of the Taiwan question by the Chinese themselves') and in principle agreed to withdraw US forces from the island (Yahuda 1978: 228–31; Spence 1999a: 595–600). In many ways the restoration of relations with the US was one of the most important legacies of the Maoist era (Pollack 1991).

What had happened to Lin Biao? According to official CCP accounts that were not made known until July 1972 Lin's conflict with Mao had come to a head in September 1971, when he and his followers attempted to engineer a coup and assassinate Mao. The plot failed and he was apparently killed when the plane he was in (possibly en route to the Soviet Union) crashed over Mongolia. The 'Lin Biao affair' is still to this day shrouded in mystery (not least because his body was never formally identified). Furthermore, a recent reassessment of Lin's role during the Cultural Revolution has questioned the official CCP view (and echoed by western observers) that Lin's overweening ambition prompted him to engage in a power struggle with Mao, claiming that Lin was thrust into national prominence only reluctantly, that his role during the Cultural Revolution was essentially passive, and that he was not a hard-line leftist in foreign or economic policy. In the final analysis, according to this reassessment, Lin was a victim of Mao's whims and the manipulations of his own family (his wife and son), who *were* ambitious on his behalf (Teiwes and Sun 1996: 4–9, 126, 131–2, 163).

Interestingly, some party historians recently have begun calling for a more balanced view of Lin's role in the revolution that would pay due credit to his achievements as a military commander during the anti-Japanese and civil wars.

What *is* clear, however, is that from being Mao's closest 'comrade-in-arms' and chosen successor, Lin Biao by 1972 was being demonized as a renegade and traitor. Not only did such a *volte-face* add to people's confusion and cynicism (especially in the wake of the grotesquely convoluted propaganda that aimed to justify it), but also destroyed popular faith in Mao's infallibility.

The period between 1971 and the death of Mao in 1976 witnessed a fierce tussle over the direction of policy between radicals and pragmatists (MacFarquhar 1991; Meisner 1999: 392–407). The radicals were led by Jiang Qing (who became a member of the Politburo in 1969) and her associates Wang Hongwen (a former Shanghai textile worker who was elected to the Politburo in 1973), Zhang Chunqiao (who rose to prominence as chairman of the Shanghai Revolutionary Committee in 1967 and was elected to the Politburo's Standing Committee in 1973) and Yao Wenyuan (a party journalist elected to the Politburo in 1969). This group was subsequently to be referred to as the 'Gang of Four' after they were purged in 1976. The pragmatists were supporters of the premier, Zhou Enlai, who had emerged unscathed from the Cultural Revolution despite Red Guard criticism of him in 1967. In 1973 Zhou was able to use his influence to have Deng Xiaoping rehabilitated, and he was appointed first vice-premier; by January 1975 he was a member of the Politburo Standing Committee.

Jiang Qing and her supporters frequently took issue with the policies of Zhou and Deng, which they saw as a deviation from the ideals of the Cultural Revolution. In particular, they criticized the policy of rehabilitating party cadres purged during the Cultural Revolution; Zhou's emphasis on economic and scientific development at the expense of ideology, illustrated by his long-term strategy of the Four Modernizations (agriculture, industry, national defence, and science and technology) that he had originally proposed in 1964 but discussed in more detail at the Fourth National People's Congress in January 1975; and the reintroduction of university entrance examinations emphasizing academic criteria. Also, in line with China's opening to the world after the diplomatic isolation of the late 1960s, Zhou and Deng implemented an economic strategy that favoured export-led growth (consisting primarily of raw materials) and the importation of technology from the capitalist world. The radicals perceived this as a betrayal of the hallowed concept of self-reliance.

The radicals were to achieve a partial victory in early 1976 when they prevented Deng from assuming the premiership after Zhou Enlai's death in January. The post of acting premier went to Hua Guofeng, a vice-premier and minister of public security who had formerly been party boss in Hunan province. Deng's policies were increasingly criticized by the party media (over which the radicals had considerable influence) and his three policy documents of autumn 1975 calling for the rationalization of industry, strengthening of managerial authority, more extensive use of foreign technology, revitalization of higher education and co-opting of intellectuals by raising their status, were referred to as the 'three poisonous weeds'. In April 1976 Deng was accused of encouraging the Tian'anmen riots, when thousands of Beijing residents angrily protested the removal of wreaths (on the orders of the radicals) that had been laid at the Monument to the Martyrs of the Revolution in Tian'anmen Square in memory of the recently deceased Zhou Enlai. Deng was once again dismissed from his posts. Victory for the radicals, however, was short lived.

The year 1976 came to be known as a year of 'natural disaster and human misfortune' (*tianzai renhuo*). The beginning of the year saw the death of Zhou Enlai, who had been premier and foreign minister since the establishment of the People's Republic. In July the death occurred of Zhu De, co-founder, with Mao, of the Red Army in the 1920s and commander of the PLA in the 1940s and early 1950s. In the same month a huge earthquake struck Tangshan (105 miles southeast of Beijing), in which over 650,000 people lost their lives. In September Mao himself died after a long illness during which he had played no significant part in policy-making. Mao's passing marked the end of an era in modern Chinese history, but his legacy was an ambivalent one. He had forged a revolutionary strategy that had brought the CCP to national power and resulted in the creation of the People's Republic of China. After decades of internal chaos, disunity and civil war, and a century of imperialist exploitation and interference, China was once again a truly independent and unified nation-state. In Mao's words China 'had at last stood up'. Yet from the mid-1950s Mao had increasingly set himself above the party, convinced that his ideas and vision alone should guide China's path to socialism. The logical outcome of this was his launching of the Cultural Revolution, which was a full-scale attack on the very party he had helped to build. Although Mao hoped to create a new socialist society the Cultural Revolution brought violence and chaos to the cities and untold misery for thousands of intellectuals, writers and artists accused of being revisionist.

In terms of the economy, the balance-sheet of the Maoist era is a mixed one. One historian believes that China's record of economic development compares favourably with Russia, Germany and Japan at comparable times in their industrialization (Meisner 1999: 417); for example, industrial output between 1952 and 1977 grew at an annual average rate of 11.3 per cent, as high a rate of growth as achieved by any country during a comparable period in modern times (ibid.: 415), although it should be noted that such an increase was at the cost of extremely high investment rates – between 1970 and 1976 investment constituted 31–34 per cent of national income (Joseph, Wong and Zweig 1991: 7). More ambivalently, the PRC by the end of the Maoist era was a nuclear power and manufacturer of intercontinental ballistic missiles (having conducted its first atomic-bomb test in 1964 and launched a satellite in 1970). The last years of the Maoist era also witnessed an expansion of foreign trade and increased importation of foreign technology; between 1969 and 1975, for example, the value of foreign trade increased from US$4 billion to US$14 billion per annum, while between 1972 and 1975 the PRC imported whole industrial plants (valued at US$2.8 billion) from Japan and Western Europe.

On the other hand, urban workers had gained very little by the time of Mao's death. By the early 1970s, for example, Cultural Revolution innovations such as the abolition of 'unreasonable' rules and red tape in factory organization and worker participation in management (through factory revolutionary committees) had been reversed. The pre-Cultural Revolution system of using exploited temporary and contract workers was still in place, as was the basic wage structure. Worker unrest was rife in the mid-1970s, with strikes and slowdowns particularly severe in the city of Hangzhou (troops had to be sent in to restore order). Official CCP trade union organizations (dismantled during the Cultural Revolution) had also been restored by 1973, replacing or absorbing workers' representative congresses that had been set up in the Cultural Revolution (Meisner 1999: 363–6).

Agricultural growth during the Maoist era was more modest than that of industry, barely keeping up with the average annual population increase (ibid.: 416). During the Cultural Revolution itself rural organization was barely affected despite the promotion of 'agrarian radicalism' at this time (Zweig 1991: 64–5). This involved an attempt to limit private plots, restrict rural markets and make the production brigade, rather than the team, the unit of account; the symbol of such 'agrarian radicalism' was the production brigade of Dazhai in Shanxi province, where workpoints were determined by public discussion and ideological commitment and whose peasant leader, Chen Yonggui, was elected to the Politburo in 1973 (significantly, with the onset of market reforms and decollectivization after 1978, the Dazhai model was to be rejected and Chen, a token representative at best, removed from the Politburo). In fact, as one study has noted, rural policy during the Cultural Revolution (in terms of organization and grain extraction) was 'remarkably stable' (Yang 1996: 241). The production team remained the unit of account, while many rural units had surreptitiously restored some form of household-responsibility system first adopted in the immediate post-Great Leap period but suppressed with the onset of the Cultural Revolution.

What *did* happen during the Cultural Revolution, however, was a revival of the Great Leap policy of industrializing the countryside (Meisner 1999: 359–61; 378–9). Small factories producing cement, pig iron and chemical fertilizers proliferated during this period. By 1976 50 per cent of all fertilizer output was being produced by rural industry as well as a significant proportion of farm machinery; by the end of the decade 800,000 rural industrial enterprises, in addition to 90,000 hydroelectric stations, employed 24 million workers and produced 15 per cent of the gross value of industrial output (Wong 1991: 183). Medical and educational resources were also shifted to rural areas, and by the mid-1970s there were over a million paramedics in the countryside; primary school enrolments also increased between 1966 and 1976 (Meisner 1999: 360–2). Since by the end of the Maoist era nearly 20 million peasants had been transformed into full-time or part-time industrial workers, it is evident that the process of 'proletarianization' amongst the peasantry that one study argues occurred only with the onset of post-Mao reforms under Deng Xiaoping (Zweig 1989) had already begun during the last years of Mao's life.

Politically, as with the case of urban workers, the Cultural Revolution did not result in a transformation of peasant life. Although tripartite committees (comprising poor peasants, cadres and demobilized PLA soldiers) had been established at the beginning of the Cultural Revolution to run communes and brigades, they were ultimately subordinated to the restored party committees, whose leadership was often identical to that of the tripartite committees. Poor and lower-middle peasant associations were also revived, but were only convened at the whim of party committees.

Mao was succeeded as party chairman by Hua Guofeng (in April 1976 he had been appointed first vice-chairman), who also retained his post as premier. The radicals evidently hoped that Hua would be a mere figurehead, allowing them to control policy. However, since the radicals were in a minority in the Politburo and their influence in the bureaucracy and the army always limited (although they retained control over certain party propaganda organs) their position was always vulnerable. Barely one month after Mao's death Hua had succeeded, with the support of the military, in having the Gang of Four arrested on charges of attempting a coup (Jiang Qing and Zhang Chunqiao had apparently tried to enlist the support of urban militia forces in Shanghai in their showdown with Hua). By July 1977 Deng Xiaoping had been restored to his posts, as well as being appointed a party vice-chairman. The stage was now set for a radical change in direction.

7

The Post-Maoist Order

After a brief 'interregnum' following Mao's death, in which his successor, Hua Guofeng, attempted to carry on with Maoist-style policies (Gardner 1982; Hsu 1990), a change in direction spearheaded by Deng Xiaoping and his allies in 1978 began a long and tortuous process of dismantling the Maoist legacy in the quest to raise living standards, enhance the party's credibility and create a vibrant and modernized economy (Lieberthal 1995: 124–7). Although some of the changes to some extent either harked back to initiatives of the early 1960s (e.g. in the realm of agriculture) or represented a consolidation of trends begun during Mao's last years (e.g. in the realm of foreign policy), the market-oriented reforms, 'open-door' policy of encouraging inward foreign investment and closer economic links with the capitalist world, and the loosening of state controls over culture, society and the economy constituted a dramatic enough transformation for one observer in the late 1980s to describe the post-Maoist period as a 'second revolution' (Harding 1987) – a phrase Deng Xiaoping himself used in 1985 – and for another in 1994, three years before the death of Deng Xiaoping, to conclude that the Maoist legacy had been well and truly 'buried' (Baum 1994).

These changes were accompanied by the rejection of other Maoist shibboleths concerning education, the nature of the PLA, and population policy. Political reform was also on the agenda during the 1980s. Mao's role in the Chinese revolution was reinterpreted to take into account what was now perceived as the 'ten bad years' of the Cultural Revolution (1966–76) and resulted in a certain 'demythologizing' of his thought. At the same time party reformers called for the implementation of 'socialist legalism', enjoining the party to conduct its activities 'within the limits permitted by the constitution and the laws of the state' (Tsou 1986: 308). Lifelong tenure for party leaders, special privileges for cadres and excessive centralization of power were condemned, while the political process itself was widened with the reinvigoration or revival of institutions such as the National People's Congress and the Chinese People's Political Consultative Conference.

The changes of the 1980s were viewed in slightly different ways by contemporary western observers. Thus one study – emphasizing the loosening of state controls, greater ideological flexibility and a certain widening of political participation – described post-Mao China as a 'consultative authoritarian regime' (Harding 1987), while another referred to a 'capitalist restoration', reviving features of the pre-1949 social and economic order (Chossudovsky 1986). The changes after 1978 were also placed in a wider twentieth-century context by highlighting continuities with earlier attempts at economic modernization, nation-building and authoritarian reform that had been a feature of all regimes from the last decade of the Qing dynasty onwards (Cohen 1988).

The reform process, nevertheless, presented the CCP with two fundamental dilemmas given its explicit assumption that the primacy of one-party rule was never to be questioned. First, how was the party to encourage participation amongst wider groups of people, invigorate moribund political institutions and clearly differentiate the party from the government without endangering overall party control; and second, how was the party to relax its control over society and the economy (in order to 'free' the productive forces) without incurring the danger of crass materialism and the dilution of the collective spirit, regional and local economic inequalities, bureaucratic corruption, a revival of 'feudal' customs and practices, and potential 'infection' by decadent western influences? The tensions caused by the reform process were to culminate in the 1989 protest movement by students and workers (although with different agendas) and its brutal suppression by the party and army. The crisis of 1989, however, did not for long halt the party's ongoing quest to modernize the economy through ever-more pervasive market-oriented reform and closer links with the capitalist world.

The 1978 'Historic Change of Direction'

For a brief period after 1976 Hua Guofeng, as Mao's 'chosen' successor, basked in the role of having saved the party and the country from the machinations of the Gang of Four – even to the extent, it was later intimated, of fostering a 'mini' personality cult of his own. Hua's heroic role was specifically praised at a Central Committee meeting of July 1977, at which the Gang of Four were formally expelled from the party as 'ultra-rightists' and 'counter-revolutionaries' (although significantly by 1979, as the process of critiquing the Cultural Revolution and questioning the Maoist legacy itself began, the Gang of Four were condemned as *ultra-leftists*). Ominously for Hua, however, the 1977 Central Committee meeting that formally approved Hua's position as Mao's successor also sanctioned the return of Deng Xiaoping – he became a member of the Politburo Standing Committee, a vice-chairman of the party, deputy premier, and chief of staff of the PLA. As one of the most prominent purgees of the Cultural Revolution and determined to effect a fundamental change in direction, Deng Xiaoping was bound to clash with Hua, who continued to identify himself with the Maoist legacy and who had risen to prominence during the Cultural Revolution – in 1966 Hua had been a junior party secretary in Hunan province, but by 1973 he was the minister for public security and a member of the party's Politburo (Harding 1987: 50–1). Although Hua officially announced the end of the Cultural Revolution in 1977, he continued to praise its achievements (e.g. in the realms of education, public health and art/literature) and even declared that there might be more Cultural Revolution-style movements in the future (ibid.: 54).

In early 1978 Hua announced an ambitious ten-year programme of industrial and agricultural development couched in Maoist terms that stressed the role of the 'revolutionary spirit' in guiding modernization (one interesting difference from the Maoist era was that Hua's plan involved making use of foreign investment from the advanced capitalist world to finance heavy industrial projects) (White 1993: 25–7; Baum 1994: 54–6).

Throughout 1978 Deng Xiaoping and his associates undermined Hua's position by implicitly criticizing blind obedience to Mao's thought, ironically using slogans such as 'practice is the sole criterion of truth' and 'seek truth from facts' that were drawn from Mao's own writings. The third plenum of the party's Eleventh Central Committee in December 1978 has been officially recognized as marking the decisive step towards the re-evaluation of the Maoist legacy and its policies. On the eve of the plenum itself the party declared that the Tian'anmen protests of April 1976, which had been condemned as 'counter-revolutionary', were in fact 'revolutionary' – a judgement that put Hua in an awkward position since he had been in charge of security at the time and responsible for clamping down on the protests (Dittmer 1991: 24). At the plenum Hua was compelled to engage in 'self-criticism' for his slavish adherence to what was known as the 'Two Whatevers' (an official editorial in 1977 had declared that 'whatever decisions Mao made we firmly support, whatever Mao instructed we unwaveringly follow', a principle that Hua himself had enunciated in October 1976), and some of Deng's associates were elevated to the Politburo. An end was also declared to 'class struggle' and the priority of 'socialist modernization' emphasized (which included adjustment to the *market* as well as to the state plan).

During the course of the third plenum backing for Deng's position had appeared in the form of the Democracy Wall Movement, when wall posters had appeared in Beijing criticizing the excesses of the Cultural Revolution and calling for party reform. A number of unofficial magazines were also published at this time. One former Red Guard activist, Wei Jingsheng, even proposed that 'democracy' be implemented as the 'Fifth Modernization' (Nathan 1985: 16–34). For Deng, ever fearful of *luan* (disorder, chaos) and the breakdown of centralized party control, which he had witnessed first-hand during the Cultural Revolution, such ideas went too far, and the movement (which may have been unofficially tolerated by Deng and his supporters at the beginning) was abruptly suppressed in March 1979; a number of activists, including Wei Jingsheng, were arrested and the unofficial magazines closed down. In October 1979 Wei was sentenced to fifteen years' imprisonment for leaking secret information to foreigners and publishing 'counter-revolutionary' statements. As in the case of the aftermath of the Hundred

Flowers campaign in 1957, the party imposed limits on potential criticism by insisting that henceforth any opinion had to uphold the Four Principles (support for the socialist road, people's democratic dictatorship, party leadership, and Marxism–Leninism–Mao Zedong Thought).

Between 1978 and 1981 Hua Guofeng's position became increasingly vulnerable. Hua's ambitious ten-year plan was virtually scrapped in 1979 (it had led to an investment rate in heavy industry that amounted to 37.5 per cent of national output in 1978, the highest for any time in the history of the People's Republic except for the Great Leap period) and more attention was paid to improving rural living standards – for example, prices paid to peasants for state grain purchases were increased and limits on the size of private plots that peasant households could cultivate were raised; earlier, in 1977, a 10 per cent wage increase had been awarded to non-agricultural workers (the first pay increase in a decade). The first steps were also taken in 1978–80 to decollectivize agriculture and introduce management autonomy in urban state enterprises. Deng Xiaoping's emphasis on 'economics in command' gained approval at the fifth plenum of the party's Eleventh Central Committee in February 1980, at which two of his key supporters – Zhao Ziyang (b. 1919), a former party secretary in Guangdong province and currently party boss in Sichuan province, and Hu Yaobang (1915–89), who had served as political commissar under Deng during the civil war – were elevated to the Politburo's Standing Committee. By August 1980, in line with Deng's proposal that party and government functions be clearly separated, Hua had resigned as premier and was replaced by Zhao Ziyang (Deng himself resigned as vice-premier at this time). During the course of 1980, also, prominent victims of the Cultural Revolution, such as Liu Shaoqi, were posthumously rehabilitated. Significantly, however, Deng's economic reform policies did not extend to political freedoms. Thus the Four Freedoms (to speak out freely, air one's views, write *dazibao* and engage in great debates), as well as the right to strike, which had been inserted into the new state constitution of 1975 (replacing the 1954 one), were deleted from the revised constitution of 1982 (Meisner 1999: 436–7).

The 1978–80 period has been described as one characterized by 'explicit discontinuation and implicit critique of the Cultural

Revolution' (Dittmer 1991: 21), but the question of Mao's own role in the movement had still to be confronted. When the Gang of Four were put on trial between November 1980 and January 1981 (to demonstrate the new era of 'socialist legality'), accused of persecuting millions of people during the Cultural Revolution, Jiang Qing defied the Special Court of thirty-five judges (attended by selected representatives from party, government and army organizations) by remaining unrepentant and insisting that she and her associates had only been following Mao's instructions. Jiang's angry exchanges with the judges were even captured on television when edited highlights of the trial were shown. The court imposed suspended two-year death sentences on Jiang Qing (she later died in prison in 1991, reportedly committing suicide) and Zhang Chunqiao and long terms of imprisonment on the others, but even to the end Jiang was defiant, shouting Maoist Cultural Revolution slogans – including *zaofan you daoli* ('to rebel is justified') – as she was dragged from the court by armed guards (Terrill 1999: 334–5).

The condemnation of the Cultural Revolution publicized at the trial further damaged Hua, but the dilemma posed by Jiang Qing's references to Mao remained. It was finally resolved at the sixth plenary session of the Eleventh Central Committee in June 1981. It was at this meeting that Deng succeeded in having his protégé, Hu Yaobang, succeed Hua as party chairman (Hua was demoted to a junior vice-chairman and by 1982 had been dropped from the Politburo). More significantly, the meeting adopted the 'Resolution on Certain Questions in the History of the People's Republic' which, while recognizing Mao's great achievements as a revolutionary and leader of the CCP, noted that from 1955 onwards he committed 'errors' as a result of being out of touch with the needs and desires of the masses. This inevitably led to the 'ten bad years' of the Cultural Revolution and the fostering of a personality cult. The resolution made clear, however, that Mao's contributions outweighed his mistakes and that his thought (now defined as the 'crystallization of the *collective* wisdom of the party') would remain the party's guide to action. It could not have been otherwise. At a time when there was widespread cynicism about the party and even questioning of the viability of socialism itself, which the official press referred to as a 'crisis of faith' (*xinyang weiji*), Mao – so closely identified with the revolution and the CCP – could not be jettisoned. This 'crisis of faith' particularly affected those in their late twenties and early thirties, many of whom were former Red Guard activists who felt they had been cynically manipulated and then rejected by the party; between 1966 and 1976, in fact, up to 17 million urban youths had been 'sent down' to rural areas and had thus missed out on higher education, becoming in effect a 'lost generation' (Meisner 1999: 369). Deng and his supporters were also keenly aware that support for the Cultural Revolution still existed among some elements of the PLA and in provinces such as Guangxi and Yunnan (Dittmer 1991: 33–4).

The 1981 Resolution, nevertheless, had rejected a number of Maoist ideological shibboleths, including the ideas that 'class struggle' might continue after the establishment of a socialist state, that a 'bureaucratic class' might emerge within the party, and that 'contradictions' might develop between the party and people. One historian argues that the Resolution represented 'the high water mark' in the repudiation of the Maoist concept of 'continuing revolution' (Dittmer 1987: 259). The principal contradiction was now perceived to be between the 'backward' productive forces (i.e. the undeveloped state of the economy) and the socialist system. In 1981 the PRC was described as being at 'the primary state of socialism'; in September 1986 premier Zhao Ziyang noted that such a stage would last a long time because of the country's low productivity and undeveloped commodity economy – any measure that enhanced the productive forces was to be considered beneficial for the socialist system (in December 1984 the official CCP newspaper *Renmin Ribao* (People's Daily), stated that 'we cannot expect the writings of Marx and Lenin of that time to provide solutions to our problems'). In 1988 an amendment to the constitution specifically declared that the state allowed the private economy to exist and develop within the limits of the law.

After 1981, also, the 'demythologization' of Mao, which had begun in the late 1970s, was given formal sanction. Copies of the 'little red book' gradually disappeared after 1978, while the use of Mao quotes on the front of newspapers went into abeyance. During the early 1980s most of Mao's portraits in pubic places were removed (although not the one adorning Tian'anmen Gate at the entrance to the Forbidden City). By the late 1980s and early 1990s, however, a form of Mao nostalgia – known as 'Mao fever' (*Mao re*) – had gripped the public, partly in response to the increasing disillusionment with growing official corruption that Deng's economic reform policies had engendered (Barmé 1996a: 4). Mao's personality cult was roundly condemned in 1981 and, significantly, Deng Xiaoping himself (although often referred to as 'China's paramount leader') never held the leading posts of party chairman or state premier. Rather like Empress-Dowager Cixi in the late nineteenth century, Deng exercised influence 'behind the screen'. This did not preclude, however, Deng's *Selected Works* from being published and widely quoted and for his thought in 1983 to be proclaimed the guiding ideology for 'building socialism with Chinese characteristics'.

The Initial Impact of Reform

It was in the realm of agriculture that the reform policies had their most significant impact. Experiments with a 'household responsibility' system, in which the individual peasant household rather than the production team became the unit of production, began in 1978 and by 1983 most peasant households had converted to the system (Meisner 1999: 460–2). Households could now sign contracts with, and lease land from, the production team; all investment and production decisions were made by the household and, after meeting its obligations to the state, could dispose of its crops in an expanded rural free market (White 1993: 100–1). Whereas in the Maoist era peasants had been compelled to concentrate on grain production, more diverse cropping patterns were now allowed. In 1979–80 state quotas were frozen to allow peasants to sell more of their annual output at higher prices for above-quota production: by 1986 18 per cent of all marketed agricultural output was sold directly by peasants in free markets (Harding 1987: 130). By 1985 mandatory state purchases of cotton and grain had been replaced by a more voluntary procurement contract system. Furthermore, new regulations in 1984 allowed land to be contracted out for up to fifteen years (as well as permitting the hiring of non-family labour), which was extended to fifty years in 1987 – by which time such contracted land could be passed on (that is to say, more or less 'inherited') to other family members instead of reverting back to the production team. The reforms also sanctioned the formation of 'specialized households' in the countryside, which engaged solely in private rural industry and commerce or provided rural services (they could 'lease' their contracted land to other peasant households). By the end of 1983 there were 25 million such 'specialized' households (Gittings 1989: 139).

These reforms resulted in an overall rise of rural incomes in the early 1980s, although inequalities inevitably developed because of the huge variety in conditions and climate from one region or locality to another (ibid.: 143). They also led to the virtual dismantlement of the commune and the subsequent decline in collective welfare services (Davis 1989); even collective-owned farm machinery such as tractors could be 'leased' to individual households.

Urban reform began with reducing the number of industrial products sold at fixed prices (state control over the price of meat, fish and vegetables was also removed) and continued with allowing more management autonomy (in areas such as wages and investment) and profit retention in state-owned enterprises. By 1985 the hallowed principle of the 'iron rice bowl (*tie wanfan*), guaranteeing permanent employment for state-sector workers, had been breached as managers were allowed more 'flexibility' in the hiring and dismissal of labour. State enterprises were now expected to be more profitable than in the past, and during the 1980s some resorted to selling shares (to employees and non-employees) in order to raise investment capital. A private enterprise sector also emerged in the urban centres, which helped to cope with unemployment as a result of the influx into the cities of 'sent down youth' returning from the countryside (in 1981 26 million urban residents were unemployed); most of the restaurants, retail stores and service shops opened after 1978 were privately owned (and could hire labour) (Dittmer 1987: 242–3). By the end of 1986 there were over 12 million private enterprises; one of the most successful was the Stone Computer Company in Beijing, and its president, Wang Runnan, was to be a prominent supporter of the student protest movement of 1989 (White 1993: 216). Increasing numbers of women were also employed in domestic service, an occupation that had hitherto been regarded as inappropriate for a socialist society.

Just as the rural reforms after 1978 had precedents in the more *laissez-faire* measures taken in the countryside during the early 1960s (as a reaction against Great Leap policies), but went much further in introducing elements of a market-oriented economy, so the 'open-door policy' after 1978 built on the shift in attitudes concerning China's relations with the outside world that occurred during the last years of Mao's life, but sanctioned measures more radical than Mao would probably have countenanced. In a move away from the Maoist concept of self-reliance and in line with Deng's that the PRC had to increase its ties with the capitalist world, a law on joint ventures was passed in 1979, allowing for direct foreign investment in Chinese enterprises such as hotels. In 1980 the first Special Economic Zones were created in Guangdong and Fujian provinces (Shenzhen, Zhuhai, Xiamen, Shantou) as export-processing regions utilizing foreign capital and technology and in which foreign-owned enterprises could be established. Foreign investors were provided with incentives such as low rates of income tax and ability to remit after-tax profits, and were assured of a cheap labour force. By 1984 fourteen coastal cities had been declared 'open' to direct foreign investment (ironically, some of them, such as Shanghai, Guangzhou, Ningbo and Fuzhou, were former treaty ports of the nineteenth century) and where foreign capital could establish fully owned subsidiaries and ventures. By the end of the 1980s the open coastal policy represented by the Special Economic Zones had been extended along the entire coast – in the process, as one analysis has pointed out, the economic meaning of 'socialism' was emptied of any substance (Crane 1996: 157–61).

China's establishment of full diplomatic relations with the US in 1979 (the US broke its official ties with Taiwan and abrogated the 1954 Mutual Defence Treaty, although arms sales to the island continued) also began a process of greater interaction with the international community (Deng himself visited the US between January and February 1979). Already, at the end of 1978, Beijing had declared it would accept direct loans and development assistance from abroad, and in the following years joined a number of world financial institutions such as the International Monetary Fund and the World Bank. Foreign policy overall became far more pragmatic after 1978; it is significant, for example, that the Theory of the Three Worlds enunciated in

1974 by Deng Xiaoping at the UN General Assembly as China's current view of the world (which identified China with the developing countries of Asia, Africa and Latin America in contradistinction to the 'First World' comprising the Soviet Union *and* the US and the 'Second World' comprising the other developed countries) (Yahuda 1978: 238–40) was rarely mentioned after 1980. Foreign trade not only increased after 1978 – for example, the ratio of exports to national output increased from less than 6 per cent in 1978 to nearly 14 per cent in 1986 – but was also increasingly directed towards the developed capitalist world in North America and East Asia (Japan and South Korea) (Harding 1987: 139–44). Such a pattern was duplicated in the destination of Chinese overseas students. Whereas most had gone to the Soviet Union to study in the 1950s, half of the 38,000 who went abroad between 1978 and 1985 went to the US, mostly to study science, technology and business management (ibid.: 155).

Military, education and population policies were also affected by the change of direction after 1978. Shortly after Deng Xiaoping's visit to the US in January–February 1979, the PLA launched an attack on communist Vietnam following a period of tension between the two countries – Vietnam's treaty with the Soviet Union in 1978 and its invasion of Cambodia later in the same year aroused fears in Beijing of the spread of Soviet 'hegemonism' in the region, while Vietnam's discriminatory treatment of its ethnic Chinese population, forcing over 100,000 to flee the country, was vehemently denounced by PRC leaders. The heavy casualties the PLA suffered by the time a ceasefire was declared in March 1979 added urgency to calls that Maoist military doctrine be revised and the PLA transformed into a modern and professionalized force. The Maoist concept of People's War, for example, with its emphasis on popular mobilization and guerrilla tactics, was now no longer considered appropriate as a response to potential invasion; instead, a streamlined, well-equipped and highly professional army that was no longer subordinate to political or ideological concerns was now deemed crucial to protect China's security (Joffe 1987: 78–81, 95). Ranks were restored in 1984 (they had been abolished in 1965) and officers were to be trained in new military academies. The militia (so dear to Mao's heart) was also abolished as a separate entity and became a reserve force for the PLA (ibid.: 121–33). The military's influence in the party was also further reduced; by September 1985, for example, the PLA had only 13 per cent of seats on the Central Committee compared to 50 per cent in 1969 (ibid.: 160–1). Interestingly, however, the priority of developing the economy meant that in addition to reducing the number of troops from 4 million to 3 million in 1985–6 there was no substantial increase in defence budgets throughout the 1980s; also, defence industries were converted into producers of civilian goods (ibid.: 102; Baum 1994: 189).

Educational policy also turned its back on the Cultural Revolution past. The *economic* role of education was emphasized and priority given to the training of a qualified elite in competitive and selective colleges and universities – a strategy that was fully endorsed by visiting international missions from UNESCO and the World Bank in 1980. Standardized national examinations (which imposed age limits, thus disadvantaging returning 'youth' from the countryside who now found themselves too old to take them) and full four-year courses were introduced, and the compulsory requirement of manual labour as part of the curriculum was abolished (Bastid 1984: 189–90). Furthermore, 98 out of the 715 higher education institutions were marked out as 'keypoint' (*zhongdian*) colleges, and had priority in choice of students and allocation of resources. These colleges, in turn, were fed by a network of keypoint primary and secondary schools, most of which were located in urban areas – thus creating a 'dual-track system' in which a better resourced elite sector coexisted with a less well endowed sector of general primary and secondary instruction (ironically, Red Guards had accused Liu Shaoqi of promoting such a system in the early 1960s). The cultural segregation of city and countryside that Mao had so often condemned was in many ways consolidated by these changes. In fact, because decollectivization had both reduced the amount of collective funds for education and created more demand for child labour, primary school enrolment actually declined from nearly 151 million in 1975 to just over 128 million in 1987 (Davis 1989: 582; Pepper 1996: 482).

On the other hand, discriminatory class labels (such as 'rightist', 'landlord' and 'rich peasant') were abolished after 1978 (Dittmer 1987: 241) and family background was no longer to be a bar to higher education, a principle that was formalized in the

1982 State Constitution which restored the provision of the 1954 Constitution (omitted in the 1975 and 1978 ones) that all citizens were equal before the law – a measure that one observer believed demonstrated the party's commitment to institutionalization and socialist democracy (Tsou 1987: 276–7). The status of intellectuals was also enhanced (in contrast to the Maoist era), with Deng declaring in 1977 that they formed an important component of the working class. It might be noted, however, that although the 1982 Constitution guaranteed for the first time the protection of the individual from 'insults, libels, false charges or frame-ups' and prohibited unlawful deprivation or restriction of a citizen's freedom of person by detention or other means, the party continued to reserve the right to label all those deemed 'guilty' of unacceptable criticism as 'counter-revolutionary'.

Family-planning policy after 1980, in contrast to previous measures adopted since the early 1960s to restrict demographic growth (White 1994), became more intrusive. In 1981 a State Family Planning Commission was established and laid down the norm of a one-child family with the aim of restricting the population to 1.2 billion by the turn of the century. The revised state constitution of 1982 also, for the first time, emphasized the duty of citizens to practise family planning (the revised marriage law of 1980, in addition to raising the legal age of marriage, likewise enjoined couples to practise birth control) (Wong 1984). It is important to note, however, that no nationwide legislation was passed to implement birth control (and it was not intended that all couples would immediately have only one child, the aim being rather to *increase the proportion* of one-child families over time); it was the provinces that drew up regulations and guidelines to implement the policy. In general, a system of incentives and penalties was used to encourage one-child families. Thus those having only one child benefited from cash bonuses, extra ration allowances, preferential health care and educational access, and larger allotments of land leased from the collective; those having a second child lost such privileges, while those having more than two children were subject to fines. Local implementation of the policy involved a pervasive and onerous intrusion by cadres into the conjugal lives of urban and rural residents (especially of women).

During the 1980s there was much popular opposition to the one-child policy, especially in rural areas where the traditional preference for sons remained strong and incentives to produce more provided by the economic reforms increased the demand for family labour. Forced sterilizations and abortions were not uncommon. At the same time first-born daughters were vulnerable and cases of female infanticide (or, more frequently, the abandoning of female babies) were reported in the 1980s, a phenomenon that may partially explain skewed sex-ratios in some areas – although this may also be due to the fact that female births were not reported or registered. During the course of the 1980s, however, various provinces introduced exceptions to the one-child norm, allowing couples to have a second (and sometimes even a third) child provided certain conditions prevailed (e.g. if the first child was a girl or if the family was facing hardship). A study of birth control implementation in Shaanxi province also notes that because of rising individual income in the rural areas and the weakening of the collective's coercive power the system of incentives and penalties became unworkable – transgressing couples, for example, could afford to pay the fines or sometimes did not pay them at all (Greenhalgh 1993). By the end of the 1990s it seemed that population growth was slowing down; in 1998 the director of the State Family Planning Commission claimed that the rate of natural increase had fallen from 2.6 per cent (in the late 1970s) to 1.06 per cent (CQ December 1998: 1088–9). The population was estimated in 1999 to total 1,259.09 billion, and the target was revised to keep the population under 1.6 billion by the middle of the twenty-first century (CQ June 2000: 607).

Family-planning policy after 1980 was not only concerned with the quantity but also with the *quality* of the population, and a recent study has noted the increasing importance of a eugenics discourse during the 1980s and 1990s (Dikotter 1998: 122 32). The first eugenics law was passed in Gansu province in 1988, prohibiting mentally disabled people from having children. Other provinces followed suit in the 1990s, while at the national level a eugenics law (euphemistically named the Maternal and Infant Health Law) in 1995 sanctioned extensive pre-marital medical check-ups and the sterilization of those deemed 'unsuitable' (ibid.: 172–4).

The Tensions of Reform and the 1989 Protest Movement

The economic reforms launched after 1978 and the ideological dismantling of Maoism led to a consumer boom in the 1980s as urban residents (at least), their appetites whetted by increasingly pervasive market advertising (hitherto taboo in Maoist China), had access to a greater variety of material goods than ever before. For example, during the 1960s China produced only 3,000 black-and-white television sets annually and in the 1970s 3,000 colour sets annually. Yet by the end of the 1980s over 90 per cent of urban households had at least one television set (Wang 1995: 158–9). Such reforms, however, were not always matched by substantial or meaningful *political* change, while at the same time the economic reforms themselves engendered problems and, especially after 1986, fomented division among the party leadership.

In general, Deng Xiaoping's political reform agenda comprised cracking down on corruption and 'bureaucratism' within the party, clearly separating party from government and limiting the former's control over economic issues, emphasizing the recruitment of younger and more educated personnel into the party (and easing out older 'veterans'), and reinvigorating previously dormant institutions like the National People's Congress (NPC) and the Chinese People's Political Consultative Conference (CPPCC) in an attempt to co-opt wider support for CCP rule (White 1993: 172–3). Thus People's Congresses (abolished during the Cultural Revolution) were restored in 1979 and the NPC began to hold an *annual* plenary session, while its Standing Committee began to meet five or six times a year (Harding 1987: 178). Hitherto treated merely as a rubber stamp for party policies and programmes, the NPC was now given wider powers to scrutinize and amend legislation (including state budgets). When once predictable unanimity prevailed at NPC meetings, there were now abstentions or even dissenting votes (ibid.: 179; Tanner 1999: 122–3). In 1983, for example, the NPC Standing Committee refused to adopt a resolution supporting the party's campaign against 'spiritual pollution' – one of several campaigns promoted in the 1980s to clamp-down on what the party perceived as the infiltration of subversive 'bourgeois' ideas and values as a result of China's greater interaction with the West. At the 7th NPC Congress in 1988 a small number of delegates even voted against the party's nomination for premier (Li Peng). The CPPCC also began to hold regular sessions, providing a platform for non-CCP members to voice reservations about government policy (such as the decrease in government education spending in the 1980s).

Party reform concentrated on enhancing efficiency and rooting out corruption rather than promoting any form of internal democracy. Overlap between top party and government posts was avoided – the one exception being Zhao Ziyang's brief occupancy of both the party chairmanship and state premier from January to October 1987 (when Li Peng became premier and Zhao was confirmed as party chairman). Other measures implemented included the creation of a Central Discipline Inspection Committee (CDIC) in 1978 to supervise party members' behaviour and rectify the party's 'work style' (*zuofeng*). At the 13th Party Congress in October 1987 a CDIC report noted that between 1982 and 1986 over 650,000 party members had been disciplined and 151,000 expelled from the party (CQ March 1988: 147). By 1987 over 200,000 cadres had been expelled (White 1993: 178), although it is only in recent years that more high-ranking officials have been charged with corruption (see Conclusion). In 1982 a Central Advisory Commission (CAC) was also established to which party elders could 'retire'. Interestingly, a suggestion was made at this time by Liao Gailong, a member of the party's Policy Research Section, to introduce a system of checks and balances by making CDIC and CAC coequal with the party Central Committee with each being able to veto the others' decisions; in fact, the former two institutions remained subordinate to the Central Committee (Dittmer 1987: 227; White 1993: 181–2; Baum 1994: 107).

Deng was also keen to fix retirement ages for government ministers (although not for party leaders) and limit periods of office. Between 1977 and 1983, in fact, 84 per cent of all state ministers were removed. As for the party itself, Deng insisted on the recruitment of younger and higher-educated technocrats to replace veteran cadres (Harding 1987: 207). Between 1982 and 1987 nearly 3 million such cadres were removed (conveniently, however, such 'retirements' were linked with the weeding out of remaining 'leftists' within the party). In 1982 nearly 60 per cent of Central Committee members who had been elected in 1977 were removed; at the same time PLA influence in the Politburo was reduced – by 1986 only three PLA officers held Politburo seats compared to thirteen in 1969 (ibid.: 217). The change in the educational profile of the party was clearly shown in 1985, when 75 per cent of those elected to the Central Committee were university-trained technocrats (compared to 57 per cent previously), while amongst party membership as a whole (totalling 46 million in 1986 and comprising 4 per cent of the population compared to 1 per cent in 1949) about 25 per cent had received a middle-school education or higher in 1985 (compared to 12.8 per cent in 1978). In recent years the party has also been keen on enrolling budding capitalists and successful entrepreneurs.

Deng himself set an example for fixed-term appointments; by October 1987 he had stepped down from the Politburo Standing Committee (having already resigned as vice-premier) and pressured other veteran leaders such as Chen Yun, Peng Zhen and Li Xian'nian to follow suit, all becoming members of CAC (ironically, it was to these veterans that Deng looked for support during the 1989 crisis). Significantly, however, Deng remained the chairman of the party's Military Affairs Commission. The Politburo was now younger and more technocratic in orientation. Zhao Ziyang, party chairman after 1986, had championed rural reform while serving as party secretary in Sichuan province during the late 1970s, while the premier, Li Peng (elected to the Politburo in 1988) was an engineering graduate and a former vice-minister of Water Conservancy and Power.

A more substantial attempt at democratizing politics *was* made at the beginning of Deng's reform programme when an Electoral Law in 1979 for the first time provided for direct elections to people's congresses above the basic township level at rural county and urban district levels. The law also allowed candidates to be nominated by non-party members and the use of secret ballots, although party-controlled supervisory committees were still to 'vet' candidates (Nathan 1985: 196–221). Elections were held in the summer and autumn of 1980, and in some constituencies such as Beijing University district (Haidian) a genuine atmosphere of electioneering prevailed as candidates displayed their 'manifestos' and participated in vigorous debates. The experience aroused consternation amongst party officials, especially as some of the candidates obliquely questioned the virtues of socialism; in some electoral districts, moreover, public opposition was voiced to the party's continued vetting of candidates. By early 1981 the official press was fulminating against the excesses of 'ultra democracy', and when further elections took place in 1984 restrictions on nominating rights and the use of campaign propaganda were implemented (Dittmer 1987: 236–7). Although the experiment with direct elections to county and district congresses was not repeated after 1984, elections of village leaders have been held in recent years, a process that began almost unnoticed in the 1980s (see Conclusion).

In addition to experimenting with elections, the party throughout the 1980s sought to consult a wider public by creating a number of policy research institutes (drawing on the expertise of party and non-party intellectuals) that drew up reform proposals and conducted public opinion surveys. A certain amount of cultural and artistic freedom was also permitted at this time, one result of which was a revived film industry after 1979, when studios were given more autonomy to produce a wider variety of films depicting the complexities of private and individual lives in urban China, gender and generational tensions, the persistence of rural traditions, the ambiguous consequences of economic reform, and the Byzantine absurdities of bureaucracy. A recent analysis, however, argues that a truly independent and autonomous film industry did not emerge in the 1980s (Pickowicz 1995: 193–206). Employing the concept, as does another recent study of contemporary popular culture in China (Barmé 1999), of the 'velvet prison' – used originally to describe the approach of post-Stalinist regimes in Eastern Europe whereby artists were 'emasculated' by state co-option and the granting of incentives to practise self-censorship – to analyse the situation of Chinese filmmakers, it is noted that all films ultimately relied on state subsidies, had to be submitted to the Film Bureau (within the Ministry of Culture, now the Ministry of Radio, Film and TV) for approval, and were totally dependent for their distribution (at least within China) on the state-owned China Film Distribution Corporation. Nevertheless, films such as *Huang Tudi* (Yellow Earth, directed by Chen Kaige in 1984), which gained international renown and is considered to have heralded a 'new wave' of Chinese cinema, dared to question the omnipotence (and even relevance) of communist propaganda when set against deeply rooted peasant beliefs and practices (the action takes place in a remote region of the Shaan–Gan–Ning Border Region in the late 1930s) that would not have been possible before 1976.

These tentative steps towards political reform and cultural freedom in the 1980s were overshadowed to a great extent by a more pressing concern among some party ideologues to prevent 'unhealthy' ideological consequences arising from the economic reforms. Ever conscious of the criticism by senior colleagues such as Chen Yun that the reforms threatened state control of the economy and diluted the socialist collective spirit, Deng himself sanctioned a number of propaganda campaigns designed to mollify conservative opposition to the market reforms. Such divisions within the reform coalition that had emerged in the wake of Hua Guofeng's fall from power have led observers to characterize politics during the 1980s as a cyclical process in which periods of advance were followed by consolidation and retrenchment (Harding 1987: 70; Baum 1994: xii). Such campaigns, however, bore little resemblance to those launched in the Maoist era, which had often caused much disruption and resulted in acts of violence (physical or psychological) against those targeted for criticism. The campaigns of the 1980s were brief affairs and, having made their point, were quickly wound down in order that the momentum of economic reform should not be halted.

The first such campaign, in 1981, promoted the virtues of 'socialist spiritual civilization' and was designed to combat widespread public cynicism after the traumas of the Cultural Revolution, a phenomenon described as a 'crisis of faith' (see earlier) and coinciding with an apparently unprecedented outbreak of juvenile crime, gratuitous muggings, corruption and unfilial behaviour that was now more openly reported in the official press (Short 1982: 69, 374), contrasting thereby with the public image of a crime-free and honest society that had been presented to the world during Mao's day. The PLA also encouraged criticism of a film script during the campaign as an example of subversive cynicism. Written (and first published in September 1979) by a PLA propaganda cadre, Bai Hua – who thus became the first officially published writer since the Cultural Revolution to be singled out for political censure (Duke 1985:

20–4) – and entitled *Ku lian* (Unrequited Love), it portrayed the life of a patriotic overseas Chinese who returns from the US in 1949 to devote himself to the new China but who subsequently suffers during the political campaigns of the 1950s and 1960s. What troubled PLA and party censors in 1981 was the script's implied criticism of the post-1949 communist state, rather than attributing China's ills to the machinations of the Gang of Four and the calamitous effects of the Cultural Revolution, as had the literature of the late 1970s (known as 'literature of the wounded' or 'scar literature') (ibid.: 64–72).

The ideological purpose of the 1981 campaign soon degenerated into an attempt to improve social behaviour (via the 'Five Stresses' of cleanliness, discipline, courtesy, decorum and appropriate morality) and to enhance the party's legitimacy by unambiguously associating it with patriotism – love of country henceforth became synonymous with support for the party, and it was no coincidence that Bai Hua's script was condemned as 'unpatriotic' (ibid.: 141; Harding 1987: 187). (The party's patriotic credentials were given a boost with the Anglo-Chinese Agreement of 1984, which allowed for the return of the British colony of Hong Kong to Chinese sovereignty in 1997 under the 'one country, two systems' arrangement preserving a certain amount of autonomy for Hong Kong.) Once Bai Hua wrote a self-criticism in October 1981, party chairman Hu Yaobang soon declared the campaign over (Baum 1994: 127–30).

In 1983 party conservatives voiced concern over damaging ideological tendencies arising from market reforms, wider contact with the capitalist world and greater relaxation in the cultural sphere. Another campaign was launched attacking 'spiritual pollution', but it again fizzled out and its latter stages were marked by acerbic barbs against current life-styles (such as disco-dancing) and mode of dress (long hair for men, make-up and high heels for women) (Harding 1987: 188), a rather fruitless exercise given the fact that the economic reforms had encouraged a consumerist culture open to foreign fashions in the first place. The prime casualty of the campaign was the deputy editor of *Renmin Ribao* (People's Daily), Wang Ruoshi, sacked for suggesting that political and economic alienation might exist in a socialist society (Nathan 1985: 99–100).

A more strident campaign against 'bourgeois liberalization' occurred in the wake of student protests and demonstrations in

December 1986 which had called for free speech, a free press, and 'democracy' (not in the sense of a multi-party system but in terms of greater government openness and accountability). Hu Yaobang himself was forced to take responsibility for the protests and was compelled to step down as party chairman in January 1987 (to be replaced by Zhao Ziyang, another of Deng's protégés), while a number of intellectuals such as Fang Lizhi, an astrophysicist and vice-president of the University of Science and Technology in Hefei (Anhui province) and Liu Binyan, an investigative journalist, who had championed the protest movement, were expelled from the party (Wills 1994: 366–71). Yet even this campaign soon ended as the new party chairman, Zhao Ziyang, stressed renewed acceleration of economic reform.

By the late 1980s, however, the problems and tensions resulting from the reforms had become serious. In the countryside inequalities between regions and even within villages increasingly widened and led to cases of violence and conflict in the competition for resources (over water rights for example), with successful rural entrepreneurs and rich peasants often the target of attack. The impoverishment of some areas had been exacerbated by decollectivization, which resulted in the reduction or abolition of collective services and welfare provision. Rural health care was especially hard hit, and it has been estimated that between 1978 and 1986 up to 3.7 million barefoot doctors, midwives and rural medical workers left their jobs (Davis 1989: 587). Paradoxically, the wealth generated amongst some rural areas as a result of the reforms led to increased investment in residential property, which encroached on potentially valuable agricultural land. The annual growth rate in agriculture fell after 1985, the result of farmers deserting grain production and the deterioration of the rural infrastructure. The rate of state investment in agriculture also declined and, combined with restrictions on credit imposed after 1988, meant that local state grain procurement departments by 1989 had to resort to giving peasants IOUs (known as 'white slips') instead of cash for their produce. Not surprisingly, peasants became increasingly reluctant to deliver their grain to state authorities (White 1993: 109–11).

After 1985, also, in the words of one account, China was characterized by considerable 'urban malaise' (Baum 1994: 200–3). In September 1985 there were student-led demonstrations against Japanese imports and Japan's 'economic aggression' (Harding 1987: 135; Gittings 1989: 172). In December 1985 Uyghur students (the Uyghurs are Turkic-speaking Muslims from Xinjiang) in Beijing and Urumqi (capital of Xinjiang) protested against nuclear-weapons testing in Xinjiang and the imposition of family-planning policies on the Uyghur community. In some cases campus unrest was fuelled by an invidious xenophobia when students staged protests against the presence of African students (accused of 'despoiling' Chinese women) in Tianjin and Beijing (1985) and in Nanjing (1985–6) (Baum 1994: 191, 239–40).

Much of the urban disaffection, however, was due to a pervasive sense amongst teachers, research workers, employees of government organs, and state-sector industrial workers that the economic reforms were passing them by (Burns 1989: 488). With their fixed salaries failing to keep up with inflation, all saw their standard of living decline in comparison with self-employed commercial and industrial workers. Urban consumers were also unhappy with increasing privatization of housing and the deregulation of rents. There were further student protests in Beijing in April 1988 against rising living costs, meagre stipends and inadequate educational budgets, while strikes and slowdowns in state-owned enterprises became a regular occurrence after 1986: 129 strikes were reported in 1987 alone (Perry 1995: 315). Discontent amongst the work force was exacerbated by lay-offs in the state sector (e.g. 400,000 were laid off from 700 factories in Shenyang province in the summer of 1988, and thousands of contract workers were made redundant in Shanghai and other cities in Hunan and Hubei provinces). Urban vagrancy increased, compounded by the continuing influx of rural migrants seeking jobs in the cities. Referred to as *youmin* (floating population) and constituting a virtual underclass since their non-urban residential status did not qualify them for welfare and educational benefits, they may have totalled over a million in Beijing on the eve of the 1989 protests (Baum 1994: 229). Even the National People's Congress expressed dissatisfaction with the reforms when, in March 1988, it criticized inflation, low pay for teachers, and the inequitable benefits accruing from the coastal developmental strategy (ibid.: 226).

Renewed calls for political reform also became more vociferous in 1986. Party intellectuals such as Su Shaozhi recommended the introduction of political pluralism, while Fang Lizhi, on a visit to college campuses in November 1986, urged students to demand rights and freedoms. The student protests that initially began at Fang's university in Hefei over tuition fees in December 1986 rapidly spread to other universities and colleges (over 150 in 17 cities). Not only were such demonstrations (calling for more party democracy and a free press) the largest since the heyday of the Cultural Revolution, but also the first since 1949 not directly sponsored or encouraged by top party officials (Wasserstrom 1991: 304).

Overshadowing grievances with the economic reforms and impatience over the lack of political reform was increasing public disillusionment with the party's inability to stem the official corruption that (ironically) the reforms had encouraged. The most notorious example of official corruption during the 1980s was the Hainan Island scandal in 1985, when party officials there smuggled luxury imports (such as cars and television sets) and resold them at high prices for their own profit (Hainan Island, part of Guangdong province, was to become a separate province and a Special Economic Zone in 1988). The official media in 1988 reported that between 1983 and 1987 there were 280,000 cases of serious 'economic crimes' (bribery, theft of public property, smuggling) of which 15 per cent originated in government organs, state enterprises and within the party (CQ September 1988: 503). Most of the 150,000 party members punished for misdemeanours in 1988 were found guilty of committing economic crimes (Baum 1994: 229–30). Such official involvement in corruption led to the coining of a new term in the 1980s: *guandao* (official profiteering), which referred specifically to cadres in state-owned enterprises taking advantage of the 'dual-track' price system that emerged after 1980 (i.e. a state sector of fixed prices for resources and goods coexisting with a free market in prices) to engage in speculative buying and selling. Government departments responsible for selling materials to state-owned enterprises, for example, often kept aside an undelivered amount for resale at higher prices on the market.

By 1985 party conservatives such as Chen Yun were linking such corruption with the open door policy, the corrosive effects of which threatened to undermine the socialist system. He also referred to the tendency for the offspring of influential party cadres (*gaogan zidi*) to make use of their connections (*guanxi*) to set up profitable private enterprises. One such person was Deng Xiaoping's own son, Deng Pufang, who headed a sprawling conglomerate (known as Kanghua) that had over a hundred subsidiaries. Kanghua was closed down in 1988 after revelations of illegal conduct (e.g. evading income-tax payments) had been made public. Kanghua was just one of several trading and investment companies (with branches in Hong Kong and abroad) run by the sons and daughters of top party leaders – referred to as *taizidang* (crown princes and princesses). Quite apart from the *taizidang*, however, during the 1980s (and even more so in the 1990s) many individual cadres, government organizations and even PLA units engaged in private business – a process known as *xiehai* (plunging into the sea). Local rural cadres also got into the act, using their official positions to guarantee that they (or their relatives) ran the most lucrative enterprises. A recent study has described the system as it developed during the 1980s as one of 'bureaucratic capitalism', defined as 'the employment of political power and influence for private gain through capitalist methods of economic activity' (Meisner 1999: 474–5), an unusual phenomenon given the fact that it emerged *after* a lengthy 'quasi-socialist' period in which the bourgeoisie had been eliminated. Another analysis refers to the emergence of 'crony capitalism', as new combinations of economic power linked entrepreneurs with bureaucrats (Naughton 1999: 37); such a relationship has also been described as an example of 'authoritarian state corporatism' (Parris 1999: 275).

By the late 1980s, too, divisions within the party leadership so dramatically illustrated by the forced resignation of Hu Yaobang as party chairman in January 1987 (blamed for letting the student unrest of 1986–7 get out of hand) were becoming more acute. Although Zhao Ziyang's call for continued economic reform gained acceptance at the 13th Party Congress (October–November 1987) and his own position was apparently strengthened with the retiral of the 'old guard' from the Politburo (including Deng Xiaoping and Chen Yun), it was also decided (ominously for Zhao) that the Politburo Standing Committee – and Zhao as party chairman – had to consult with Deng and Chen on all political and economic matters (suggesting a less than total confidence in Zhao's judgement) (Baum 1994:

218). At the same time, Zhao's insistence on deeper structural reform of the economy (such as extending the coastal developmental strategy and privatizing state-owned enterprises) clashed with the more cautious approach of Li Peng, premier and Politburo Standing Committee member since 1987 (ibid.: 226–7).

Interestingly, a television documentary aired in the summer of 1988 that questioned the nation's fundamental goals and values was later cited by Zhao's conservative opponents within the party as a devious attempt to promote his radical open door policy (Barmé 1999: 23–4). Entitled *Heshang* (River Elegy), the documentary – the script of which has now been translated into English (Su 1991: 101–269) – used the Yellow River as a metaphor for the unbroken cultural continuity and conservatism of Chinese civilization, and contrasted the backwardness of hinterland China (especially in the north) with the dynamic regions of the coastal littoral. In a sense the programme unleashed new ways of imagining China, pitting a pluralist south open to outside influences against a more insular and static north (Friedman 1996: 169–82). In the process both Confucian chauvinism and revolutionary Maoism (associated with the rural north) were called into question. For the programme's critics, however, the programme was guilty of unabashedly praising western technology and values (Baum 1994: 231–2). Further showings of the six-part documentary were banned in November 1988, indicating yet further a growing cleavage amongst the party leadership (some of Zhao's supporters were associated with the programme).

Matters came to a head following the sudden death of the disgraced Hu Yaobang in April 1989 (Wills 1994: 372–7). As in the case of Zhou Enlai's death in 1976, public mourning soon ignited a wider movement. Using the opportunity of Hu's death and the gathering of thousands of mourners in Tian'anmen Square, students addressed a petition to the NPC Standing Committee calling for a correct evaluation of Hu, public knowledge of the salaries earned by top leaders and their offspring, freedom of the press and public expression, and increased stipends and salaries for students and teachers (Baum 1994: 247). The students' ability to appropriate or mimic official rituals was illustrated by their staging of a mock ceremonial remonstrance on the steps of the Great Hall of the People (where the

NPC met) on the day of Hu's official funeral, when they presented their petition in the manner of traditional 'loyal' officials. Also, with the imminent official celebration of the 70th anniversary of the May Fourth Movement students sought to contest the CCP's interpretation of its significance (which identified May Fourth with the founding of the CCP and its subsequent leadership of the anti-imperialist and anti-feudal revolution). Thus twelve days before Hu's death student activists in Beijing displayed a poster (entitled 'An Open Letter to Beijing University Authorities') calling attention to the fact that May Fourth symbolized above all else democracy and science (Han 1990: 16–19).

The students' petition was rejected by party authorities, with Li Peng denouncing the protest as 'turmoil' (*dongluan*), a term that conjured up Cultural Revolution images of youthful disorder and anarchy, and criticizing the students as 'unpatriotic' (Baum 1994: 249). Meanwhile, workers – with grievances of their own – added their voices to the protest, and on 20 April the newly formed Beijing Workers' Autonomous Federation (Gongzilian) issued a manifesto blaming corrupt bureaucrats for China's social ills. Students in Beijing also established their own autonomous federation on 26 April and the following day up to 100,000 marched on Tian'anmen Square (joined by many other residents of Beijing). By 4 May there were over 150,000 students in the square (by which time class boycotts were widespread), increasingly impatient with continuing official refusal to engage in dialogue. Similar demonstrations broke out in Shanghai, Changsha, Nanjing and Wuhan; it has been estimated that between 4 May and 19 May over 1.5 million students and university staff from 500 higher education institutions in 80 cities joined the protest (ibid.: 253). One of the leading student activists was Wang Dan, a history undergraduate at Beida and the son of a university professor. In late 1988 and early 1989 he had organized 'democracy salons' at Beida to foster debate, a process that occurred on other campuses in the city, although a recent analysis emphasizes the more important link between ordinary patterns of campus social life and student protest (Wasserstrom and Liu 1995: 363).

Zhao Ziyang, who had been away in early May on an official visit to North Korea, described the students' demands as 'reasonable' on his return, angering his more hardline colleagues.

He further alienated the 'old guard' (and especially Deng Xiaoping) when he revealed in a talk with visiting Soviet President Mikhail Gorbachev that all decisions were referred to Deng and his senior colleagues on the Central Affairs Commission, a procedure that was supposed to be kept secret. Gorbachev's visit (from 15 May to 18 May) proved embarrassing in other ways – not only did he have to be received outside the city centre because of the students' occupation of Tian'anmen Square, but also his own reform policies (known as *glasnost*) were hailed by the students as an example that China's leaders should follow.

With some students embarking on a hunger strike on 13 May, State President Yang Shangkun instructed the Military Affairs Commission to make preparations for assembling troops. A meeting on 18 May between Li Peng and student leaders, at which the former would not yield to the latter's strident demand that the current protest movement be treated as a 'patriotic' democracy movement (Han 1990: 242–6), proved fruitless. Following an abortive attempt by Zhao Ziyang on 19 May to persuade students to abandon their hunger strike (his last public act as party chairman), his colleagues on the Politburo voted to impose martial law on 20 May (although it should be noted that martial law had already been declared in Tibet in February 1989 following demonstrations against the Han Chinese presence there). Zhao himself was ousted as party chairman a few days later, accused by hardliners of encouraging a treacherous 'anti-party clique'.

By the time the first contingent of unarmed PLA units advanced on Tian'anmen – soon withdrawn when students 'welcomed' them in an attempt to persuade them of the justness of their cause – the student encampment on the square was, in the words of one study, 'a state within a state' complete with its own communications centre, security apparatus and sanitation department (Baum 1994: 266). Although workers were now a highly visible part of the movement – by the beginning of June the Gongzilian comprised 20,000 members (Perry 1995: 317) – their agenda was not completely the same as that of the students. Whereas the students in general believed the reforms had not gone far enough, protesting workers – for the most part employees of state-owned enterprises (electronics, steel, automobiles) – perceived the urban economic reforms as directly responsible for their declining standard of living and the cause of the bureaucratic corruption that oppressed them. Furthermore, the students, reflecting the traditional elitism of the scholar class, held aloof from the workers and were initially reluctant to let them into the square; even when they were, at the end of May, students and workers remained separate (the centre of the square was always occupied by students only). Workers, however, were not the only group to join the protest movement. An internal enquiry after the crackdown revealed that more than 10,000 cadres from central party and government departments took part in the May demonstrations (Baum 1994: 276). Overall, 800,000 cadres may have taken part in rallies in 123 cities during the course of 1989.

The final crackdown occurred on the evening and early morning of 3–4 June when armed troops – totalling 200,000 from twelve group armies (and three military regions) – were ordered to retake the square (Brook 1998: 108–50). The exact number of casualties in the wake of the suppression is still not known. Outside reports of civilian deaths have ranged from 2,000 to 7,000 (Baum 1994: 276; Brook 1998: 151–69; Meisner 1999: 510–11). Later, Chinese government sources put the number of deaths at 300. Most of those who died were ordinary Beijing residents outside Tian'anmen Square, crushed by tanks on their way to the square; thirty-six students in the square and several dozen soldiers and police also died. Casualties were reported in the cities of Shanghai and Changsha following similar military and police crackdowns there.

The suppression was quickly followed by mass arrests for what the party condemned as 'counter-revolutionary rebellion' (*fan geming baoluan*), a verdict that was reaffirmed in 1991 and that still holds today. By the spring of 1991 the party confirmed that over 2,500 arrests had been made. Forty student leaders and dissident intellectuals escaped and fled into exile (mostly to the US and western Europe). Even intellectuals such as Fang Lizhi who had no direct involvement in the movement (although in January 1989 he had addressed an open letter to Deng Xiaoping calling for the release of political prisoners) were considered masterminds behind the protest. Fang himself took refuge in the US embassy in Beijing before eventually (in 1990) being allowed to go into exile abroad. Surprisingly, few cadres known to have sympathized with the movement (1,179 out of 800,000) were punished (Baum 1994: 316). Individuals who suffered the severest treatment tended to be workers since, in the eyes of the party, the willingness of urban workers to join the protest constituted a more threatening challenge to party rule than that posed by intellectuals or party cadres.

The 1989 protest movement represented the most serious challenge to CCP rule since the establishment of the PRC, but one study notes that 'political meltdown' was avoided after 4 June because of PLA discipline and its responsiveness to civilian command (even though some in the foreign media at the time believed that elements within the PLA might disobey party orders), divisions within the student movement (a phenomenon that became clear when student activists who fled abroad became competing dissidents), student reluctance to ally with workers, a deep-seated fear of *luan* (disorder) and previous economic growth giving the party a certain amount of credibility (ibid.: 307).

Recent work on the background and context of the 1989 protest movement has also provided a more nuanced understanding of its nature. At the time the foreign media described the events of May–June 1989 as a heroic protest in the cause of democracy, graphically symbolized by a 35-feet high statue dubbed the 'Goddess of Democracy' (*minzhu nushen*); constructed by students from the Beijing Central Arts Academy, it made its first appearance in the square on 30 May. Student participants later tended to 'mythologize' the events of 1989, casting themselves in the roles of either tragic or romantic heroes driven by a pure spirit and untainted motives (Wasserstrom 1994: 283–8).

A more balanced assessment argues that the movement was certainly not a manifestation of *luan* reminiscent of the Cultural Revolution – even though Deng Xiaoping may have seen it in these terms (Young 1994: 24–5) – since the students maintained order throughout, did not produce anti-western rhetoric, and did not express any devotional loyalty to a living CCP leader. On the other hand, neither was the movement a manifestation of 'bourgeois liberalism' in the sense of promoting western-style democracy. Students elevated the principle of unity above that of majority rule, while their conception of democracy (*minzhu*) did not allow for a free competition of divergent ideas and was itself tinged with elitism. In many ways students in 1989, like the traditional Confucian scholar class, continued to assume that the leading role in society should be played by a virtuous and educated elite (Esherick and Wasserstrom 1994: 33–6). Such elitism was also evident in the attitude of Chinese students towards their worker compatriots during the work-study movement in France at the end of the First World War (Bailey 1988: 454–5). Thus a student poster of 24 April, after referring to a long tradition of dictatorship that would make it difficult for people to adjust quickly to a democratic society, revealingly continued: 'at least urban citizens, intellectuals and Communist Party members are as ready for democracy as any of the citizens who already live in democratic societies. Thus we should implement complete democracy within the Communist Party and within the urban areas' (Han 1990: 35). In defining democracy, the poster mentioned a check on corruption, limited privatization, freedom of speech and 'equality' – the latter, apparently, not to apply (at least immediately) to large segments of the population. In this respect it might be noted that gender inequalities in Chinese society did not figure prominently in student discourse and it is no coincidence that Chai Ling was the only conspicuous female student leader (Feigon 1994: 127–8).

Furthermore, students consistently described themselves as 'patriotic' whose demands reflected a sincere desire for *national development and unity*. As an open letter to the Central Committee written by a student from Wuhan University on 28 April noted, such unity was being undermined by growing corruption that threatened the close relationship between party and people (Han 1990: 51–6). In essence students wanted to be *recognized* by the state and were not necessarily alienated from it (Perry 1994: 80). It has also been argued that although Chinese intellectuals had always tended to view the ingrained 'feudal' values of a 'backward' peasantry as the principal brake on political progress, it was, in fact, urban intellectuals and students-with their elitism and 'exclusionist style of protest' – who constituted the greatest fetter on further development of the Tian'anmen movement (ibid.: 75–7, 88).

Finally, the events of 1989 have also been described as an exercise in 'political theatre' in which students drew on familiar 'protest scripts' (e.g. hunger strikes) and state rituals (e.g. deferential petitioning, solemn funeral marches) that symbolically undermined the regime's legitimacy and moved other groups to action (Wasserstrom 1991: 312–16; Esherick and Wasserstrom 1994: 37–8). Students were not the only ones, however, to appropriate past symbols and practice. One citizens' group during the protest carried a banner using a modernized version of a Boxer invulnerabilty chant: 'Knives and halberds won't penetrate us, nor electric batons shock us' (*daoqiang buru, diangun buchu*). When activist workers heard that PLA units were advancing on Tian'anmen they jogged down Chang'an Avenue chanting the slogan (Cohen 1997: 215).

The Accession of Jiang Zemin and the Consolidation of Deng Xiaoping's Reform Strategy

The ousted Zhao Ziyang was replaced by Jiang Zemin (b. 1926), who had been elected to the Politburo in 1987 and was Shanghai party secretary during the 1989 protest movement. From an intellectual family in Jiangsu province, Jiang had studied industrial technology in Nanjing during the anti-Japanese War before joining the communist underground in Shanghai in 1946. In 1955–6 he studied in Moscow (at the Stalin Autoworks) and in subsequent years worked in power plants and at the First Ministry of Machine-Building before becoming Minister of Electronics Industry in 1983 (by which time he had joined the party's Central Committee). In 1985 Jiang was appointed mayor of Shanghai and took a hardline stand against the 1985–6 student protests in the city (for which he was promoted to Shanghai party secretary in 1987) (Gilley 1998). After June 1989 Jiang gradually amassed increasing power (with Deng's tacit support). He succeeded Deng as chairman of the party's Military Affairs Commission in November 1989 and by 1993 had succeeded Yang Shangkun as state president (Yang's attempt to distance himself from the 1989 crackdown may have spurred Deng on to push for his retirement). Jiang thus became the first leader since Mao to hold all three top positions.

Jiang set about restoring economic growth and political stability in the wake of the 1989 crisis (martial law was lifted in January 1990), a task that one study believes had been largely achieved by the time of Deng Xiaoping's death in February 1997 (ibid.: 4). Thus although international sanctions had been imposed on Beijing after June 1989, China's international trade links were soon restored and foreign investment revived. Official figures from 1997 and 1998 forecasts estimated that direct foreign investment during the 1990s would total US$250 billion (compared to US$15 billion in the 1980s) (ibid.: 4). After 1993, moreover, China became the recipient of more loans from the World Bank than any other country (CQ December 1998: 1,090). Tourism, also, picked up after a short blip. In 1996 51.13 million tourists visited China (10 per cent more than in 1995); by 1999 the numbers had increased to 72 million (CQ June 2000: 607). At the same time Jiang launched a movement of patriotic indoctrination after 1989 to counter the 'evils' of 'bourgeois liberalism'; interestingly, however, the resurrection in 1990 of Lei Feng as an ideological model in a new campaign to promote collective values was short-lived. The party's view that students in 1989 had been corrupted by western influences was reflected in comments made by the official press on the 90th anniversary of the Boxer uprising, which stressed vigilance against imperialist aggression and emphasized the 'sham' nature of western civilization (Cohen 1997: 221).

The party's appeal to nativist sentiment (further illustrated by the unremitting publicity it gave to the Beijing-hosted Asian Games in 1990 and to the fact that most of the gold medals were won by Chinese athletes) struck a chord in society (especially amongst some intellectuals) as a certain amount of disenchantment with the West set in after 1989. Even the popular Mao cult of the early 1990s (which reached a crescendo on the anniversary of his birth in 1993) – manifested in the appearance of all kinds of kitsch memorabilia (Mao t-shirts, cigarette lighters, playing cards), as well as Mao good-luck talismans (*guawu*) hung in temples and in the cars of taxi-drivers, and Mao's poems set to rock music – contained a certain anti-foreign tone. While nostalgia for the Mao era may have reflected public disillusionment with the corruption of the present, it also tapped into the notion that Mao had instilled a sense of pride and self-worth amongst the Chinese people, now lost as a result of the open door policy (Barmé 1996a: 16–47; 1996b: 186–9). An analysis of contemporary rock music has also demonstrated that while it played a subversive role during the 1989 movement, in the 1990s it became highly 'commodified', emphasizing the pleasures of private consumption and appealing to nativist pride; in the case of Cui Jian, a rock hero to the students in 1989, this meant elevating the virtues of northern Chinese rock music above that being imported from Hong Kong and Taiwan (Jones 1994: 149, 158–61).

Perhaps the most significant development after 1989, however, was the continuation of the economic reform agenda, which some party conservatives questioned in the aftermath of the 1989 crisis. They could point, for example, to the ongoing destabilizing effects of the reforms in urban areas where, in 1990–1, more than 50,000 workers engaged in strikes, slowdowns and rallies (Perry 1995: 321) and unemployment affected (according to government figures) 200 million people in March 1993 (Baum 1994: 378). By 1990, also, more than 70 million transients (*youmin*) had setteld into urban areas (Davis 1995: 1). Against this background of uncertainty within the party Deng Xiaoping took the initiative by staging his last significant political act in January 1992, when he began a month's tour of the southeast coastal development regions and the Special Economic Zones. Hitherto content to advise and guide behind the scenes in the unprepossessing manner of the traditional Confucian bureaucrat, Deng for the first time made extensive use of television to publicize the tour, which aimed to highlight the success of the open door policy and market reforms (Pye 1993: 414–15). In Shenzhen, for example, he made a point of supporting its fledgling stock market. At the same time, to pre-empt conservative criticism that market reforms would inexorably lead to a capitalist system (referred to as the danger of 'peaceful evolution'), Deng insisted there was no necessary link between market economics and capitalism (Baum 1994: 341–3).

By the time of the 14th Party Congress in October 1992 the need to press forward with the economic reforms was generally accepted when the reform agenda of transforming China from 'a socialist planned commodity economy' into 'a socialist market economy' was formally ratified; the following year, at the 8th NPC, the definition of China's economy as 'a socialist market economy' was codified (ibid.: 361, 375). This gave the green light, for example, to further deregulation of the now anti-quated state-owned industrial sector by freeing it from central planning and subjecting it to the market – the effects of which were to be problematic over the following years (see Conclusion). The reform cause was also strengthened at the congress when three activist reformers were elected to the Politburo

Standing Committee (one of whom was Zhu Rongji, a former mayor of Shanghai who was to succeed Li Peng as premier in 1998) and the decision taken to abolish the Central Affairs Commission (CAC), the stronghold of veteran leaders who had often baulked at modernizing change. Over the coming years they all passed from the scene: Li Xian'nian, who had been state president from 1983 to 1988, died in 1992; Chen Yun, the foremost economic planner during the 1950s and chairman of CAC, died in 1995; and Peng Zhen, mayor of Beijing from 1951 to 1966 and chairman of the NPC Standing Committee in the 1980s, died in 1997.

The year 1997 also witnessed the death of Deng Xiaoping, just over four months before the British colony of Hong Kong was formally returned to Chinese sovereignty in July under an arrangement ('one country, two systems') that he had pioneered (Yahuda 1993: 561). Although Deng had been declared 'Man of the Year' by *Time* in 1979 and 1985, and by *The Financial Times* in 1992 (Gittings 1996: 8), his role in the suppression of the 1989 protest movement meant that his reputation at home and abroad would always be controversial. Nevertheless, as with the case of Mao Zedong, Deng's role and his ideas were lauded by the CCP (in 1993 Deng Xiaoping Thought was held to represent 'modern Chinese Marxism'), and it was made clear by Party Chairman Jiang Zemin (who would gain increasing influence and authority in subsequent years) that Deng's vision of China as an economically vibrant power under disciplined CCP rule would continue to guide the country's future.

Conclusion

Just as the twentieth century opened with the Qing dynasty attempting to strengthen the foundations and legitimacy of dynastic rule by embarking on an ambitious state-building programme, so the twentieth century closed with the CCP – itself a beneficiary of the disorder and the crisis in political authority set in motion by the fall of the dynasty in 1911 – seeking to maintain the legitimacy of its rule with a similarly ambitious programme of economic reform designed to improve general living standards and enhance China's role on the world stage. Yet while the 15th National Party Congress in 1997 legitimized Jiang Zemin's authority (Baum 1998: 141–56; Meisner 1999: 523–4) and produced a consensus for his reform programme, serious problems of social disorder, popular unrest and corruption continued to plague the country. At the same time, disagreements with the US and lack of progress over the 'Taiwan question' marred China's increasingly productive interaction with the international community (the latest manifestation of which is the country's imminent acceptance into the World Trade Organization). Furthermore, recent attempts to elevate Jiang's ideological status and to portray him as the direct heir of Mao Zedong and Deng Xiaoping in following the policy of CCP-controlled development are clearly designed to prevent any change of direction once Jiang steps down as chairman in 2002. Thus a billboard (seen by the author in Jinan, the capital of Shandong province, in October 2000) portrayed the faces of Mao, Deng and Jiang against the background of the Chinese national flag and high-rise apartments and accompanied by the slogan *san'nian dai lingxiu da jueci* (Three Generations of Leaders Following the Grand Policy of Development).

One source of social disorder lay in growing urban unemployment as a result of the restructuring of state-owned enterprises (which meant, in effect, laying off state-employed workers or closing down unprofitable enterprises). As the end of 1997 there were a reported 5.768 million jobless, in addition to the 6.343 million laid off from state-owned enterprises (CQ September 1998: 707). In March 2000 it was reported by the minister of labour and social security that an expected 5 million lay-offs from the state sector would bring the total number of displaced workers to 11.5 million (CQ June 2000: 600). By the end of the 1990s, too, urban areas were home to 130 million 'surplus' rural labourers and migrants (CQ Sept. 1998: 707). As temporary residents (i.e. without formal urban registration) such migrants constituted an underclass with no access to welfare facilities; residing in their own segregated communities (and often treated with disdain or hostility by permanent urban residents), they added to a growing 'floating population' that sought work on construction sites or in the repair trades (Solinger 1995: 114–15; 1999: 233). Most migrants were uneducated male peasants, although the government in 1991 also admitted the presence of 4 million child labourers (Solinger 1995: 119–20).

Other manifestations of widespread malaise can be seen in increasing rates of criminality (e.g. narcotics smuggling, especially on China's southwestern borders) and drug addiction. One alarming consequence of the economic reforms has been the 'commodification' of women (Evans 2000); with a growing 'market' for potential wives and female labour there has been a resurgence of the abduction and selling of women and children. A 1995 report noted that between 1991 and 1994 there were nearly 70,000 of such abductions, leading to the arrest of 100,000 criminals (ibid.: 225). It might be noted here that since the beginning of the reform process there has also been a steady increase in prostitution (ibid.: 225; Hershatter 1996).

As China enters the twenty-first century the government continues to face ethnic unrest in Tibet and Xinjiang, where a growing Han Chinese presence arouses resentment. In Xinjiang, for example, home to the Uyghurs (a Turkish-speaking and

Muslim people) who constitute nearly 50 per cent of the population, the Han Chinese presence has grown from 6.3 per cent of the population in 1949 to 38 per cent today; furthermore, all the top party positions are monopolized by Han Chinese. A ban (since 1990) on all religious activity for those under eighteen years of age is also bitterly opposed. In recent years a separatist movement has emerged (paralleling the growth of a Tibetan opposition movement that originated with the escape of the Dalai Lama to India in 1959) that derives its inspiration from the East Turkestan Republic briefly established in 1944–9 at a time when Guomindang rule was crumbling.

Beijing takes this threat seriously – after all, Xinjiang is not only of crucial strategic importance as far as Beijing is concerned but is also the location of China's nuclear weapons sites and is a rich source of coal, iron and natural gas – and this was illustrated by the fact (according to Amnesty International documented reports) that 210 death sentences were imposed and 190 executions carried out in the region between January 1997 and April 1999; most of those executed were Uyghurs convicted of terrorist or subversive acts. The state media itself has noted that in 2000 (up to September) Xinjiang courts sentenced to death at least 24 Uyghur separatists (FEER 7 September 2000: 22–4). Fears of a nationalist/Islamic separatist movement in Xinjiang partially explained Beijing's fierce opposition to NATO action in Kosovo in 1999, which was seen as a dangerous precedent for possible western (especially US) intervention in the affairs of other countries to help persecuted Muslim minorities.

The CCP leadership today is attempting to solve the problem in two ways. First, Jiang Zemin has sought the co-operation of Russia and the newly independent Central Asian states (Kazakhstan, Kirgyzstan, Tajikstan) in co-ordinating security measures for the suppression of all separatist activities; in July 2000 a summit of the so-called 'Group of Five' to discuss such matters was held in Tajikistan. Second, the CCP announced an ambitious programme in March 2000 (and formally inaugurated by a huge fireworks display in October) to encourage economic development and greater investment in China's western regions (including Xinjiang). Such an initiative reflected a growing awareness of the widening economic gulf between the prosperous eastern and coastal provinces and the much poorer western provinces where most of those living in rural poverty are located; those living in 'abject rural poverty', according to the government's own reports, comprise 50 million people (Oi 1999:617). A recent study has even surmised that social and economic inequality in today's China is more extreme than during Mao's day, when a relatively egalitarian society existed (Meisner 1999:533). As far as Xinjiang and Tibet are concerned, economic development is seen as an effective way to undercut separatist feelings.

Perhaps the most serious problem Chinese leaders currently have to confront, and potentially the most damaging to CCP legitimacy, is the increasing levels of corruption. During the 1980s and most of the 1990s most corruption cases involved low-ranking cadres and officials. This all changed in September 1997 when Chen Xitong, the mayor and party secretary of Beijing, became the first high-level official to be charged with corruption when he was dismissed from the Politburo and later (in February 1998) formally arrested; he was subsequently sentenced to 16 years imprisonment (CQ December 1998: 1,085). The party leadership hoped that such a high-profile case would stem the tide of corruption that affected all levels of party and government administration, but to no avail. Despite propaganda campaigns such as 'The Three Stresses' (*sanzhong*) emphasizing the importance of study, correct political consciousness and correct conduct – the latest appeal to which was made by Premier Zhu Rongji at the 9th NPC in March 2000 – an official report in 1999 noted that procuratorial organs had investigated 38,383 cases of abuses of power (embezzlement, bribery, dereliction of duty). Amongst those implicated were 3 provincial-level, 136 prefectural-level and 2,200 county-level officials (CQ June 2000: 601).

Two of the most recent cases of corruption indicate its alarming extent. In September 2000 Cheng Kejie, former governor of Guangxi province, Politburo member and vice-chairman of the NPC Standing Committee, was executed for bribery and embezzlement. Although the official media gave prominence to the case, the second one, known as the Yuanhua Smuggling Scandal, has not been given publicity because of its damaging implications. In 2000 trials began in Xiamen and other cities in Fujian province that were likely to result in the execution of twelve senior officials (including the vice-minister of public security) accused of being involved in a huge smuggling operation worth an estimated US$10 billion. Over six years (1993–9) the head of the Yuanhua Company in Xiamen (who has now fled the country) was apparently able to bribe military, police, customs, municipal and party officials to smuggle goods into the country (including computer chips, crude oil, automobiles, petrochemical products and building materials) and invest the profits in a bewildering array of office buildings, apartments and night clubs (SCMP 16 Sept. 2000: 17).

Such official corruption has a particularly explosive effect in rural areas, where peasant farmers have to endure the imposition of arbitrary taxes and levies, and where bloated bureaucracies (and the transferral of funds destined for agriculture to township enterprises run by cadres or their relatives) have left local governments unable to pay cash for the peasants' grain deliveries. Not surprisingly, rural disturbances and riots have increased over the last decade (Bernstein 1999: 213, 217). In 1993 alone, a government report noted 1.7 million cases of 'resistance' in the countryside, of which 6,230 were 'disturbances' (*naoshi*) resulting in damage to persons or property (Perry 1993: 314). One of the most recent 'disturbances' occurred in Jiangxi province in August 2000, when up to 20,000 farmers from several villages clashed with police in protest against arbitrary levies; three peasants were killed and fifty arrested, but not before several government offices were ransacked (SCMP 5 Sept. 2000: 8). A letter from a concerned township party secretary in Hubei province addressed to the State Council, and published in an official journal the same month, noted that in addition to land fees (200 *yuan* per hectare) each household had to pay a variety of levies imposed on other family members which could amount to several thousand *yuan* a year – a huge amount given the fact that the annual net income for some peasant farmers might not exceed 1,000 *yuan* (SCMP 4 Sept. 2000: 8). Man-made problems for peasants were exacerbated by natural disasters towards the end of the 1990s. In July–August 1998 severe floods (the worst since 1954) affected large areas of the central/southern Yangzi region and of the northeast. Thirteen million hectares of crops were lost and 13.4 million people compelled to move (CQ December 1998: 1,084). Ironically, the mammoth Yangzi Gorge project designed to prevent flooding and given the go-ahead in 1992 will necessitate the compulsory relocation of nearly a million people (Gittings 1996: 108).

One possible solution to the problem of rural discontent is the further development of direct village-level elections, a process that began informally and spontaneously when the residents of a few villages in Guangxi province decided to elect their own leaders in late 1980 and early 1981 (O'Brien and Li 2000: 465–89). Over subsequent years the practice was gradually enshrined in national law, despite the misgivings of party leaders and the reluctance of local cadres. One of the most prominent supporters of village-level elections was Peng Zhen, the chairman of the NPC during the 1980s; he argued that such elections would increase support for the CCP by eliminating corrupt and incompetent cadres (elected officials would also be in a better position to impose unpopular state policies). In 1987 the NPC passed the Organic Law of Village Committees, which sanctioned the election of village committees (to comprise from three to seven members) for three-year periods; the policy was endorsed by the party's Central Committee in 1990 (Li and O'Brien 1999: 129–30). In November 1998 an additional law made it mandatory that villages hold elections every three years, in which village committee members were all to be directly nominated by the villagers themselves, the numbers of candidates were to exceed the number of positions, and all voting was to be done in secret (the local party branch, however, was still to constitute the village's 'leadership core'). Party officials now claim that at least one round of elections has been carried out in 80 per cent of China's villages; other estimates put it at between 10 per cent and 30 per cent (ibid.: 140). Despite the fact that the party leadership clearly sees no incompatibility between grassroots democracy and strong state control, a recent assessment argues that the scope for more autonomous action by local people and peasant farmers has been considerably enhanced (O'Brien and Li 2000: 486–9). For example, it is often villagers themselves who force reluctant township officials to hold elections (Li and O'Brien 1999: 137–9).

The question of village autonomy touches on the wider issue of whether a 'civil society' has emerged (or is emerging) in China, a debate sparked off by the market reforms of the 1980s (Wakeman 1993). Some western scholars detected in the market reforms of the 1980s a re-emergence of civil society (in the shape of non-state economic groups and quasi-independent research institutes) that had first become evident during the last years of the Qing, when officially sanctioned mobilization of gentry and merchant elites allowed them to form professional and voluntary associations and gave them greater influence in education, public security and economic development (Rankin and Esherick 1990: 337–8; Wakeman 1993: 110, 113). Optimism has been more guarded since the suppression of the 1989 protest movement. Thus a recent analysis of urban life has detected a more vibrant and (at least economically) autonomous city life in which an increasingly diverse population is able to converse (privately and publicly) on a growing range of subjects, noting that 'Chinese urbanites may already be psychologically pre-pared for radical and successful confrontation against CCP hegemony in the near future' (Davis 1995: 2–9); nevertheless, it is argued, no 'societal' association has emerged with the moral and institutional clout to *limit* state coercion *consistently* (ibid.: 15). Another scholar surmises that although there has been continuing expansion of the 'public realm' since the turn of the century this has not led to 'the habituated assertion of civic power against the state' (Wakeman 1993: 133). Still, it is highly significant that many people have sought to take advantage of the Administrative Procedure Law of 1990 allowing citizens to bring suit against arbitrary officials; in 1995 a reported 70,000 filed suit against individual officials or government agencies (Goldman and MacFarquhar 1999: 14). Furthermore, official reports in 1996 noted the existence of 186,666 'social organiza-tions' (*shehui tuanti*, referring to legally registered autonomous organizations and those set up by state agencies to carry out social welfare activities). A recent analysis of these organiza-tions surmises they have the potential to influence the policy-making process or vigorously champion the interests of their members (Saich 2000: 125–6).

Certainly the party–state has been able to squash any inde-pendent political activity. Thus in June 1998, taking advantage of a brief period of government relaxation (coinciding with the visit of US President Clinton to China in June–July), a group of dissi-dents attempted to form a legal opposition party (called the China Democracy Party). Within six months it had 200 members and 'branches' in 24 provinces. Declared illegal by the authori-ties, party members were arrested by the end of the year and all 34 of its leaders are now in jail (SCMP 5 Sept. 2000: 7). Other 'troublesome' dissidents have simply been allowed to go into exile. Wei Jingsheng, for example, who was imprisoned after the 1979 Democracy Wall Movement, released in 1983, and sentenced to a further 15 years imprisonment in 1995, was finally released in November 1997 and forced into exile to the US. A similar fate befell Wang Dan, a student leader of the 1989 movement, in April 1998 (after being imprisoned until 1993 and resentenced to 11 years imprisonment in 1996). The party's coercive power has also been recently demonstrated by the suppression of the Falungong, a religious group founded in 1992 that adhered to an amalgam of Buddhist and Daoist beliefs and practised traditional breathing and health exercises (*qigong*). After a sit-in demonstration by 10,000 of its followers outside Zhongnanhai (the official residence of top CCP leaders) in April 1999 the organization was banned and condemned as a superstitious and dangerous religious 'cult'. Ironically, although *qigong* has been promoted by the state as a unique Chinese tradition, authorities remain suspicious of the social networks such activity gives rise to, as well as of their charismatic leaders such as Li Hongzhi, the founder of the Falungong (Chen 1995: 347–59).

Such coercive power notwithstanding, the party–state may in the future find it more difficult to control ever growing public access to outside sources of information (via the internet). By the beginning of 2000 nearly 10 million people had access to the internet, and the number is set to increase dramatically over the next few years. Even in the realm of print publications the party will continue to experience problems of control. In the wake of the 1989 protests, for example, the authorities confiscated 31 million books and magazines and closed down 41 publishing houses; yet two years later, in 1991, officials discovered an underground publishing 'network' comprising 257 editing, publishing and distributional units scattered over 85 cities (Wang 1995: 171).

Finally, while the CCP could point to continued economic growth (the *sine qua non* of maintaining its monopoly on power), there was clearly concern about the party's credibility as the 16th Party Congress approached in 2002. In early 2000 Jiang Zemin launched a formal campaign (accompanied by a booklet entitled 'A Great Programme For Comprehensively Strengthening Party-Building') designed to raise the moral stature of party members (and boost his status as an ideological heavyweight). Yet there was a touch of unreality to Jiang's idea that the party must represent the most advanced part of the economy, the most advanced culture, and the basic interests of the masses ('the three represents'), given the fact that the non-state sector was rapidly becoming the most dynamic component of the economy and that the party's economic reforms fostered inequalities and corruption. There is also something fundamentally dishonest about the way the party continues to legitimize its rule. On the one hand, it clearly disassociates itself from the pre-1978 period, thereby avoiding responsibility for the disasters of the 1950s and 1960s (blamed on Mao or the Gang of Four); on the other, it boosts its patriotic credentials by insisting on the regime's continuity with the Maoist period when, it is held, Mao and his other patriotic colleagues dedicated themselves to the national interest and economic development (completely overlooking, of course, the bitter conflicts within the party leadership brought on by Mao's differences with those same colleagues).

It may be the case, as one scholar notes, that the PRC continues to exhibit the characteristics of a 'mature Leninist state' and that the regime is more resilient than outside observers believe (Burns 1999: 580–94). Others point to a growing dichotomy between China's economic growth and an increasingly fragile party–state, the result of accelerating decentralization that enables local governments to make economic decisions and facilitate the money-making capacities of private enterprise while ignoring central government injunctions against corruption and labour exploitation (Goldman and MacFarquhar 1999: 8, 17). The fact remains, however, that CCP rule is justified on the grounds that it alone guarantees social stability and economic progress. As my wife and I mingled with an animated and joyous crowd that packed Tian'anmen Square on the eve of National Day (1 October, the anniversary of the founding of the PRC), which basked in the satisfaction of knowing that China had come third in the gold medal table at the recent Sydney 2000 Olympics and looked forward to a week's holiday that the government for the first time had granted, it was hard to believe that only eleven years earlier the square had been the centre of a widespread protest movement. Beijing, however, is not China. How the party–state meets the enormous challenge of improving the lives of all its citizens will largely determine whether the party survives into the twenty-first century.

Glossary of Chinese Terms

baihua 'Vernacular speech'; promoted by cultural radicals during the May Fourth movement.

chun 'A group' or the act of grouping together; a term used by Liang Qichao in the late nineteenth century to refer to a new national community based on collective dynamism.

da yuejin 'The Great Leap Forward.'

danwei 'Work unit'; a state-owned workplace (school, factory, government agency, hospital) to which all urban employees were assigned after 1949, and which was responsible for the political, social and economic well-being of its members.

'daoqiang buru, diangun buchu' 'Knives and halberds won't penetrate us, nor electric batons shock us'; an updated version of a Boxer invulnerability chant used by Beijing citizens during the 1989 protest movement.

datong 'World community'; a Confucian utopian ideal to which Kang Youwei referred in his reformist writings of the late nineteenth and early twentieth centuries.

dazibao 'Big character poster'; posters first displayed by students on university campuses during the 100 Flowers movement of 1956–7 expressing criticism of bureaucratism and elitism. Also used during the Cultural Revolution and the Democracy Wall movement of 1979.

difang zizhi   'Local self government'; a term introduced from the Japanese in the 1890s.

dongluan   'Turmoil'; a term used by premier Li Peng and the official press to describe the student demonstrations of April–May 1989.

fan geming baoluan   'Counter-revolutionary rebellion'; the official CCP description of the 1989 protest movement.

fanshen   Lit. 'to turn the body over'; used in connection with land reform of the late 1940s in which tenants and poor peasants were said to have emancipated themselves from their lowly class status.

feiguo   'Bandit nation'; a description of China used by the Chinese press in the 1920s.

fengjian   'Enfeoffment'; originally a reference to a system of feudal rule, but used from the seventeenth century onwards to describe local gentry participation in the administration of their home areas.

fengshui   'Wind and water'; refers to the unseen forces that are believed to guarantee the natural harmony of the environment (geomancy).

'fuQing mie yang'   'Uphold the Qing and eliminate the foreigner'; a slogan used by the Boxers in 1899–1900.

gaogan zidi   Offspring of high-level cadres.

guandao   'Official profiteering'; a term that came into common use in the 1980s to describe the negative effects of the economic reforms.

guanxi   'Connections', a key attribute for getting on in life.

guawu   Mao good-luck talismans that appeared in the late 1980s and early 1990s and hung in the cars of taxi drivers, private residences and temples.

Guofu   'Father of the Nation'; an honorific title bestowed on Sun Yatsen after his death by the Guomindang.

hongdengzhao   The Red Lanterns, a separate detachment of young women in the Boxer movement and believed to possess magical powers.

hongweibing The Red Guards.

huiguan Native-place association, providing charity and security for sojourners in cities such as Shanghai who came from the same region or locale.

hukou Household registration system dating from the mid-1950s aiming to clearly differentiate urban and rural populations.

hutong A Beijing traditional-style street alleyway or lane, fast disappearing as a result of changes in the contemporary urban landscape.

jiangshen futi Lit. 'spirits descending and attaching themselves to the body'; a form of spirit possession practised by the Boxers.

jieji diren Class enemy; a term often used in the mass campaigns of the 1950s and 1960s.

jieji douzheng Class struggle.

jingshi School of Practical Statecraft; refers to a body of ideas on administrative reform advocated by a number of late eighteenth and early nineteenth century bureaucrats and scholars.

jinshi Metropolitan scholar; also refers to the highest level of degree in the traditional civil service examinations.

luan Disorder, chaos.

Mao re 'Mao fever'; refers to the popular Mao cult of the late 1980s and early 1990s that combined nostalgia with kitsch commercialism.

Mao Zedong Sixiang 'Mao Zedong Thought'; referred to as the CCP's ideological guide at its 7th Congress (April–June 1945).

minquan 'People's rights', a concept popularized in Liang Qichao's reformist writings in the early years of the twentieth century.

minzhu nushen 'Goddess of Democracy', a statue constructed by Beijing students during the Tian'anmen protest.

naoshi 'Disturbance'; used in connection with peasant riots and demonstrations during the 1990s.

qingyi 'Pure speech'; refers to the approach adopted by a number of fundamentalist officials and scholars in the late nineteenth century who insisted that only the revival of Confucian principles (rather than technological change *per se*) could deflect the western threat.

renmin gongshe   People's communes; the first one appeared in Henan in April 1958.

sanfan   'The Three Antis', a mass campaign of 1951 targeting CCP members, bureaucrats and factory managers accused of waste and corruption.

sanlunche   A three-wheeled motor vehicle that served as a makeshift taxi in the early days of economic reform (the early 1980s), now supplanted by imported western and Japanese automobiles.

san'nian dai lingxiu da jueci   'Three generations of leaders following the grand policy of development'; a contemporary propaganda slogan proclaiming that Mao Zedong, Deng Xiaoping and Jiang Zemin all adhered (or adhere) to the programme of economic modernization.

sanmin zhuyi   The 'Three People's Principles'; the revolutionary programme of Sun Yatsen's anti-Manchu movement advocating nationalism, democracy and the improvement of the people's livelihood.

sanxian   'The third front'; a secret policy followed after 1965 (until the early 1970s) that reallocated resources for state-controlled industry in remote inland provinces for strategic and developmental reasons.

sanzhong   'The three stresses'; a propaganda campaign of the late 1990s aimed at enhancing CCP prestige and morale, calling for an emphasis on study, correct political consciousness and correct conduct.

shangwu zhuyi   Lit. 'honour the military-ism'; used in connection with the promotion of a martial spirit in the modern schools established in the last years of the Qing dynasty.

shangxia yixin   'Ruler and people of one mind'; the official rationale used to justify constitutionalism in the Qing dynasty's reform programme of the early twentieth century.

shangzhan 'Commercial warfare'; a term used during the latter half of the nineteenth century in reference to competition with foreign economic interests in China.

shehui tuanti Social organization; a legally registered autonomous organization or a state agency in contemporary China that fulfills social welfare functions.

shenshang 'Gentry-merchant'; a term used in the late nineteenth century to describe a new hybrid class of gentry investing in commercial or industrial enterprises.

shouhui liquan 'Retrieval of economic rights'; a key aim of the Self-Strengthening movement of the late nineteenth century, which sought to reduce foreign economic privilege in China.

shuyuan Traditional Confucian academy where scholars researched and discussed classical texts.

taizidang 'Crown princes and princesses'; contemporary term referring to the sons and daughters of party and governmemt leaders using their connections to gain political and economic advantages.

tianzai renhuo 'Natural disaster and human misfortune'; refers to the year 1976, which witnessed the deaths of Mao Zedong, Zhou Enlai and Zhu De, and an earthquake that caused the deaths of over half a million people.

tie wanfan 'Iron rice bowl'; refers to the system of permanent employment in state-owned factories after 1949, now being dismantled by market-oriented reform.

Tongmenghui Alliance League; Sun Yatsen's revolutionary organization founded in Tokyo in 1905.

waihuipiao Foreign exchange certificate; a 'foreign' version of the domestic currency with which foreign consumer goods in China had to be purchased in the 1980s.

wuchan jieji wenhua da geming 'Great Proletarian Cultural Revolution.'

wufan 'The Five Antis'; mass campaign of 1952 denouncing industrialists and businessmen accused of bribery, tax evasion and theft of state property.

xiafang   'Going down to the countryside'; a policy first used in 1942–4 to transfer Communist Party cadres and intellectuals to rural areas, where they engaged in manual work.

xiehai   'Plunging into the sea'; refers to the process whereby individual cadres/officials or state organizations enter private business.

Xin Qingnian   'New Youth'; a radical journal founded by Chen Duxiu in 1915, and one of the most important publications of the May Fourth Movement.

Xingzhonghui   Revive China Society; Sun Yatsen's first revolutionary organization, founded in Hawaii in late 1894.

xinmin   'New citizen'; a term used by Liang Qichao in the early twentieth century in his call for a self-reliant, disciplined and public-spirited Chinese people.

xinyang weiji   'Crisis of faith'; a term used by the official media in the early 1980s to describe widespread public cynicism and disillusionment.

xinzheng   'New policies'; refers to the reform programme sanctioned by the Qing dynasty in its last years.

xuechao   'Student tide'; refers to the wave of unrest and strikes in the modern schools during the early years of the twentieth century.

xuehui   'Study association'; a new form of voluntary association founded by gentry during the late nineteenth and early twentieth centuries to promote western learning or champion reform projects.

Yihequan   The Boxers (lit. 'Boxers United in Righteousness').

youmin   'Floating population'; contemporary description of rural migrants in the cities.

youyi shangdian   Friendship Store; state-owned department store selling imported consumer goods to foreigners and highly placed cadres during the 1980s.

zaofan you daoli   'To rebel is justified'; a Cultural Revolution slogan first used by Mao Zedong in his encouragement of Beijing University students to criticize university authorities in 1966.

zhongdian 'Keypoint'; refers to the elite schools and universities in post-1949 China that receive the lion's share of resources.

zili gengsheng 'Self-reliance'; a Maoist ideal first enunciated during the Yanan period (1936–47) and then during the Great Leap Forward.

zuofeng 'Work-style.'

Bibliography

Ahn, Byung-joon 1976: *Chinese Politics and the Cultural Revolution.* Seattle: University of Washington Press.

Alitto, G. 1979: *The Last Confucian: Liang Shu-ming and the Chinese Dilemma of Modernity.* Berkeley: University of California Press.

Anagnost, A. 1997: *National Past-Times.* Durham, NC: Duke University Press.

Andors, P. 1983: *The Unfinished Liberation of Chinese Women 1949–1980.* Bloomington: Indiana University Press.

Apter, D. 1995: 'Discourse as Power: Yan'an and the Chinese Revolution.' In T. Saich and H. Van de Ven (eds) *New Perspectives on the Chinese Communist Revolution.* New York: M. E. Sharpe, 193–234.

Atwell, P. 1985: *British Mandarins and Chinese Reformers.* Hong Kong: Oxford University Press.

Averill, S. 1990: 'Local Elites and Communist Revolution in the Jiangxi Hill Country.' In J. Esherick and M. Rankin (eds) *Chinese Local Elites and Patterns of Dominance.* Berkeley: University of California Press, 282–304.

Bachman, D. 1991: *Bureaucracy, Economy and Leadership in China: The Institutional Origins of the Great Leap Forward.* Cambridge: Cambridge University Press.

Bailey, P. 1988: 'The Chinese Work-Study Movement in France.' *China Quarterly,* 115, 441–61.

Bailey, P. 1990: *Reform the People: Changing Attitudes Towards Popular Education in Early Twentieth Century China.* Edinburgh: Edinburgh University Press.

Bailey, P. 1992: 'Voltaire and Confucius: French Attitudes Towards China in the Early Twentieth Century.' *History of European Ideas,* 14: 6, 817–37.

Bailey, P. (trans. and intro.) 1998: *Strengthen the Country and Enrich the People: The Reform Writings of Ma Jianzhong (1845–1900)*. Richmond: Curzon Press.

Bailey, P. 2000: 'From Shandong to the Somme: Chinese Indentured Labour in France During World War One.' In A. Kershen (ed.) *Language, Labour and Migration*. Aldershot: Ashgate Press, 179–96.

Bailey, P. 2001: 'Active Citizen or Efficient Housewife? The Debate Over Women's Education in Early Twentieth Century China.' In G. Peterson, R. Hayhoe and Yongling Lu (eds) *Education, Culture and Identity in Twentieth-Century China*. Ann Arbor: University of Michigan Press.

Barmé, G. 1996a: *Shades of Mao*. New York: M. E. Sharpe.

Barmé, G. 1996b: 'To Screw Foreigners is Patriotic: China's Avant-Garde Nationalists.' In J. Unger (ed.) *Chinese Nationalism*. New York: M. E. Sharpe, 183–208.

Barmé, G. 1999: *In the Red: On Contemporary Chinese Culture*. New York: Columbia University Press.

Bastid, M. 1980: 'Currents of Social Change.' In J. Fairbank and K. C. Liu (eds) *The Cambridge History of China, vol. 11: Late Ch'ing 1800–1911*. Cambridge: Cambridge University Press, 536–602.

Bastid, M. 1984: 'Chinese Educational Policies in the 1980s and Economic Development.' *China Quarterly*, 98, 189–219.

Bastid, M. 1987: 'Official Conceptions of Imperial Authority at the End of the Qing Dynasty.' In S. Schram (ed.) *Foundations and Limits of State Power in China*. Hong Kong: Chinese University Press, 147–85.

Bastid, M. 1988: *Educational Reform in Early Twentieth-Century China*, trans. P. Bailey. Ann Arbor: Center for Chinese Studies, University of Michigan.

Baum, R. 1975: *Prelude to Revolution: Mao, the Party, and the Peasant Question 1962–1966*. New York: Columbia University Press.

Baum, R. 1994: *Burying Mao: Chinese Politics in the Age of Deng Xiaoping*. Princeton, NJ: Princeton University Press.

Baum, R. 1998: 'The Fifteenth National Party Congress: Jiang Takes Command?' *China Quarterly*, 153, 141–52.

Bays, D. 1978: *China Enters the Twentieth Century: Chang Chih-tung and the Issues of a New Age 1895–1909*. Ann Arbor: University of Michigan Press.

Beahan, C. 1975: 'Feminism and Nationalism in the Chinese Women's Press.' *Modern China*, 1, 379–416.

Beasley, W. 1989: 'The Foreign Threat and the Opening of the Ports.' In M. Jansen (ed.) *The Cambridge History of Japan, vol. 5: The Nineteenth Century*. Cambridge: Cambridge University Press, 259–307.

Bedeski, R. 1981: *State-Building in Modern China*. Berkeley: Institute of East Asian Studies, University of California.

Benedict, C. 1996: *Bubonic Plague in Nineteenth-Century China.* Stanford, CA: Stanford University Press.

Benton, G. 1992: *Mountain Fires: The Red Army's Three-year War in South China 1934–1938.* Berkeley: University of California Press.

Benton, G. 1999: *New Fourth Army.* Richmond: Curzon Press.

Benton, G. and Hunter, A. (eds) 1995: *Wild Lily, Prairie Fire: China's Road to Democracy, Yanan to Tian'anmen 1942–1989.* Princeton, NJ: Princeton University Press.

Bergère, M.-C. 1968: 'The Role of the Bourgeoisie.' In M. Wright (ed.) *China in Revolution: The First Phase 1900–1913.* New Haven, CT: Yale University Press, 229–96.

Bergère, M.-C. 1983: 'The Chinese Bourgeoisie, 1911–1937.' In J. Fairbank (ed.) *The Cambridge History of China, vol. 12: Republican China 1912–1949.* Cambridge: Cambridge University Press, 722–827.

Bergère, M.-C. 1989: *The Golden Age of the Chinese Bourgeoisie 1911–1937.* Cambridge: Cambridge University Press.

Bergère, M.-C. 1997: 'Civil Society and Urban Change in Republican China.' *China Quarterly*, 150, 309–28.

Bergère, M.-C. 1998. *Sun Yat-Sen.* Stanford, CA: Stanford University Press.

Bernal, M. 1976: *Chinese Socialism to 1907.* Ithaca, NY: Cornell University Press.

Bernhardt, K. 1992: *Rents, Taxes, and Peasant Resistance: The Lower Yangzi Region 1840–1950.* Stanford, CA: Stanford University Press.

Bernstein, T. 1977: *Up to the Mountains and Down to the Villages.* New Haven, CT: Yale University Press.

Bernstein, T. 1999: 'Farmer Discontent and Regime Responses.' In M. Goldman and R. MacFarquhar (eds) *The Paraodox of China's Post-Mao Reforms.* Cambridge, MA: Harvard University Press, 197–219.

Bianco, L. 1971: *Origins of the Chinese Revolution 1915–1949.* Stanford, CA: Stanford University Press.

Bianco, L. 1995: 'Peasant Responses to CCP Mobilization Policies, 1937–1945.' In T. Saich and H. Van de Ven (eds) *New Perspectives on the Chinese Communist Revolution.* New York: M. E. Sharpe, 175–87.

Billingsley, P. 1988: *Bandits in Republican China.* Stanford, CA: Stanford University Press.

Borthwick, S. 1983: *Education and Social Change in China.* Stanford, CA: Hoover Institution Press.

Boyle, J. 1972: *China and Japan at War 1937–1945.* Stanford, CA: Stanford University Press.

Brandt, C. 1958: *Stalin's Failure in China 1924–1927.* Cambridge, MA: Harvard University Press.

Brandt, L. 1997: 'Reflections on China's Late Nineteenth Century and Early Twentieth Century Economy.' *China Quarterly*, 150, 282–308.
Breslin, S. 1998: *Mao*. London: Addison Wesley Longman.
Brook, T. 1998: *Quelling the People*. Stanford, CA: Stanford University Press.
Brugger, B. 1981: *China: Liberation and Transformation 1942–1962*. London: Croom Helm.
Bunker, G. 1971: *The Peace Conspiracy: Wang Ching-wei and the China War 1937–1941*. Cambridge, MA: Harvard University Press.
Burns, J. 1989: 'China's Governance: Political Reform in a Turbulent Environment.' *China Quarterly*, 119, 481–518.
Burns, J. 1999: 'The People's Republic at 50: National Political Reform.' *China Quarterly*, 159, 580–94.
Chan, A. 1982: *Arming the Chinese: The Western Armaments Trade in Warlord China*. Vancouver: University of British Columbia Press.
Chan, A., Madsen, R. and Unger, J. 1992: *Chen Village Under Mao and Deng*. Berkeley: University of California Press.
Chan, W. 1977: *Merchants, Mandarins and Modern Enterprise in Late Ch'ing China*. Cambridge, MA: East Asian Research Center, Harvard University.
Chang, Hao 1971: *Liang Ch'i-ch'ao and Intellectual Transition in China 1890–1907*. Cambridge, MA: Harvard University Press.
Chang, Hao 1980: 'Intellectual Change and the Reform Movement'. In J. Fairbank and K. C. Liu (eds) *The Cambridge History of China, vol. 11: Late Ch'ing 1800–1911*. Cambridge: Cambridge University Press, 274–338.
Chang, Hao 1987: *Chinese Intellectuals in Crisis: Search for Order and Meaning (1890–1911)*. Berkeley: University of California Press.
Chang, M. 1985: *The Chinese Blue Shirt Society: Fascism and Developmental Nationalism*. Berkeley: Institute of East Asian Studies, University of California.
Chang, P. 1975: *Power and Policy in China*. University Park: Pennsylvania State University Press.
Ch'en, J. 1961: *Yuan Shih-k'ai, 1859–1916*. London: George Allen and Unwin.
Ch'en, J. 1965: *Mao and the Chinese Revolution*. Oxford: Oxford University Press.
Ch'en, J. 1983: 'The Chinese Communist Movement to 1927.' In J. Fairbank (ed.) *The Cambridge History of China, vol. 12: Republican China 1911–1949*. Cambridge: Cambridge University Press, 505–26.
Chen, J. 1971: *The May Fourth Movement in Shanghai*. Leiden: Brill.
Chen, N. 1995: 'Urban Spaces and Experiences of Qigong.' In D. Davis, R. Kraus, B. Naughton and E. Perry (eds) *Urban Spaces in Contemporary China*. Cambridge: Cambridge University Press, 347–61.

Chen, T. 1981: *Chinese Education Since Mao: Academic and Revolutionary Models*. Oxford: Pergamon Press.

Chen, Yung-fa 1986: *Making Revolution: The Communist Movement in Eastern and Central China 1937–1945*. Berkeley: University of California Press.

Chen, Yung-fa 1995: 'The Blooming Poppy Under the Red Sun: The Yan'an Way and the Opium Trade.' In T. Saich and H. Van de Ven (eds) *New Perspectives on the Chinese Communist Revolution*. New York: M. E. Sharpe, 263–98.

Chesneaux, J. 1968: *The Chinese Labour Movement 1919–1927*. Stanford, CA: Stanford University Press.

Chesneaux, J. 1969: 'The Federalist Movement in China 1920–1923.' In J. Gray (ed.) *Modern China's Search for a Political Form*. Oxford: Oxford University Press, 96–137.

Ch'i, Hsi-sheng 1976: *Warlord Politics in China 1916–1928*. Stanford, CA: Stanford University Press.

Ch'i, Hsi-sheng 1982: *Nationalist China at War: Military Defeats and Political Collapse 1937–1945*. Ann Arbor: University of Michigan Press.

Chi, M. 1970: *China Diplomacy 1914–1918*. Cambridge, MA: East Asian Research Center, Harvard University.

Chossudovsky, M. 1986: *Towards Capitalist Restoration? Chinese Socialism After Mao*. Basingstoke: Macmillan.

Chow, Kai-wing 1997: 'Imagining Boundaries of Blood: Zhang Binglin and the Invention of the Han "Race" in Modern China.' In F. Dikotter (ed.) *The Construction of Racial Identities in China and Japan*. London: Hurst, 34–52.

Chow, Tse-tsung 1960: *The May Fourth Movement: Intellectual Revolution in Modern China*. Cambridge, MA: Harvard University Press.

Chu, S. 1980: 'The New Life Movement Before the Sino-Japanese Conflict: A Reflection of Kuomintang Limitations in Thought and Action.' In G. Chan (ed.) *China at the Crossroads: Nationalists and Communists 1927–1949*. Boulder, CO: Westview Press, 37–68.

Clifford, N. 1979: *Shanghai 1925: Urban Nationalism and the Defense of Foreign Privilege*. Ann Arbor: Center for Chinese Studies, University of Michigan.

Coble, P. 1980: *The Shanghai Capitalists and the Nationalist Government 1927–1937*. Cambridge, MA: Council on East Asian Studies, Harvard University.

Coble, P. 1991: *Facing Japan: Chinese Politics and Japanese Imperialism 1931–1937*. Cambridge, MA: Council on East Asian Studies, Harvard University.

Cochran, S. 1980: *Big Business in China: Sino-Foreign Rivalry in the Cigarette Industry 1890–1930*. Cambridge, MA: Harvard University Press.

Cochran, S. and Hsieh, A. (trans. and eds) 1983: *One Day in China: May 21 1936.* New Haven, CT: Yale University Press.

Cohen, P. 1974: *Between Reform and Tradition: Wang T'ao and Reform in Late Ch'ing China.* Cambridge, MA: Harvard University Press.

Cohen, P. 1988: 'The Post-Mao Reforms in Historical Perspective.' *Journal of Asian Studies*, 47: 3, 518–40.

Cohen, P. 1992: 'The Contested Past: The Boxers as History and Myth.' *Journal of Asian Studies*, 51: 1, 81–113.

Cohen, P. 1997: *History in Three Keys: The Boxers as Event, Experience and Myth.* New York: Columbia University Press.

Compton, B. (trans. and ed.) 1966: *Mao's China: Party Reform Documents 1942–1944.* Seattle: University of Washington Press.

Crane, G. 1996: ' "Special Things in Special Ways": National Identity and China's Special Economic Zones.' In J. Unger (ed.) *Chinese Nationalism.* New York: M. E. Sharpe, 148–68.

Crossley, P. Kyle 1990: *Orphan Warriors: Three Manchu Generations and the End of the Qing World.* Princeton, NJ: Princeton University Press.

Crossley, P. Kyle 1994: 'Manchu Education.' In B. Elman and A. Woodside (eds) *Education and Society in Late Imperial China, 1600–1900.* Berkeley: University of California Press, 340–78.

Crossley, P. Kyle 1997: *The Manchus.* Oxford: Blackwell Publishers.

Davin, D. 1976: *Woman-Work: Women and the Party in Revolutionary China.* Oxford: Clarendon Press.

Davin, D. 1999: *Internal Migration in Contemporary China.* Basingstoke: Macmillan.

Davis, D. 1989: 'Chinese Social Welfare: Policies and Outcomes.' *China Quarterly*, 119, 577–97.

Davis, D. 1995: 'Introduction: Urban China.' In D. Davis, R. Kraus, B. Naughton and E. Perry (eds) *Urban Spaces in Contemporary China.* Cambridge: Cambridge University Press, 1–19.

Des Forges, R. 1973: *Hsi-liang and the Chinese National Revolution.* New Haven, CT: Yale University Press.

Diamant, N. 2000: *Revolutionizing the Family: Politics, Love and Divorce in Urban and Rural China, 1949–1968.* Berkeley: University of California Press.

Diamond, N. 1975: 'Women Under Kuomintang Rule: Variations on the Feminine Mystique.' *Modern China*, 1, 3–45.

Dikotter, F. 1992: *The Discourse of Race in Modern China.* London: Hurst.

Dikotter, F. 1997: 'Racial Discourse in China: Continuities and Permutations.' In F. Dikotter (ed.) *The Construction of Racial Identities in China and Japan.* London: Hurst, 12–33.

Dikotter, F. 1998: *Imperfect Conceptions: Medical Knowledge, Birth Defects and Eugenics in China.* London: Hurst.

Dirlik, A. 1975: 'The Ideological Foundations of the New Life Movement.' *Journal of Asian Studies*, 34: 4, 945–80.

Dirlik, A. 1989: *The Origins of Chinese Communism.* Oxford: Oxford University Press.

Dirlik, A. 1991: *Anarchism in the Chinese Revolution.* Berkeley: University of California Press.

Dittmer, L. 1987: *China's Continuing Revolution: The Post-Liberation Epoch 1949–1981.* Berkeley: University of California Press.

Dittmer, L. 1991: 'Learning from Trauma: The Cultural Revolution in Post-Mao Politics.' In W. Joseph, C. Wong and D. Zweig (eds) *New Perspectives on the Cultural Revolution.* Cambridge, MA: Council on East Asian Studies, Harvard University, 19–39.

Dittmer, L. 1998: *Liu Shaoqi and the Chinese Cultural Revolution,* revd edn. New York: M. E. Sharpe.

Dolozelova-Velingerova, M. 1977: 'The Origins of Modern Chinese Literature.' In M. Goldman (ed.) *Modern Chinese Literature in the May Fourth Era.* Cambridge, MA: Harvard University Press, 17–35.

Domenach, J.-L. 1995: *The Origins of the Great Leap Forward: The Case of One Chinese Province.* Boulder, CO: Westview Press.

Duara, P. 1988: *Culture, Power and the State: Rural North China 1900–1942.* Stanford, CA: Stanford University Press.

Duara, P. 1995: *Rescuing History From the Nation: Questioning Narratives of Modern China.* Chicago: University of Chicago Press.

Duiker, W. 1977: *Ts'ai Yuan-p'ei: Educator of Modern China.* University Park: Pennsylvania State University Press.

Duke, M. 1985: *Blooming and Contending: Chinese Literature in the Post-Mao Era.* Bloomington: Indiana University Press.

Duus, P. 1989: 'Japan's Informal Empire in China 1895–1937: An Overview.' In P. Duus, R. Myers and M. Peattie (eds) *The Japanese Informal Empire in China 1895–1937.* Princeton, NJ: Princeton University Press, xi–xxix.

Eastman, L. 1974: *The Abortive Revolution: China Under Nationalist Rule 1927–1937.* Cambridge, MA: Harvard University Press.

Eastman, L. 1980: 'Facets of an Ambivalent Relationship: Smuggling, Puppets and Atrocities During the War 1937–1945.' In A. Iriye (ed.) *The Chinese and the Japanese: Essays in Political and Cultural Interactions.* Princeton, NJ: Princeton University Press, 275–303.

Eastman, L. 1984: *Seeds of Destruction: Nationalist China in War and Revolution 1937–1949.* Stanford, CA: Stanford University Press.

Elleman, B. 1994: 'The Soviet Union's Secret Diplomacy Concerning the Chinese Eastern Railway 1924–1925.' *Journal of Asian Studies,* 53: 2, 459–86.

Elvin, M. 1969: 'The Gentry Democracy in Chinese Shanghai 1905–1914.' In J. Gray (ed.) *Modern China's Search For a Political Form.* Oxford: Oxford University Press, 41–65.

Elvin, M. 1996: 'Mandarins and Millenarians: Reflections on the Boxer Uprising of 1899–1900.' In *Another History: Essays on China From a European Perspective*. Sydney: Wild Peony, 197–226.

Esherick, J. 1976: *Reform and Revolution in China: The 1911 Revolution in Hunan and Hubei*. Berkeley: University of California Press.

Esherick, J. 1987: *The Origins of the Boxer Uprising*. Berkeley: University of California Press.

Esherick, J. 1995: 'Ten Theses on the Chinese Revolution.' *Modern China*, 1, 45–76.

Esherick, J. and Wasserstrom, J. 1994: 'Acting Out Democracy: Political Theater in Modern China.' In J. Wasserstrom and E. Perry (eds) *Popular Protest and Political Culture in Modern China*, 2nd edn. Boulder CO: Westview Press, 32–69.

Evans, H. 2000: 'Marketing Femininity: Images of the Modern Chinese Woman.' In T. Weston and L. Jensen (eds) *China Beyond the Headlines*. Lanham: Rowman and Littlefield.

Feigon, L. 1983: *Chen Duxiu: Founder of the Chinese Communist Party*. Princeton, NJ: Princeton University Press.

Feigon, L. 1994: 'Gender and the Chinese Student Movement.' In J. Wasserstrom and E. Perry (eds) *Popular Protest and Political Culture in Modern China*. Boulder, CO: Westview Press, 125–35.

Feuerwerker, A. 1968: *The Chinese Economy 1912–1949*. Ann Arbor: Center for Chinese Studies, University of Michigan.

Feuerwerker, A. 1983a: 'Economic Trends 1912–1949.' In J. Fairbank (ed.) *The Cambridge History of China, vol. 12: Republican China 1911–1949*. Cambridge: Cambridge University Press, 28–127.

Feuerwerker, A. 1983b: 'The Foreign Presence in China', In J. Fairbank (ed.) *The Cambridge History of China, vol. 12: Republican China 1911–1949*. Cambridge: Cambridge University Press, 128–207.

Feuerwerker, A. 1989: 'Japanese Imperialism in China: A Commentary.' In P. Duus, R. Myers and M. Peattie (eds) *The Japanese Informal Empire in China 1895–1937*. Princeton, NJ: Princeton University Press, 431–8.

Fewsmith, J. 1985: *Party, State and Local Elites in Republican China: Merchant Organizations and Politics in Shanghai 1890–1930*. Honolulu: University of Hawaii Press.

Fincher, J. 1981: *Chinese Democracy: The Self-Government Movement in Local, Provincial and National Politics 1905–1914*. New York: St. Martin's Press.

Fitzgerald, J. 1996: *Awakening China: Politics, Culture and Class in the Nationalist Revolution*. Stanford, CA: Stanford University Press.

Friedman, E. 1996: 'A Democratic Chinese Nationalism?' In J. Unger (ed.) *Chinese Nationalism*. New York: M. E. Sharpe, 169–82.

Fu, P. 1993: *Passivity, Resistance and Collaboration: Intellectual Choices in Occupied Shanghai 1937–1945*. Stanford, CA: Stanford University Press.

Fung, E. 1980: *The Military Dimension of the Chinese Revolution: The New Army and its Role in the Revolution of 1911*. Vancouver: University of British Columbia Press.

Galbiati, F. 1985: *P'eng P'ai and the Hai-Lu-Feng Soviet*. Stanford, CA: Stanford University Press.

Gao, Yuan 1987: *Born Red: A Chronicle of the Cultural Revolution*. Stanford, CA: Stanford University Press.

Gardner, J. 1982: *Chinese Politics and the Succession to Mao*. London: Macmillan.

Gasster, M. 1969: *Chinese Intellectuals and the Revolution of 1911*. Seattle: University of Washington Press.

Gasster, M. 1980: 'The Republican Revolutionary Movement.' In J. Fairbank and K. C. Liu (eds) *The Cambridge History of China, vol. 11: Late Ch'ing 1800–1911*. Cambridge: Cambridge University Press, 463–534.

Gaubatz, P. 1995: 'Urban Transformation in Post-Mao China: Impacts of the Reform Era on China's Urban Form'. In D. Davis, R. Kraus, B. Naughton and E. Perry (eds) *Urban Spaces in Contemporary China*. Cambridge: Cambridge University Press, 28–60.

Gaulton, R. 1981: 'Political Mobilization in Shanghai 1949–1951.' In C. Howe (ed.) *Shanghai: Revolution and Development in an Asian Metropolis*. Cambridge: Cambridge University Press, 35–65.

Gernet, J. 1996: *A History of Chinese Civilization*, 2nd edn. Cambridge: Cambridge University Press.

Gilley, B. 1998: *Tiger on the Brink: Jiang Zemin and China's New Elite*. Berkeley: University of California Press.

Gillin, D. 1964: '"Peasant Nationalism" in the History of Chinese Communism.' *Journal of Asian Studies*, 23: 2, 269–89.

Gillin, D. 1967: *Warlord: Yen Hsi-shan in Shansi Province, 1911–1949*. Princeton, NJ: Princeton University Press.

Gilmartin, C. 1995: *Engendering the Chinese Revolution: Radical Women, Communist Politics and Mass Movements in the 1920s*. Berkeley: University of California Press.

Gittings, J. 1967: *The Role of the Chinese Army*. London: Oxford University Press.

Gittings, J. 1968: *Survey of the Sino-Soviet Dispute: A Commentary and Extracts from the Recent Polemics 1963–1967*. London: Oxford University Press.

Gittings, J. 1974: *The World and China 1922–1972*. London: Eyre Methuen.

Gittings, J. 1989: *China Changes Face: The Road From Revolution, 1949–1989.* Oxford: Oxford University Press.

Gittings, J. 1996: *Real China: From Cannibalism to Karaoke.* London: Simon and Schuster.

Godley, M. 1981: *The Mandarin-Capitalists From Nanyang: Overseas Chinese Enterprise in the Modernization of China 1893–1911.* Cambridge: Cambridge University Press.

Goldman, M. 1973: 'The Chinese Communist Party's "Cultural Revolution" of 1962–1964.' In C. Johnson (ed.) *Ideology and Politics in Contemporary China.* Seattle: University of Washington Press, 219–54.

Goldman, M. 1981: *China's Intellectuals: Advise and Dissent.* Cambridge, MA: Harvard University Press.

Goldman, M. and MacFarquhar, R. 1999: 'Dynamic Economy, Declining Party–State.' In M. Goldman and R. MacFarquhar (eds) *The Paradox of China's Post-Mao Reforms.* Cambridge, MA: Harvard University Press, 3–29.

Goodman, B. 1995: *Native Place, City and Nation: Regional Networks and Identities in Shanghai 1853–1937.* Berkeley: University of California Press.

Greenhalgh, S. 1993: 'The Peasantization of the One-Child Policy in Shaanxi.' In D. Davis and S. Harrell (eds) *Chinese Families in the Post-Mao Era.* Berkeley: University of California Press, 219–50.

Grieder, J. 1970: *Hu Shih and the Chinese Renaissance: Liberalism in the Chinese Revolution 1917–1937.* Cambridge, MA: Harvard University Press.

Grieder, J. 1981: *Intellectuals and the State in Modern China.* New York: Free Press.

Han, Minzhu 1990: *Cries for Democracy: Writings and Speeches From the 1989 Chinese Democracy Movement.* Princeton, NJ: Princeton University Press.

Hao, Yen-p'ing 1969: 'Cheng Kuan-ying: The Comprador as Reformer.' *Journal of Asian Studies,* 29: 1, 15–22.

Hao, Yen-p'ing and Wang, Erh-min 1980: 'Changing Chinese Views of Western Relations, 1840–1895.' In J. Fairbank and K. C. Liu (eds) *The Cambridge History of China, vol. 11: Late Ch'ing 1800–1911.* Cambridge: Cambridge University Press, 142–201.

Harding, H. 1981: *Organizing China: The Problem of Bureaucracy 1949–1976.* Stanford, CA: Stanford University Press.

Harding, H. 1987: *China's Second Revolution: Reform After Mao.* Washington, DC: Brookings Institution.

Harding, H. 1991: 'The Chinese State in Crisis.' In R. MacFarquhar and J. Fairbank (eds) *The Cambridge History of China, vol. 15: The People's Republic.* Cambridge: Cambridge University Press, 107–217.

Harrell, P. 1992: *Sowing the Seeds of Change: Chinese Students, Japanese Teachers 1895–1905*. Stanford, CA: Stanford University Press.

Harrell, S. 1992: 'Introduction: Civilizing Projects and the Reaction to Them.' In S. Harrell (ed.) *Cultural Encounters on China's Ethnic Frontiers*. Seattle: University of Washington Press, 3–36.

Harrison, J. 1972: *The Long March to Power: A History of the Chinese Communist Party, 1921–1972*. New York: Praeger.

Hartford, K. and Goldstein, S. 1989: 'Introduction: Perspectives on the Chinese Communist Revolution.' In K. Hartford and S. Goldstein (eds) *Single Sparks: China's Rural Revolutions*. New York: M. E. Sharpe, 3–33.

Henriot, C. 1993: *Shanghai, 1927–1937: Municipal Power, Locality and Modernization*. Berkeley: University of California Press.

Hershatter, G. 1986: *The Workers of Tianjin 1900–1949*. Stanford, CA: Stanford University Press.

Hershatter, G. 1996: 'Chinese Sex Workers in the Reform Period.' In E. Perry (ed.) *Putting Class in its Place: Worker Identities in East Asia*. Berkeley: Institute of East Asian Studies, University of California, 199–224.

Hershatter, G. 1997: *Dangerous Pleasures: Prostitution and Modernity in Twentieth-Century Shanghai*. Berkeley: University of California Press.

Hershatter, G., Honig, E. and Stross, R. 1996: 'Introduction.' In G. Hershatter, E. Honig, J. Lipman and R. Stross (eds) *Remapping China: Fissures in Historical Terrain*. Stanford, CA: Stanford University Press, 1–9.

Hevia, J. 1992: 'Leaving a Brand on China: Missionary Discourse in the Wake of the Boxer Movement.' *Modern China*, 3, 304–32.

Hevia, J. 1995: *Cherishing Men From Afar: Qing Guest Ritual and the Macartney Embassy of 1793*. Durham, NC: Duke University Press.

Hinton, W. 1966: *Fanshen: A Documentary of Revolution in a Chinese Village*. New York: Vintage Books.

Hinton, W. 1972: *Hundred Day War: The Cultural Revolution at Tsinghua University*. New York: Monthly Review Press.

Ho, Pint-ti 1959: *Studies on the Population of China, 1368–1953*. Cambridge, MA: Harvard University Press.

Hofheinz, R. 1977: *The Broken Wave: The Chinese Communist Peasant Movement 1920–1928*. Cambridge, MA: Harvard University Press.

Holm, D. 1991: *Art and Ideology in Revolutionary China*. Oxford: Clarendon Press.

Honig, E. 1986: *Sisters and Strangers: Women in the Shanghai Cotton Mills 1919–1949*. Stanford, CA: Stanford University Press.

Honig, E. 1992: *Creating Chinese Ethnicity: Subei People in Shanghai 1850–1980*. New Haven, CT: Yale University Press.

Howard, R. 1969: 'The Chinese Reform Movement of the 1890s: A Symposium: Introduction.' *Journal of Asian Studies*, 29: 1, 7–14.

Howland, D. 1996: *Borders of Chinese Civilization: Geography and History at Empire's End*. Durham, NC: Duke University Press.

Hsia, C. T. 1978: 'Yen Fu and Liang Ch'i-ch'ao as Advocates of New Fiction.' In A. Rickett (ed.) *Chinese Approaches to Literature From Confucius to Liang Ch'i-ch'ao*. Princeton, NJ: Princeton University Press, 221–57.

Hsiao, Kung-ch'uan 1975: *A Modern China and a New World: K'ang Yu-wei, Reformer and Utopian 1858–1927*. Seattle: University of Washington Press.

Hsieh, W. 1975: *Chinese Historiography on the Revolution of 1911*. Stanford, CA: Hoover Institution Press.

Hsiung, J. and Levine, S. (eds) 1992: *China's Bitter Victory: The War With Japan 1937–1945*. New York: M. E. Sharpe.

Hsu, I. 1990: *China Without Mao: The Search for a New Order*, 2nd edn. Oxford: Oxford University Press.

Hsu, I. 2000: *The Rise of Modern China*, 6th edn. Oxford: Oxford University Press.

Huang, P. 1995: 'Class Struggle in the Chinese Revolution.' *Modern China*, 1, 105–43.

Hucker, C. 1975: *China's Imperial Past: An Introduction to Chinese History and Culture*. Stanford, CA: Stanford University Press.

Hung, Chang-tai 1994: *War and Popular Culture: Resistance in Modern China 1937–1945*. Berkeley: University of California Press.

Hunt, M. 1972: 'The American Remission of the Boxer Indemnity: A Reappraisal.' *Journal of Asian Studies*, 31: 3, 539–59.

Hunt, M. 1973: *Frontier Defense and the Open Door: Manchuria in Chinese–American Relations 1895–1911*. New Haven, CT: Yale University Press.

Hunt, M. 1983: *The Making of a Special Relationship: The United States and China to 1914*. New York: Columbia University Press.

Hunt, M. 1996: *The Genesis of Chinese Communist Foreign Policy*. New York: Columbia University Press.

Hunter, A. and Sexton, J. 1999: *Contemporary China*. London: Macmillan.

Ichiko, Chuzo 1980: 'Political and Institutional Reform, 1901–1911.' In J. Fairbank and K. C. Liu (eds) *The Cambridge History of China, vol. 11: Late Ch'ing 1800–1911*. Cambridge: Cambridge University Press, 375–415.

Iriye, A. 1965: *After Imperialism: The Search for a New Order in the Far East 1921–1931*. Cambridge, MA: Harvard University Press.

Iriye, A. 1967: 'Public Opinion and Foreign Policy: The Case of Late Ch'ing China.' In A. Feuerwerker, R. Murphey and M. Wright (eds)

Approaches to Modern Chinese History. Berkeley: University of California Press, 216–38.

Irons, N. 1983: *The Last Emperor*. London: House of Fans.

Isaacs, H. 1961: *The Tragedy of the Chinese Revolution*, 2nd revd edn. Stanford, CA: Stanford University Press.

Israel, J. 1998: *Lianda: A Chinese University in War and Revolution*. Stanford, CA: Stanford University Press.

Israel, J. and Klein, D. 1976: *Rebels and Bureaucrats: China's December 9ers*. Berkeley: University of California Press.

Jacobs, D. 1981: *Borodin: Stalin's Man in China*. Cambridge, MA: Harvard University Press.

Jansen, M. 1954: *The Japanese and Sun Yat-sen*. Cambridge, MA: Harvard University Press.

Jansen, M. 1975: *Japan and China: From War to Peace 1894–1972*. Chicago: Rand McNally.

Jansen, M. 1980: 'Japan and the Revolution of 1911.' In J. Fairbank and K. C. Liu (eds) *The Cambridge History of China, vol. 11: Late Ch'ing 1800–1911*. Cambridge: Cambridge University Press, 339–74.

Jansen, M. 1984: 'Japanese Imperialism: Late Meiji Perspectives.' In R. Myers and M. Peattie (eds) *The Japanese Colonial Empire 1894–1945*. Princeton, NJ: Princeton University Press, 61–79.

Jenner, W. 1992: *The Tyranny of History: The Roots of China's Crisis*. London: Lane, Penguin Press.

Joffe, E. 1987: *The Chinese Army After Mao*. Cambridge, MA: Harvard University Press.

Johnson, C. 1962: *Peasant Nationalism and Communist Power: The Emergence of Revolutionary China*. Stanford, CA: Stanford University Press.

Johnson, K. Ann 1983: *Women, the Family, and Peasant Revolution in China*. Chicago: University of Chicago Press.

Jones, A. 1994: 'The Politics of Popular Music in Post-Tiananmen China.' In J. Wasserstrom and E. Perry (eds) *Popular Protest and Political Culture in Modern China*, 2nd edn. Boulder, CO: Westview Press, 148–65.

Jordan, D. 1976: *The Northern Expedition: China's National Revolution of 1926–1928*. Honolulu: University Press of Hawaii.

Jordan, D. 1991: *Chinese Boycotts Versus Japanese Bombs: The Failure of China's 'Revolutionary Diplomacy' 1931–1932*. Ann Arbor: University of Michigan Press.

Joseph, W., Wong, C. and Zweig, D. 1991: 'Introduction: New Perspectives on the Cultural Revolution.' In W. Joseph, C. Wong and D. Zweig (eds) *New Perspectives on the Cultural Revolution*. Cambridge, MA: Council on East Asian Studies, Harvard University, 1–16.

Judge, J. 1996: *Print and Politics: Shibao and the Culture of Reform in Late Qing China*. Stanford, CA: Stanford University Press.

Kapp, R. 1973: *Szechuan and the Chinese Republic: Provincial Militarism and Central Power 1911–1938*. New Haven, CT: Yale University Press.

Kataoka, T. 1974: *Resistance and Revolution in China: The Communists and the Second United Front*. Berkeley: University of California Press.

Keenan, B. 1977: *The Dewey Experiment in China: Educational Reform and Political Power in the Early Republic*. Cambridge, MA: Council on East Asian Studies, Harvard University.

Kim, I. 1973: *The Politics of Chinese Communism: Kiangsi Under the Soviets*. Berkeley: University of California Press.

Kirby, W. 1984: *Germany and Republican China*. Stanford, CA: Stanford University Press.

Kirby, W. 1997: 'The Internationalization of China: Foreign Relations At Home and Abroad in the Republican Era.' *China Quarterly*, 150, 433–58.

Kuhn, P. 1975: 'Local Self-Government Under the Republic.' In F. Wakeman and C. Grant (eds) *Conflict and Control in Late Imperial China*. Berkeley: University of California Press, 257–98.

Kuhn, P. 1978: 'The Taiping Rebellion.' In J. Fairbank (ed.) *The Cambridge History of China, vol. 10: Late Ch'ing 1800–1911*. Cambridge: Cambridge University Press, 264–317.

Kwan, D. 1997: *Marxist Intellectuals and the Chinese Labor Movement*. Seattle: University of Washington Press.

Kwong, L. 1984: *A Mosaic of the Hundred Days: Personalities, Politics and Ideas of 1898*. Cambridge, MA: Council on East Asian Studies, Harvard University.

Lary, D. 1974: *Region and Nation: The Kwangsi Clique in Chinese Politics 1925–1937*. Cambridge: Cambridge University Press.

Lary, D. 1985: *Warlord Soldiers: Chinese Common Soldiers 1911–1937*. Cambridge: Cambridge University Press.

Lee, Chong-sik 1983: *Revolutionary Struggle in Manchuria: Chinese Communism and Soviet Interest 1922–1945*. Berkeley: University of California Press.

Lee, Leo Ou-fan 1987: *Voices From the Iron House: A Study of Lu Xun*. Bloomington: Indiana University Press.

Lee, Leo Ou-fan 1999: *Shanghai Modern: The Flowering of a New Urban Culture in China 1930–1945*. Cambridge, MA: Harvard University Press.

Lee, Leo Ou-fan 2000: 'The Cultural Construction of Modernity in Urban Shanghai: Some Preliminary Explorations.' In Wen-hsin Yeh (ed.) *Becoming Chinese*. Berkeley: University of California Press, 31–61.

Lee, Leo Ou-fan and Nathan, A. 1985: 'The Beginnings of Mass Culture: Journalism and Fiction in the Late Ch'ing and Beyond.' In

D. Johnson, A. Nathan and E. Rawski (eds) *Popular Culture in Late Imperial China.* Berkeley: University of California Press, 360–95.

Lee, Lily Xiao Hong and Wiles, S. 1999: *Women of the Long March.* St. Leonards, NSW: Allen and Unwin.

Levenson, J. 1964: *Confucian China and its Modern Fate, vol. 2: The Problem of Monarchical Decay.* London: Routledge and Kegan Paul.

Levich, E. 1993: *The Kwangsi Way in Kuomintang China 1931–1939.* New York: M. E. Sharpe.

Levine, S. 1987: *Anvil of Victory: The Communist Revolution in Manchuria 1945–1948.* New York: Columbia University Press.

Lewis, C. 1976: *Prologue to the Chinese Revolution: The Transformation of Ideas and Institutions in Hunan Province 1891–1907.* Cambridge, MA: Harvard University Press.

Li, Lianjiang and O'Brien, K. 1999: 'The Struggle Over Village Elections.' In M. Goldman and R. MacFarquhar (eds) *The Paradox of China's Post-Mao Reforms.* Cambridge, MA: Harvard University Press, 129–44.

Liang, Heng and Shapiro, J. 1983: *Son of the Revolution.* London: Chatto and Windus.

Lieberthal, K. 1980: *Revolution and Tradition in Tientsin 1949–1952.* Stanford, CA: Stanford University Press.

Lieberthal, K. 1993: 'The Great Leap Forward and the Split in the Yan'an leadership 1958–1965.' In R. MacFarquhar (ed.) *The Politics of China 1949–1989.* Cambridge: Cambridge University Press, 87–147.

Lieberthal, K. 1995: *Governing China: From Revolution Through Reform.* London: Norton.

Liew, K. S. 1971: *Struggle For Democracy: Sung Chiao-jen and the 1911 Chinese Revolution.* Berkeley: University of California Press.

Lifton, R. 1968: *Revolutionary Immortality: Mao Tse-tung and the Chinese Cultural Revolution.* New York: Random House.

Lin, Yu-sheng 1979: *The Crisis of Chinese Consciousness: Radical Antitraditionalism in the May Fourth Era.* Madison: University of Wisconsin Press.

Litzinger, C. 1996: 'Rural Religion and Village Organization in North China: The Catholic Challenge in the Late Nineteenth Century.' In D. Bays (ed.) *Christianity in China: From the Eighteenth Century to the Present.* Stanford, CA: Stanford University Press, 41–52.

Louis, W. 1971: *British Strategy in the Far East 1919–1939.* Oxford: Clarendon Press.

Luk, M. 1990: *The Origins of Chinese Bolshevism: An Ideology in the Making 1920–1928.* Oxford: Oxford University Press.

Lupher, M. 1995: 'Revolutionary Little Red Devils: The Social Psychology of Rebel Youth 1966–1967.' In A. Kinney (ed.)

Chinese Views of Childhood. Honolulu: University of Hawaii Press, 321–43.

Lyell, W. 1976: *Lu Hsun's Vision of Reality.* Berkeley: University of California Press.

Lyell, W. (trans.) 1990: *Diary of a Madman and Other Stories.* Honolulu: University of Hawaii Press.

McCord, E. 1993: *The Power of the Gun: The Emergence of Modern Chinese Warlordism.* Berkeley: University of California Press.

McCormack, G. 1977: *Chang Tso-lin in Northeast China 1911–1928: China, Japan and the Manchurian Idea.* Stanford, CA: Stanford University Press.

McDonald, A. 1978: *The Urban Origins of Rural Revolution: Elites and Masses in Hunan Province, China 1911–1927.* Berkeley: University of California Press.

MacFarquhar, R. 1960: *The Hundred Flowers Campaign and the Chinese Intellectuals.* New York: Praeger.

MacFarquhar, R. 1974: *The Origins of the Cultural Revolution, vol. 1: Contradictions Among the People 1956–1957.* New York: Columbia University Press.

MacFarquhar, R. 1983: *The Origins of the Cultural Revolution, vol. 2: The Great Leap Forward 1958–1960.* Oxford: Oxford University Press.

MacFarquhar, R. 1991: 'The Succession to Mao and the End of Maoism.' In R. MacFarquhar and J. Fairbank (eds) *The Cambridge History of China, vol. 15: The People's Republic.* Cambridge: Cambridge University Press, 305–41.

MacFarquhar, R. 1997: *The Origins of the Cultural Revolution, vol. 3: The Coming of the Cataclysm 1961–1966.* Oxford: Oxford University Press.

Mackinnon, S. 1980: *Power and Politics in Late Imperial China: Yuan Shikai in Beijing and Tianjin 1901–1908.* Berkeley: University of California Press.

Mancall, M. 1984: *China at the Center: 300 Years of Foreign Policy.* New York: Free Press.

Mann Jones, S. and Kuhn, P. 1978: 'Dynastic Decline and the Roots of Rebellion.' In J. Fairbank (ed.) *The Cambridge History of China, vol. 10: Late Ch'ing 1800 1911.* Cambridge: Cambridge University Press, 107–62.

Marks, R. 1984: *Rural Revolution in South China: Peasants and the Making of History in Haifeng County 1570–1930.* Madison: University of Wisconsin Press.

Marshall, J. 1976: 'Opium and the Politics of Gangsterism in Nationalist China 1927–1945.' *Bulletin of Concerned Asian Scholars*, 8, 19–48.

Martin, B. 1996: *The Shanghai Green Gang: Politics and Organized Crime 1919–1937.* Berkeley: University of California Press.

Meienberger, N. 1980: *The Emergence of Constitutional Government in China (1905–1908)*. Bern: P. Lang.

Meijer, M. 1983: 'Legislation on Marriage and Family in the Chinese Soviet Republic.' In W. Butler (ed.) *The Legal System of the Chinese Soviet Republic 1931–1934*. New York: Transnational Publishers, 95–106.

Meisner, M. 1967: *Li Ta-chao and the Origins of Chinese Marxism*. Cambridge, MA: Harvard University Press.

Meisner, M. 1999: *Mao's China and After: A History of the People's Republic*, 3rd edn. New York: Free Press.

Miles, J. 1996: *The Legacy of Tiananmen: China in Disarray*. Ann Arbor: University of Michigan Press.

Min, Tu-ki 1989: *National Polity and Local Power: The Transformation of Late Imperial China*. Cambridge, MA: Council on East Asian Studies, Harvard University.

Moore, B. 1966: *Social Origins of Dictatorship and Democracy: Lord and Peasant in the Making of the Modern World*. Boston: Beacon Press.

Nathan, A. 1985: *Chinese Democracy*. New York: Alfred A. Knopf.

Naughton, B. 1991: 'Industrial Policy During the Cultural Revolution: Military Preparation, Decentralization and Leaps Forward.' In W. Joseph, C. Wong and D. Zweig (eds) *New Perspectives on the Cultural Revolution*. Cambridge, MA: Council on East Asian Studies, Harvard University Press, 153–81.

Naughton, B. 1999: 'China's Transition in Economic Perspective.' In M. Goldman and R. MacFarquhar (eds) *The Paradox of China's Post-Mao Reforms*. Cambridge, MA: Harvard University Press, 30–44.

Nee, V. 1969: *The Cultural Revolution at Peking University*. London: Monthly Review Press.

O'Brien, K. and Li, Lianjiang 2000: 'Accommodating "Democracy" in a One-Party State: Introducing Village Elections in China.' *China Quarterly*, 162, 465–89.

Ogata, S. 1964: *Defiance in Manchuria: The Making of Japanese Foreign Policy 1931–1932*. Berkeley: University of California Press.

Oi, J. 1999: 'Two Decades of Rural Reform in China: An Overview and Assessment.' *China Quarterly*, 159, 616–28.

Ono, K. 1989: *Chinese Women in a Century of Revolution 1850–1950*. Stanford, CA: Stanford University Press.

Ownby, D. 1996: *Brotherhoods and Secret Societies in Early and Mid-Qing China: The Formation of a Tradition*. Stanford, CA: Stanford University Press.

Parris, K. 1999: 'The Rise of Private Business Interests.' In M. Goldman and R. MacFarquhar (eds) *The Paradox of China's Post-Mao Reforms*. Cambridge, MA: Harvard University Press, 262–82.

Paulson, D. 1989: 'Nationalist Guerrillas in the Sino-Japanese War: The "Die-Hards" of Shandong Province.' In K. Hartford and S. Goldstein (eds) *Single Sparks: China's Rural Revolutions*. New York: M. E. Sharpe, 128–50.

Peattie, M. 1975: *Ishiwara Kanji and Japan's Confrontation With the West*. Princeton, NJ: Princeton University Press.

Pepper, S. 1978: *Civil War in China: The Political Struggle 1945–1949*. Berkeley: University of California Press.

Pepper, S. 1986: 'The KMT–CCP Conflict, 1945–1949.' In J. Fairbank and A. Feuerwerker (eds) *The Cambridge History of China, vol. 13: Republican China 1912–1949*. Cambridge: Cambridge University Press, 723–88.

Pepper, S. 1991: 'Education.' In R. MacFarquhar and J. Fairbank (eds) *The Cambridge History of China, vol. 15: The People's Republic*. Cambridge: Cambridge University Press, 540–93.

Pepper, S. 1996: *Radicalism and Education Reform in the Twentieth Century*. Cambridge: Cambridge University Press.

Perry, E. 1993: *Shanghai on Strike: The Politics of Chinese Labor*. Stanford, CA: Stanford University Press.

Perry, E. 1994: 'Casting a Chinese "Democracy" Movement: The Roles of Students, Workers, and Entrepreneurs.' In J. Wasserstrom and E. Perry (eds) *Popular Protest and Political Culture in Modern China*, 2nd edn. Boulder, CO: Westview Press, 74–92.

Perry, E. 1995: 'Labor's Battle For Political Space: The Role of Worker Associations in Contemporary China.' In D. Davis, R. Kraus, B. Naughton and E. Perry (eds) *Urban Spaces in Contemporary China*. Cambridge: Cambridge University Press, 302–25.

Perry, E. 1999: 'Crime, Corruption and Contention.' In M. Goldman and R. MacFarquhar (eds) *The Paradox of China's Post-Mao Reforms*. Cambridge, MA: Harvard University Press, 308–29.

Perry, E. and Li, Xun 1997: *Proletarian Power: Shanghai in the Cultural Revolution*. Boulder, CO: Westview Press.

Peyrefitte, A. 1993: *The Collision of Two Civilizations: The British Expedition to China in 1792–1794*. London: Harvill.

Pickowicz, P. 1995: 'Velvet Prisons and the Political Economy of Chinese Filmmaking.' In D. Davis, R. Kraus, B. Naughton and E. Perry (eds) *Urban Spaces in Contemporary China*. Cambridge: Cambridge University Press, 193–220.

Pickowicz, P. 2000: 'Victory as Defeat: Postwar Visualizations of China's War of Resistance.' In Wen-hsin Yeh (ed.) *Becoming Chinese*. Berkeley: University of California Press, 365–98.

Polachek, J. 1983: 'The Moral Economy of the Kiangsi Soviet (1928–1934).' *Journal of Asian Studies*, 42: 4, 805–29.

Pollack, J. 1991: 'The Opening to China.' In R. MacFarquhar and J. Fairbank (eds) *The Cambridge History of China, vol. 15: The People's Republic*. Cambridge: Cambridge University Press, 402–72.

Pong, D. 1985: 'The Vocabulary of Change: Reformist Ideas of the 1860s and 1870s.' In D. Pong and E. Fung (eds) *Ideal and Reality: Social and Political Change in Modern China, 1860–1949*. Lanham: University Press of America, 25–60.

Pong, D. 1994: *Shen Pao-chen and China's Modernization in the Nineteenth Century*. Cambridge: Cambridge University Press.

Prazniak, R. 1999: *Of Camel Kings and Other Things: Rural Rebels Against Modernity in Late Imperial China*. Lanham: Rowman and Littlefield.

Price, D. 1974: *Russia and the Roots of the Chinese Revolution 1896–1911*. Cambridge, MA: Harvard University Press.

Pye, L. 1971: *Warlord Politics: Conflict and Coalition in the Modernization of Republican China*. New York: Praeger.

Pye, L. 1993: 'An Introductory Profile: Deng Xiaoping and China's Political Culture.' *China Quarterly*, 135, 412–43.

Rankin, M. 1975: 'The Emergence of Women at the End of the Ch'ing: The Case of Ch'iu Chin.' In M. Wolf and R. Witke (eds) *Women in Chinese Society*. Stanford, CA: Stanford University Press, 39–66.

Rankin, M. 1986: *Elite Activism and Political Transformation in China: Zhejiang Province, 1865–1911*. Stanford, CA: Stanford University Press.

Rankin, M. 1997: 'State and Society in Early Republican Politics 1912–1918.' *China Quarterly*, 150, 260–81.

Rankin, M. and Esherick, J. 1990: 'Concluding Remarks.' In J. Esherick and M. Rankin (eds) *Chinese Local Elites and Patterns of Dominance*. Berkeley: University of California Press, 305–45.

Rawski, E. 1996: 'Re-envisioning the Qing: The Significance of the Qing Period in Chinese History.' *Journal of Asian Studies*, 55: 4, 829–50.

Rawski, E. 1998: *The Last Emperors: A Social History of Qing Imperial Institutions*. Berkeley: University of California Press.

Rawski, T. 1989: *Economic Growth in Prewar China*. Berkeley: University of California Press.

Reardon-Anderson, J. 1980: *Yenan and the Great Powers: The Origins of Chinese Communist Foreign Policy 1944–1946*. New York: Columbia University Press.

Reynolds, D. 1993: *China 1898–1912: The Xinzheng Revolution and Japan*. Cambridge, MA: Council on East Asian Studies, Harvard University.

Rhoads, E. 1975: *China's Republican Revolution: The Case of Kwangtung 1895–1913*. Cambridge, MA: Harvard University Press.

Rice, E. 1972: *Mao's Way*. Berkeley: University of California Press.

Robinson, T. 1991: 'China Confronts the Soviet Union: Warfare and Diplomacy on China's Inner Asian Frontiers.' In R. MacFarquhar and J. Fairbank (eds) *The Cambridge History of China, vol. 15: The People's Republic*. Cambridge: Cambridge University Press, 218–301.

Rowe, W. 1989: *Hankow: Conflict and Community in a Chinese City, 1796–1895*. Stanford, CA: Stanford University Press.

Rowe, W. 1994: 'Education and Empire in Southwest China.' In B. Elman and A. Woodside (eds) *Education and Society in Late Imperial China 1600–1900*. Berkeley: University of California Press, 417–57.

Rue, J. 1966: *Mao Tse-tung in Opposition 1927–1935*. Stanford, CA: Stanford University Press.

Saich, T. 2000: 'Negotiating the State: The Development of Social Organizations in China.' *China Quarterly*. 161, 124–41.

Scalapino, R. and Yu, G. 1985: *Modern China and its Revolutionary Process: Recurrent Challenges to the Traditional Order 1850–1920*. Berkeley: University of California Press.

Schaller, M. 1979: *The US Crusade in China 1938–1945*. New York: Columbia University Press.

Schiffrin, H. 1968: *Sun Yat-sen and the Origins of the Chinese Revolution*. Berkeley: University of California Press.

Schoppa, R. Keith. 1982: *Chinese Elites and Political Change: Zhejiang Province in the Early Twentieth Century*. Cambridge, MA: Harvard University Press.

Schram, S. (ed.) 1963: *The Political Thought of Mao Tse-tung*. New York: Praeger.

Schram, S. 1966: *Mao Tse-tung*. Harmondsworth: Penguin.

Schram, S. 1973: 'The Cultural Revolution in Historical Perspective.' In S. Schram (ed.) *Authority, Participation and Cultural Change in China*. Cambridge: Cambridge University Press, 1–108.

Schram, S. (ed.) 1974: *Mao Tse-tung Unrehearsed: Talks and Letters 1956–1971*. Harmondsworth: Penguin.

Schram, S. 1987: 'Party Leader or True Ruler? Foundations and Significance of Mao Zedong's Personal Power.' In S. Schram (ed.) *Foundations and Limits of State Power in China*. Hong Kong: Chinese University Press, 203 56.

Schram, S. 1989: *The Thought of Mao Tse-tung*. Cambridge: Cambridge University Press.

Schrecker, J. 1969: 'The Reform Movement, Nationalism and China's Foreign Policy.' *Journal of Asian Studies*, 29: 1, 43–53.

Schrecker, J. 1971: *Imperialism and Chinese Nationalism: Germany in Shantung*. Cambridge, MA: Harvard University Press.

Schurmann, F. 1968: *Ideology and Organization in Communist China*. Berkeley: University of California Press.

Schwarcz, V. 1986: *The Chinese Enlightenment: Intellectuals and the Legacy of the May Fourth Movement of 1919*. Berkeley: University of California Press.

Schwartz, B. 1951: *Chinese Communism and the Rise of Mao*. Cambridge, MA: Harvard University Press.

Schwartz, B. 1964: *In Search of Wealth and Power: Yen Fu and the West*. Cambridge, MA: Harvard University Press.

Seagrave, S. 1985: *The Soong Dynasty*. London: Sidgwick and Jackson.

Selden, M. 1971: *The Yenan Way in Revolutionary China*. Cambridge, MA: Harvard University Press.

Selden, M. 1995a: *China in Revolution: The Yenan Way Revisited*. New York: M, E. Sharpe.

Selden, M. 1995b: 'Yan'an Communism Reconsidered.' *Modern China*, 1, 8–44.

Shaffer, L. 1982: *Mao and the Workers: The Hunan Labor Movement 1920–1923*. New York: M. E. Sharpe.

Sheehan, J. 1998: *Chinese Workers: A New History*. London: Routledge.

Sheel, K. 1989: *Peasant Society and Marxist Intellectuals in China: Fang Zhimin and the Origins of a Revolutionary Movement in the Xinjiang Region*. Princeton: Princeton University Press.

Sheng, M. 1997: *Battling Western Imperialism: Mao, Stalin and the US*. Princeton, NJ: Princeton University Press.

Sheridan, J. 1966: *Chinese Warlord: The Career of Feng Yu-hsiang*. Stanford, CA: Stanford University Press.

Sheridan, J. 1977: *China in Disintegration: The Republican Era in Chinese History 1912–1949*. New York: Free Press.

Sheridan, J. 1983: 'The Warlord Era: Politics and Militarism Under the Peking Government 1916–1928.' In J. Fairbank (ed.) *The Cambridge History of China, vol. 12: Republican China 1912–1949*. Cambridge: Cambridge University Press, 284–321.

Shirk, S. 1982: *Competitive Comrades: Career Incentives and Student Strategies in China*. Berkeley: University of California Press.

Short, P. 1982: *The Dragon and the Bear: Inside China and Russia Today*. London: Hodder and Stoughton.

Short, P. 1999: *Mao: A Life*. London: Hodder and Stoughton.

Shue, V. 1980: *Peasant China in Transition: The Dynamics of Development Towards Socialism 1949–1956*. Berkeley: University of California Press.

Shum, K. K. 1985: 'The Chinese Communist Party's Strategy for Galvanizing Popular Support, 1930–1945.' In D. Pong and E. Fung (eds) *Ideal and Reality: Social and Political Change in Modern China, 1860–1949*. Lanham: University Press of America, 327-54.

Shum, K. K. 1988: *The Chinese Communists' Road to Power: The Anti-Japanese National United Front*. Oxford: Oxford University Press.

Sigel, L. 1976: 'Foreign Policy Interests and Activities of the Treaty Port Chinese Community.' In P. Cohen and J. Schrecker (eds) *Reform in Nineteenth Century China*. Cambridge, MA: East Asian Research Center, Harvard University, 272–81.

Sigel, L. 1985: 'The Treaty Port Commercial Community and the Diplomacy of Chinese Nationalism 1900–1911.' In D. Pong and E. Fung (eds) *Ideal and Reality: Social and Political Change in Modern China 1860–1949*. Lanham: University Press of America, 221–49.

Sigel, L. 1992: 'Business–Government Cooperation in Late Qing Foreign Policy.' In J. Kate Leonard and J. Watt (eds) *To Achieve Security and Wealth: The Qing Imperial State and the Economy 1644–1911*. Ithaca, NY: East Asia Program, Cornell University, 157–81.

Solinger, D. 1995: 'The Floating Population in the Cities: Chances For Assimilation?' In D. Davis, R. Kraus, B. Naughton and E. Perry (eds) *Urban Spaces in Contemporary China*. Cambridge: Cambridge University Press, 113–39.

Solinger, D. 1999: 'China's Floating Population.' In M. Goldman and R. MacFarquhar (eds) *The Paradox of China's Post-Mao Reforms*. Cambridge, MA: Harvard University Press, 220–40.

Solomon, R. 1971: *Mao's Revolution and the Chinese Political Culture*. Berkeley: University of California Press.

Spence, J. 1982: *The Gate of Heavenly Peace: The Chinese and Their Revolution 1895–1980*. London: Faber and Faber.

Spence, J. 1999a: *The Search for Modern China*, 2nd edn. London: W. W. Norton.

Spence, J. 1999b: *Mao Zedong*. New York: Viking Penguin.

Stacey, J. 1983: *Patriarchy and Socialist Revolution in China*. Berkeley: University of California Press.

Storry, R. 1979: *Japan and the Decline of the West in Asia 1894–1943*. London: Macmillan.

Stranahan, P. 1983: *Yan'an Women and the Communist Party*. Berkeley: Institute of East Asian Studies, University of California.

Stranahan, P. 1998: *Underground: The Shanghai Communist Party and the Politics of Survival 1927–1937*. Lanham: Rowman and Littlefield.

Strand, D. 1989: *Rickshaw Beijing: City People and Politics in the 1920s*. Berkeley: University of California Press.

Strand, D. 1995: 'Conclusion: Historical Perspectives.' In D. Davis, R. Kraus, B. Naughton and E. Perry (eds) *Urban Spaces in Contemporary China*. Cambridge: Cambridge University Press, 394–426.

Strauss, J. 1997: 'The Evolution of Republican Government.' *China Quarterly*, 150, 329–51.

Stross, R. 1996: 'Field Notes From the Present.' In G. Hershatter, E. Honig, J. Lipman and R. Stross (eds) *Remapping China: Fissures in Historical Terrain*. Stanford, CA: Stanford University Press, 261–74.

Su, Xiaokang 1991: *Deathsong of the River: A Reader's Guide to the Chinese TV Series Heshang*. Ithaca, NY: East Asia Program, Cornell University.

Sutton, D. 1980: *Provincial Militarism and the Chinese Republic: The Yunnan Army, 1905–1925*. Ann Arbor: University of Michigan Press.

Sweeten, A. 1996: 'Catholic Converts in Jiangxi Province: Conflict and Accommodation 1860–1900.' In D. Bays (ed.) *Christianity in China: From the Eighteenth Century to the Present*. Stanford, CA: Stanford University Press, 24–40.

Tang, Xiaobing 1996: *Global Space and the Nationalist Discourse of Modernity: The Historical Thinking of Liang Qichao*, Stanford, CA: Stanford University Press.

Tanner, M. 1999: 'The National People's Congress.' In M. Goldman and R. MacFarquhar (eds) *The Paradox of China's Post-Mao Reforms*. Cambridge, MA: Harvard University Press, 100–28.

Teiwes, F. and Sun, W. 1996: *The Tragedy of Lin Biao: Riding the Tiger During the Cultural Revolution 1966–1971*. Honolulu: University of Hawaii Press.

Terrill, R. 1999: *Madame Mao: The White-Boned Demon*, revd edn. Stanford, CA: Stanford University Press.

Thaxton, R. 1983: *China Turned Rightside Up: Revolutionary Legitimacy in the Present*. New Haven, CT: Yale University Press.

Thaxton, R. 1997: *Salt of the Earth: The Political Origins of Peasant Protest and Communist Revolution in China*. Berkeley: University of California Press.

Thompson, L. (ed. and trans.) 1958: *Ta T'ung Shu: The One World Philosophy of K'ang Yu-wei*. London: Allen and Unwin.

Thompson, R. (trans. and intro.) 1990: *Report From Xunwu*. Stanford, CA: Stanford University Press.

Thompson, R. 1995: *China's Local Councils in the Age of Constitutional Reform 1898–1911*. Cambridge, MA: Council on East Asian Studies, Harvard University.

Thorne, C. 1972: *The Limits of Foreign Policy: The West, the League and the Far Eastern Crisis of 1931-1933*. London: Hamilton.

Thornton, R. 1969: *The Comintern and the Chinese Communists 1928–1931*. Seattle: University of Washington Press.

Townsend, J. 1996: 'Chinese Nationalism.' In J. Unger (ed.) *Chinese Nationalism*. New York: M. E. Sharpe, 1–30.

Trocki, C. 1999: *Opium, Empire and the Global Political Economy: A Study of the Asian Opium Trade*. London: Routledge.

Tsai, Shih-Shan Henry 1983: *China and the Overseas Chinese in the US 1968–1911*. Fayetteville: University of Arkansas Press.

Tsou, Tang 1986: *The Cultural Revolution and Post-Mao Reforms: A Historical Perspective*. Chicago: University of Chicago Press.

Tsou, Tang, 1987: 'Marxism, the Leninist Party, the Masses and the Citizens in the Rebuilding of the Chinese State.' In S. Schram (ed.) *Foundations and Limits of State Power in China*. Hong Kong: Chinese University Press, 257–89.

Tuchman, B. 1971: *Stilwell and the American Experience in China*. New York: Macmillan.

Tucker, N. 1983: *Patterns in the Dust: Chinese–American Relations and the Recognition Controversy 1949–1950*. New York: Columbia University Press.

Unger, J. 1982: *Education Under Mao: Class and Competition in Canton Schools 1960–1980*. New York: Columbia University Press.

Van de Ven, H. 1991: *From Friend to Comrade: The Founding of the Chinese Communist Party 1920–1927*. Berkeley: University of California Press.

Van de Ven, H. 1997: 'The Military in the Republic.' *China Quarterly*, 150, 352–74.

Van Slyke, L. 1986: 'The Chinese Communist Movement During the Sino-Japanese War 1937–1945.' In J. Fairbank and A. Feuerwerker (eds) *The Cambridge History of China, vol. 13: Republican China 1912–1949*. Cambridge: Cambridge University Press, 609–722.

Vogel, E. 1969: *Canton Under Communism: Programs and Politics in a Provincial Capital 1949–1968*. Cambridge, MA: Harvard University Press.

Wakeman, F. 1975: *The Fall of Imperial China*. New York: Free Press.

Wakeman, F. 1993: 'The Civil Society and Public Sphere Debate: Western Reflections on Chinese Political Culture.' *Modern China*, 2, 108–38.

Wakeman, F. 1995: *Policing Shanghai 1927–1937*. Berkeley: University of California Press.

Wakeman, F. 1996: *The Shanghai Badlands: Wartime Terrorism and Urban Crime 1937–1941*. Cambridge: Cambridge University Press.

Wakeman, F. 1997: 'A Revisionist View of the Nanjing Decade: Confucian Fascism.' *China Quarterly*, 150, 395–432.

Wakeman, F. 2000: '*Hanjian* (Traitor)! Collaboration and Retribution in Wartime Shanghai.' In Wen-hsin Yeh (ed.) *Becoming Chinese*. Berkeley: University of California Press, 298–341.

Walder, A. 1991: 'Cultural Revolution Radicalism: Variations on a Stalinist Theme.' In W. Joseph, C. Wong and D. Zweig (eds) *New Perspectives on the Cultural Revolution*. Cambridge, MA: Council on East Asian Studies, Harvard University, 41–61.

Waldron, A. 1995: *From War to Nationalism: China's Turning Point 1924–1925*. Cambridge: Cambridge University Press.

Waley-Cohen, J. 1993: 'China and Western Technology in the Late Eighteenth Century.' *American Historical Review*, 98: 5, 1525–44.

Wang, David Der-Wei 1997: *Fin-de-Siècle Splendor: Repressed Modernities of Late Qing Fiction 1849–1911*. Stanford, CA: Stanford University Press.

Wang, Shaoguang 1995: 'The Politics of Private Time: Changing Leisure Patterns in Urban China.' In D. Davis, R. Kraus, B. Naughton and E. Perry (eds) *Urban Spaces in Contemporary China*. Cambridge: Cambridge University Press, 149–72.

Wang, Yeh-chien 1973: *Land Taxation in Imperial China*. Cambridge, MA: Harvard University Press.

Wang, Zheng 1999: *Women in the Chinese Enlightenment: Oral and Textual Histories*. Berkeley: University of California Press.

Wasserstrom, J. 1987: ' "Civilization" and its Discontents: The Boxers and Luddites as Heroes and Villains.' *Theory and Society*, 5, 675–707.

Wasserstrom, J. 1991: *Student Protests in Twentieth-Century China: The View From Shanghai*. Stanford, CA: Stanford University Press.

Wasserstrom, J. 1994: 'History, Myth, and the Tales of Tiananmen.' In J. Wasserstrom and E. Perry (eds) *Popular Protest and Political Culture in Modern China*, 2nd edn. Boulder, CO: Westview Press, 272–308.

Wasserstrom, J. and Liu, Xinyong 1995: 'Student Associations and Mass Movements.' In D. Davis, R. Kraus, B. Naughton and E. Perry (eds) *Urban Spaces in Contemporary China*. Cambridge: Cambridge University Press, 363–93.

Westad, O. 1993: *Cold War and Revolution: Soviet–American Rivalry and the Origins of the Chinese Civil War*. New York: Columbia University Press.

White, G. 1993: *Riding the Tiger: The Politics of Economic Reform in Post-Mao China*. Basingstoke: Macmillan.

White, L. 1989: *Policies of Chaos: The Organizational Causes of Violence in China's Cultural Revolution*. Princeton, NJ: Princeton University Press.

White, L. 1991: 'The Cultural Revolution as an Unintended Result of Administrative Policies.' In W. Joseph, C. Wong and D. Zweig (eds) *New Perspectives on the Cultural Revolution*. Cambridge, MA: Council on East Asian Studies, Harvard University, 83–104.

White, T. 1994: 'The Origins of China's Birth Planning Policy.' In C. Gilmartin, G. Hershatter, L. Rofel and T. White (eds) *Engendering China: Women, Culture and the State*. Cambridge, MA: Harvard University Press.

Whiting, A. 1954: *Soviet Policies in China 1917–1924*. New York: Columbia University Press.

Whiting, A. 1960: *China Crosses the Yalu: The Decision to Enter the Korean War*. Ann Arbor: University of Michigan Press.

Wilbur, C. Martin 1968: 'Military Separatism and the Process of Reunification Under the Nationalist Regime, 1922–1937.' In Ho Ping-ti and Tsou Tang (eds) *China In Crisis, vol. 1.* Chicago: University of Chicago Press, 203–63.

Wilbur, C. Martin 1976: *Sun Yat-sen: Frustrated Patriot.* New York: Columbia University Press.

Wilbur, C. Martin 1983: 'The Nationalist Revolution: From Canton to Nanking 1923–1928.' In J. Fairbank (ed.) *The Cambridge History of China, vol. 12: Republican China 1912–1949.* Cambridge: Cambridge University Press, 527–720.

Wilbur, C. Martin and How, J. 1989: *Missionaries of Revolution: Soviet Advisers and Nationalist China 1920–1927.* Cambridge, MA: Harvard University Press.

Wills, J. 1994: *Mountain of Fame: Portraits in Chinese History.* Princeton, NJ: Princeton University Press.

Womack, B. 1982: *The Foundations of Mao Zedong's Political Thought 1917–1935.* Honolulu: University of Hawaii Press.

Wong, C. 1991: 'The Maoist "Model" Reconsidered: Local Self-Reliance and the Financing of Rural Industrialization.' In W. Joseph, C. Wong and D. Zweig (eds) *New Perspectives on the Cultural Revolution.* Cambridge, MA: Council on East Asian Studies, Harvard University, 183–96.

Wong, Siu-lun 1984: 'Consequences of China's New Population Policy.' *China Quarterly,* 98, 220–40.

Wou, O. 1978: *Militarism in Modern China: The Career of Wu P'ei-fu, 1916–1939.* Folkestone: Dawson.

Wou, O. 1994: *Mobilizing the Masses: Building Revolution in Henan.* Stanford, CA: Stanford University Press.

Wright, M. 1957: *The Last Stand of Chinese Conservatism: The T'ung-chih Restoration 1862–1874.* Stanford, CA: Stanford University Press.

Wright, M. 1968: 'Introduction: The Rising Tide of Change.' In M. Wright (ed.) *China in Revolution: The First Phase 1900–1913.* New Haven, CT: Yale University Press, 1–63.

Wright, T. 1984: *Coal Mining in China's Economy and Society 1895–1937.* Cambridge: Cambridge University Press.

Wu, Tian-wei 1976: *The Sian Incident: A Pivotal Point in Modern Chinese History.* Ann Arbor: Center for Chinese Studies, University of Michigan.

Wylie, R. 1980: *The Emergence of Maoism: Mao Tse-tung, Ch'en Po-ta and the Search for Chinese Theory.* Stanford, CA: Stanford University Press.

Xiao, Zhiwei 1997: 'Anti-Imperialism and Film Censorship During the Nanjing Decade 1927–1937.' In S. Hsiao-peng Lu (ed.) *Transnational Chinese Cinemas: Identity, Nationhood, Gender.* Honolulu: University of Hawaii Press, 35–57.

Yahuda, M. 1978: *China's Role in World Affairs.* London: Croom Helm.

Yahuda, M. 1993: 'Deng Xiaoping: The Statesman.' *China Quarterly*, 135, 551–72.

Yang, Dali 1996: *Calamity and Reform in China: State, Rural Society, and Institutional Change Since the Great Famine*. Stanford, CA: Stanford University Press.

Yang, Rae 1997: *Spider Eaters: A Memoir*. Berkeley: University of California Press.

Yeh, Wen-hsin 1996: *Provincial Passages: Culture, Space and the Origins of Chinese Communism*. Berkeley: University of California Press.

Yeh, Wen-hsin 1998: 'Urban Warfare and Underground Resistance: Heroism in the Chinese Secret Service During the War of Resistance.' In Wen-hsin Yeh (ed.) *Wartime Shanghai*. London: Routledge, 111–32.

Yick, J. 1995: *Making Urban Revolution in China: The CCP–GMD Struggle for Beiping–Tianjin 1945–1949*. New York: M. E. Sharpe.

Yip, Ka-che 1996: *Health and National Reconstruction in Nationalist China: The Development of Modern Health Services 1928–1937*. Ann Arbor: Association for Asian Studies.

Young, E. 1968: 'Yuan Shih-k'ai's Rise to the Presidency.' In M. Wright (ed.) *China in Revolution: The First Phase 1900–1913*. New Haven, CT: Yale University Press, 420–42.

Young, E. 1976: 'The Hung-Hsien Emperor as a Modernizing Conservative.' In C. Furth (ed.) *The Limits of Change: Essays on Conservative Alternatives in Republican China*. Cambridge, MA: Harvard University Press, 171–90.

Young, E. 1977: *The Presidency of Yuan Shih-k'ai: Liberalism and Dictatorship in Early Republican China*. Ann Arbor: University of Michigan Press.

Young, E. 1983: 'Politics in the Aftermath of Revolution: The Era of Yuan Shih-k'ai 1912–1916.' In J. Fairbank (ed.) *The Cambridge History of China, vol. 12: Republican China 1912–1949*. Cambridge: Cambridge University Press, 208–55.

Young, E. 1994: 'Imagining the Ancien Régime in the Deng Era.' In J. Wasserstrom and E. Perry (eds) *Popular Protest and Political Culture in Modern China*, 2nd edn. Boulder, CO: Westview Press, 18–31.

Yu, G. 1966: *Party Politics in Republican China: The Kuomintang 1912–1924*. Berkeley: University of California Press.

Yu, Ying-shih 1994: 'The Radicalization of China in the Twentieth Century.' In Tu Wei-ming (ed.) *China in Transformation*. Cambridge, MA: Harvard University Press, 125–50.

Zarrow, P. 1990: *Anarchism and Chinese Political Culture*. New York: Columbia University Press.

Zweig, D. 1989: *Agrarian Radicalism in China 1968–1981*. Cambridge, MA: Harvard University Press.

Zweig, D. 1991: 'Agrarian Radicalism as a Rural Development Strategy 1968–1978.' In W. Joseph, C. Wong and D. Zweig (eds) *New Perspectives on the Cultural Revolution*. Cambridge, MA: Council on East Asian Studies, Harvard University, 63–81.

Index